THINQ, GRADES 1–3

Inquiry-based learning in the classroom

Jill Colyer
Shannon Simpson
Marie Swift
Liz Davis
Teresa Cariglia-Bull

Series Editors
Jill Colyer, Jennifer Watt

Solution Tree | Press
a division of Solution Tree

American version published in the United States by Solution Tree Press

555 North Morton Street
Bloomington, IN 47404
800.733.6786 (toll free) / 812.336.7700
FAX: 812.336.7790
email: info@SolutionTree.com
SolutionTree.com

Visit **go.SolutionTree.com/instruction** to download the free reproducibles in this book.

Printed in the United States of America

Library of Congress Cataloging-in-Publication Data

Names: Colyer, Jill, author, editor. | Watt, Jennifer, 1965- editor.
Title: THINQ, Grades 1-3 : inquiry-based learning in the classroom / Jill Colyer, Teresa Cariglia-Bull, Liz Davis, Shannon Simpson, Marie Swift ; Jill Colyer, (editor), Jennifer Watt, (editor).
Description: Bloomington, IN : Solution Tree Press, [2024] | Series: THINQ | Includes bibliographical references and index.
Identifiers: LCCN 2024007663 (print) | LCCN 2024007664 (ebook) | ISBN 9781962188258 (paperback) | ISBN 9781962188265 (ebook)
Subjects: LCSH: Inquiry-based learning. | Education, Elementary.
Classification: LCC LB1027.23 .C648 2024 (print) | LCC LB1027.23 (ebook) | DDC 372.13--dc23/eng/20240513
LC record available at https://lccn.loc.gov/2024007663
LC ebook record available at https://lccn.loc.gov/2024007664

Solution Tree
Jeffrey C. Jones, CEO
Edmund M. Ackerman, President

Solution Tree Press
President and Publisher: Douglas M. Rife
Associate Publishers: Todd Brakke and Kendra Slayton
Editorial Director: Laurel Hecker
Art Director: Rian Anderson
Copy Chief: Jessi Finn
Senior Production Editor: Miranda Addonizio
Proofreader: Evie Madsen
Acquisitions Editors: Carol Collins and Hilary Goff
Assistant Acquisitions Editor: Elijah Oates
Content Development Specialist: Amy Rubenstein
Associate Editor: Sarah Ludwig
Editorial Assistant: Anne Marie Watkins

Acknowledgments

I would like to thank the teachers and students from Richland Academy, whose work is profiled in *THINQ, Grades 1–3*. Seeing inquiry in action, across grade levels, has helped me continue to grow as an educational leader and evolve my thinking around inquiry-based learning and assessment. Thank you to my writing partners Terry, Liz, Marie and Shannon. And a special thank you to my long-term collaborator and friend, Jennifer Watt, who made this process such a joy. My deep gratitude for the love and support of my husband David, and the amazing children in our life: Sam, Jack and Emma.

—Jill Colyer

Thanks to all those who said to me, "I enjoyed your books." I probably didn't respond with adequate enthusiasm since I was somewhat embarrassed by your compliment. But I really, truly appreciate your support and your amazing efforts in inquiry learning.

To my husband Barry, you are amazing. To the rest of my family, Emma, Sean, Matt, Elisha Mom, and Marion, you bring me joy. My deep gratitude to the remarkable Jill and David for bringing the book to life. Thanks also to my brilliant writing partners.

—Jennifer Watt

I want to extend my deepest gratitude to the extraordinary teachers and students who have allowed me to learn with and from them throughout their inquiry journey. I feel fortunate to have worked with so many remarkable individuals who have impacted my learning. To my colleagues, to my sister Sarah, and to my mentor Linda, thank you for always pushing my thinking and encouraging my passion for inquiry. Thank you to my family: to Scott for your support, and to Liam and Bryn for your wonder and inspiration and for being my why, thank you. Finally, I am grateful to Jill and David for the opportunity to be a part of this work.

—Shannon Simpson

I would like to thank all those teachers who allowed me a window into their classrooms, sharing their dedication to inquiry through practical examples. To my colleagues, who continue to inspire me, and especially to Shannon, for encouraging me to take on this project, I wish to express my gratitude. Thanks to my husband Chris for all your support. Our sons, Alexander and Brendan, continue to inspire me with their sense of wonder and curiosity. Thank you, Jill and David, for this exciting opportunity.

—Marie Swift

I would like to thank teachers Allison Bonner, Elinor Crowe, Gillian Madeley, Stacia Snow, Jilian Stambolich and Alana Young for their contributions and their unwavering belief in our students. I would also like to thank my co-writing partner and vice principal, Terry Cariglia-Bull, for her strength, her insights, and her questions! Thank you to Jill for the opportunity to share in this incredible work.

—Liz Davis

I would like to gratefully acknowledge the learning and efforts of colleagues in York Region who have been part of this journey. A special thank you to Morning Glory Public School teachers Alana Young, Allison Bonner and Elinor Crowe, for welcoming us into their classrooms to learn and grow with them and their students, and to my cowriter and mentor Liz Davis, for her passion for learning and her unwavering belief in me. Thank you to Jill for this incredible opportunity, and to my family for their support, love and encouragement.

—Teresa Cariglia-Bull

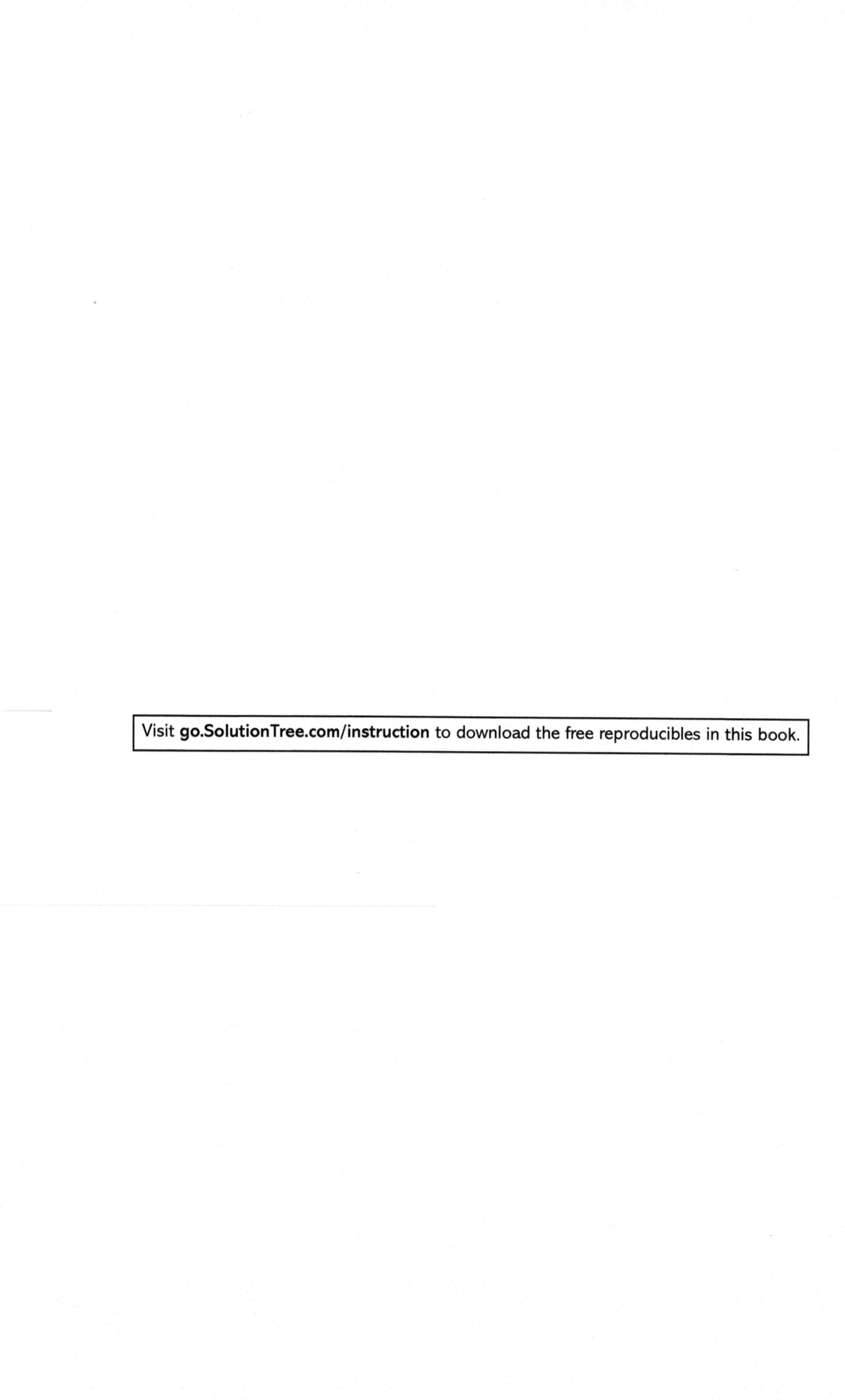

Visit **go.SolutionTree.com/instruction** to download the free reproducibles in this book.

Table of Contents

MAKING SENSE: Helping primary students synthesize, consolidate and reflect 111

REFLECTING AND SHARING: Pushing learning to a deeper level 139

WRAPPING IT UP: What matters most 153

About the Series Editors

Jill Colyer has worked in educational leadership positions for twenty years. Throughout her career, Jill has been committed to improving student outcomes and supporting teacher growth. She has worked as a classroom teacher, coordinator, and principal in both public and private school systems. As a principal, Jill led one of her schools through the International Baccalaureate (IB) authorization process and the school became an IB World School in the Primary Years Program. Jill also worked in the curriculum and assessment division of the Ontario Ministry of Education.

Jill was the national coordinator of The Historical Thinking Project, a pan-Canadian history education reform initiative. Established by Professor Peter Seixas of the University of British Columbia, The Historical Thinking Project worked with provincial education authorities, teaching associations, and publishers to embed critical historical thinking skills into curriculum documents, educational resources, and pedagogical practice.

Jill has written over fifteen student books and numerous professional learning resources for teachers. She has published with Oxford University Press, McGraw-Hill Ryerson, and Nelson. She also served as the editor for the Canadian Broadcasting Corporation educational current affairs program News in Review. In addition to working as a principal, she currently acts as a consultant to educational publishers and gives workshops to teachers and administrators across Canada. Jill, with her writing partner Jennifer Watt, are the creators and consultants of the THINQ professional learning series.

Visit www.linkedin.com/in/jill-colyer-0046b531 to learn more about Jill's work.

Jennifer Watt was the Program Coordinator for literacy for beginning teachers and their mentors at the Toronto District School Board. She has been a history, politics, social science, and English teacher and a consultant and coordinator for over thirty years. Throughout her career, she has supported both new and experienced classroom teachers at all grade levels and subject areas in thinking about how to share their knowledge, experience, and practices to improve student learning and establish professional communities. She is president of Intersectional Inquiry Educational Consulting (www.intersectional-inquiry.ca).

Jennifer has a master's degree focusing on the assessment of teacher practice. She is the author of several books, as well as exemplars and curriculum units. Her most recent publication is My Best Idea: Culturally Relevant Pedagogy, Rubicon-A Savvas Company (2023).

Visit www.linkedin.com/in/jennifer-watt-canada or www.intersectional-inquiry.ca to learn more about Jennifer's work.

About the Authors

Shannon Simpson was a teacher with the Simcoe County District and Upper Grand District school boards in Ontario. Passionate about innovation, critical thinking, and deep learning, she has been in education for over thirty years as a secondary school teacher, instructional resource teacher, and assessment facilitator. Shannon has delivered a variety of workshops and presentations and has been a writer of curriculum materials and teacher resources.

Marie Swift has been a K–3 classroom teacher for the majority of her career. She was a K–12 technology resource teacher and a literacy resource teacher for K–8 in the Simcoe County District in Ontario. She continued to support student inquiry in her role as teacher librarian in the same district and again while employed at an American international school in Dubai. Marie has done a wide variety of workshops, presentations, and webinars on various topics to support educators, teacher candidates, administrators, and students.

Elizabeth "Liz" Davis is the proud mother of two and a Superintendent in York Region District School Board in Ontario. She is passionate about school improvement work with a particular interest in resilience and working to improve outcomes for students in underperforming/underserved schools. She feels fortunate to have been a member of several school teams working to improve student achievement and well-being for over twenty years as a classroom teacher, special education resource teacher, literacy teacher mentor, and administrator.

Elizabeth has a master's degree in education focused on language and learning. In addition to contributions to this book, she contributed a chapter in *The Principal Reader: Narratives of Experience* edited by Darrin Griffiths and Scott Lowrey (2017). Her collaboration with the Ontario Humane Society working with youth from vulnerable communities resulted in a paper titled *Building a Bright Future: Humane Education From Theory to Practice* delivered at a conference at Oxford University in 2019. This paper was also presented at the Unesco Conference in May 2021.

Teresa Cariglia-Bull began her investigation of cognitive and instructional strategies as a graduate student working under the direction of Michael Presley at the University of Western Ontario. She coauthored a number of academic publications during this time.

While working under Maureen Lovett at the Learning Disabilities Research Program at The Hospital for Sick Children in Toronto, Ontario, Teresa was struck by the need to better understand how to accelerate learning in students with learning disabilities in a regular school setting. As a result, she returned to university to complete her bachelor's degree in education at the University of Toronto. Teresa's passion for cultivating optimal learning environments was evident as a homeroom teacher, performance plus teacher, special education resource teacher, reading recovery teacher, autism spectrum disorder classroom teacher and literacy lead. In 2013, she was recognized as the York Region District School Board Elementary Teacher of the Year. In 2016, she continued her instructional leadership as a vice-principal. She has facilitated many presentations and workshops at the school, area, and board level.

Foreword

by Kath Murdoch

There is a wonderful *Calvin and Hobbes* cartoon I often share with teachers and parents. In it, the two characters are playing outdoors when they come across a snake. They are fascinated and begin to ask all kinds of questions: "Why do they smell with their tongue?" "Do snakes have eyelids?" "How do they swallow something bigger than their head?" The friends eagerly decide to go home and find out more before suddenly realizing (with some horror) they want to *learn*. "But we are on vacation, we don't want to *learn* anything!" They finally agree that, given no one is *making* them do the learning, it's OK to learn! The last frame of the cartoon depicts them pouring over a book to find out more.

This cartoon struck a chord with me. In my early years as a primary teacher, I learned much more about how to teach effectively in the classroom from watching children learning outside it. Back then, I was heavily involved in the environmental education movement. Observing children connecting with nature offered powerful and sometimes confronting insights into learning and teaching. I saw first-hand the value of authentic contexts for learning, the driving force of great questions, the potency of curiosity and the true agency developed in children when teachers got out of their way. I was unsettled by the contrast between these experiences and the kind of learning that was, at the time, happening within the daily routine of my classroom.

Despite wanting things to be different, my classroom was not dissimilar to those in which I myself had been taught. Like so many of my colleagues, my identity as a teacher was acutely bound to my own memories of schooling. Our teaching was most often an act of knowledge transmission, and that knowledge was presented as fixed and unproblematic with, as the authors of this wonderful book put it, little "tolerance for ambiguity." We were diligent and caring, and our classrooms were warm and supportive, but *we* were the ones who decided what, how, when, where and with whom learning would occur. We were the ones who asked most of the questions. For the most part, our children were passive players in the game of school. School was about listening to the teacher, doing activities, doing the right thing and getting the work done.

Like *Calvin and Hobbes,* what went on in the classroom seemed a long way short of what happened when we took the learning outdoors. I knew I had to bridge the gap. I needed to bring that passionate, curious, adept, creative approach to learning to *everything* we did. I needed to allow my students to be the inquirers I knew they could be! Even as a young teacher, this meant some rethinking and unlearning of deeply embedded ways of seeing my role as a teacher, seeing curriculum and seeing my students. An inquiry approach offered me a way to turn my teaching around and place both my learners and learning itself at the centre. I've never looked back.

Several decades later, I find myself regularly engaged in vigorous conversations with teachers wrestling with the same dilemma. As I write, I am acutely aware of the gradual but necessary paradigm shift in education that raises important questions about what school is for. Now well into the 21st century, we are increasingly aware of the need to place learning processes at the heart of all we do. As Michael Wesch (2017) reminds us, our learners need to move from being simply knowledgeable to being knowledge-*able*: "It becomes less important for students to know, memorize, or recall information, and more important for them to be able to find, sort, analyze, share, discuss, critique, and create information."

Our learners need to be inquirers.

While excited by the possibilities of this shift, many teachers I meet report feeling overwhelmed and under prepared for the challenge of using an inquiry based approach. Resources in the field are often highly theorised and inaccessible or over simplified and flippant — leading to shallow, sham inquiry that can give it a bad name.

Not so this book. Like the other books in this excellent series, *THINQ, Grades 1–3* is a perfect blend of the theoretical and practical. The table of contents is a thorough summary of the questions teachers so often ask when grappling with this approach. The pages that follow lead us into elegant explanations that honor the complexity of the approach while making it abundantly clear and accessible. Research in the field is deftly woven into the text. The authors have been careful to acknowledge the comprehensive work that has been done in this field by many educators all over the world and their diligent reference to this background research gives the book depth *and* breadth. The photos, case studies, diagrams, charts and pull out boxes are fabulous provocations for the reader and provide excellent go-to reminders of the essential big ideas identified throughout. Whether a novice or experienced inquiry teacher, there is so much here for the reader to pore over, try out, reflect on, connect with and be inspired by.

Of course, one of the most compelling aspects of this book is the fact that it is written with a very specific target audience in mind. While inquiry can be used throughout K–12, it is not a one-size-fits-all approach. Its implementation necessarily evolves and changes as children progress through their schooling. Learners in their primary years are at a unique stage in their development. This is a phase of strong identity construction. These are the years in which the child's sense of *who they are as a learner* and indeed their view of learning itself are rapidly forming. The authors of *THINQ, Grades 1–3* challenge us to build this learner identity by focusing on key dispositions. Inquiry is not simply a process children use to explore their questions; it is a way of being for both teachers and learners. By consciously nurturing open-mindedness, hopefulness, curiosity, reflection and resiliency, teachers can create a community of inquiry that is deeply committed to what Peter H. Johnston (2004) calls the *agentive dimension* of the child's identity. The examples so generously provided throughout the book mean that any teacher of primary aged learners can immediately find case studies, explanations, strategies and resources for immediate application. Questions posed throughout the book provide a wonderful scaffold for collaborative teacher inquiry into inquiry.

Primary classrooms are habitats in which learning can either thrive or wither and in which curiosity and wonder are either nurtured or dismissed. It is the approaches we use as teachers (and our understanding of those approaches) that largely determines the health of that habitat. Young learners in contemporary classrooms deserve to learn and grow in communities in which their questions and interests are nurtured and valued. And, in turn, teachers need the kind of resources that help address *their* burning questions. This book, filled with such thoughtful, thorough guidance and the obvious wisdom of the authors' experience, does just that.

Introduction
About THINQ

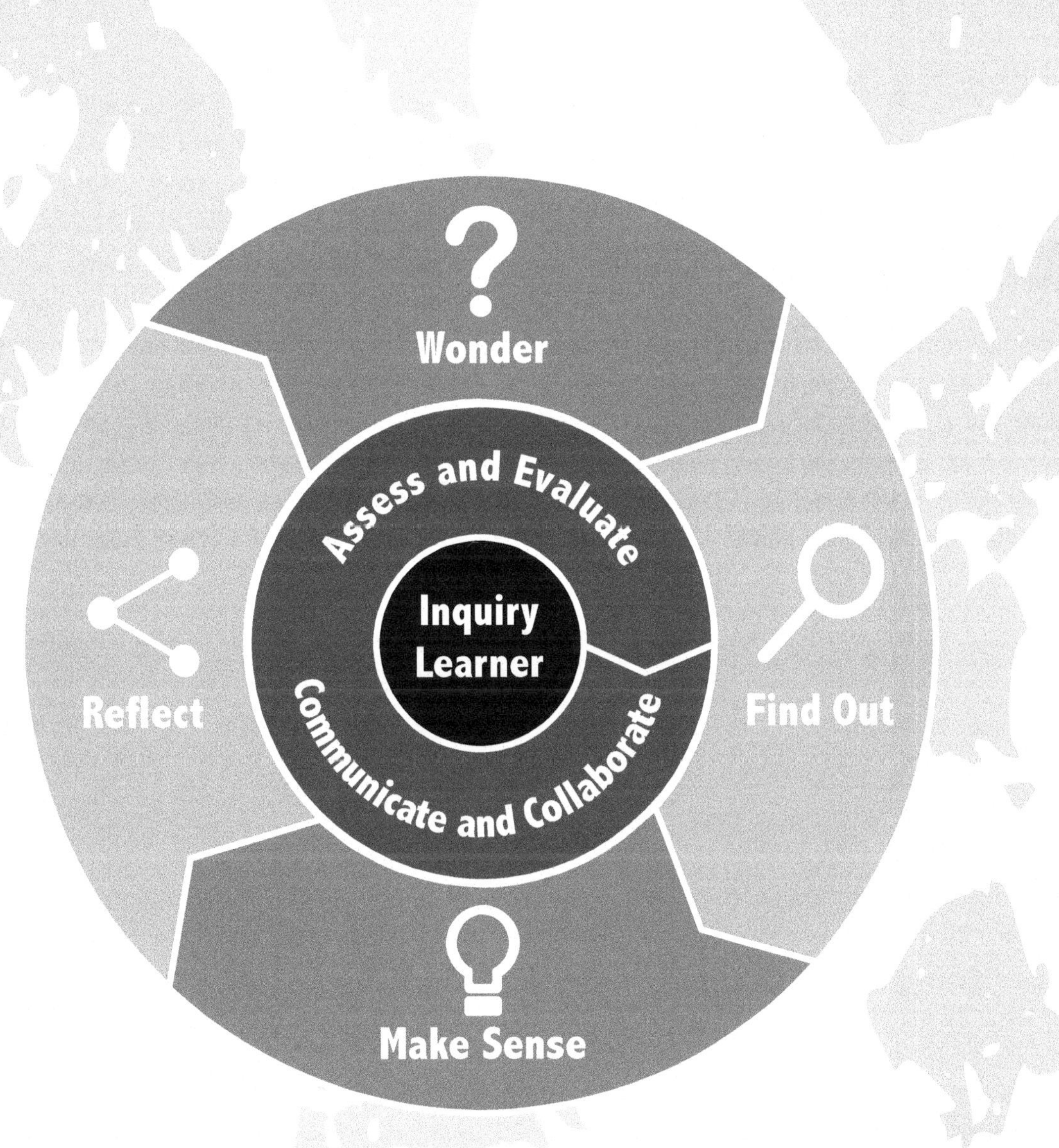

What if our schools could train students to be better lifelong learners and better adapters to change, by enabling them to be better questioners?

—Warren Berger

An ever increasing number of educators are exploring the potential of inquiry-based pedagogies to build a bridge to teaching, learning and assessment in a digital age. They instinctively understand that asking questions and seeking answers is a natural way of being a learner in the world. However, translating this basic truth into daily instructional practice is no small thing. This is the focus of *THINQ* — to help make inquiry-based learning a practical reality for every classroom, teacher and student. The title originates from the concept that student thinking is the driving force behind the inquiry process, and this belief is encapsulated by a portmanteau of think and inquiry: THINQ.

We wrote the *THINQ* professional learning series from a teacher perspective with an empathetic and realistic appreciation of a teacher's daily challenges. *THINQ* is designed to help teachers see how, over time, they can realistically integrate more inquiry-based learning into the context of their own classrooms.

THINQ resources are designed to:

- encourage teachers to do more inquiry.
- explore the big ideas of inquiry in an accessible and reader-friendly way.
- make explicit what inquiry can look, feel and sound like.
- demonstrate how inquiry-based learning can be assessed and evaluated.
- pose deep questions for teacher self-reflection and discussion with colleagues.
- provide case studies that introduce practical strategies with contextual examples.
- address common teacher questions and misconceptions about inquiry.

THINQ emphasizes the big ideas that underpin inquiry-based learning regardless of grades and disciplines. We also apply them to the specific needs and characteristics of learners at different ages and developmental stages: *THINQ, Kindergarten*, *THINQ, Grades 1–3*, *THINQ, Grades 4–6* and *THINQ, Grades 7–9*. We recognize that school jurisdictions organize their schools and grade divisions differently, but all of us share the understanding that there are distinct developmental learning stages. So while "junior learner" may not be the designation for grades 4–6 in your system, we feel confident, based on our work with teachers, that the students, issues and challenges are the same.

In this introduction, we offer an explanation of the Five Cs approach, a way to reflect, take action and assess progress on your professional journey to do more inquiry. We also provide book study questions to support you and your colleagues in your learning path.

Professional learning – a personal journey

We believe that transforming the daily assessment and instructional practice of teachers is the single most important consideration in transitioning the traditional education system to digital-age teaching and learning models. But because change is hard, it is only really achievable if and when educators, individually and in collaborative communities, believe passionately in its benefits. They must choose voluntarily (not through coercion or compliance) to take up the challenge to change classroom practice and school culture. This is what *THINQ* is all about — helping educators reflect upon and move forward along their individual professional learning paths.

We believe that integrating more inquiry rests, in part, upon a deep **conviction** that inquiry-based learning is needed and a personal **commitment** to persist until classrooms and schools begin to operate differently. Building the **capacity** to implement more inquiry in the **context** of one's own classroom and school is only sustainable if positive outcomes are **confirmed** by evidence and shared with others. Margin prompts throughout this book use these five Cs to provoke reflection, individually or with your colleagues, about your journey into inquiry-based learning (see figure I.1). We have also included throughout the book recurring features that encourage self-reflection and group discussion. These features include THINQ Questions, Inquiry in Action, Big Ideas and Educators Ask. In addition to these text features, we offer suggestions to launch a book study.

Aristotle said, "For the things we have to learn before we can do them, we learn by doing them." When it comes to inquiry-based teaching and learning, Aristotle was right—there is really is only one way to learn. We hope that whatever else you may take away from our resource, you will be motivated to try and do and learn.

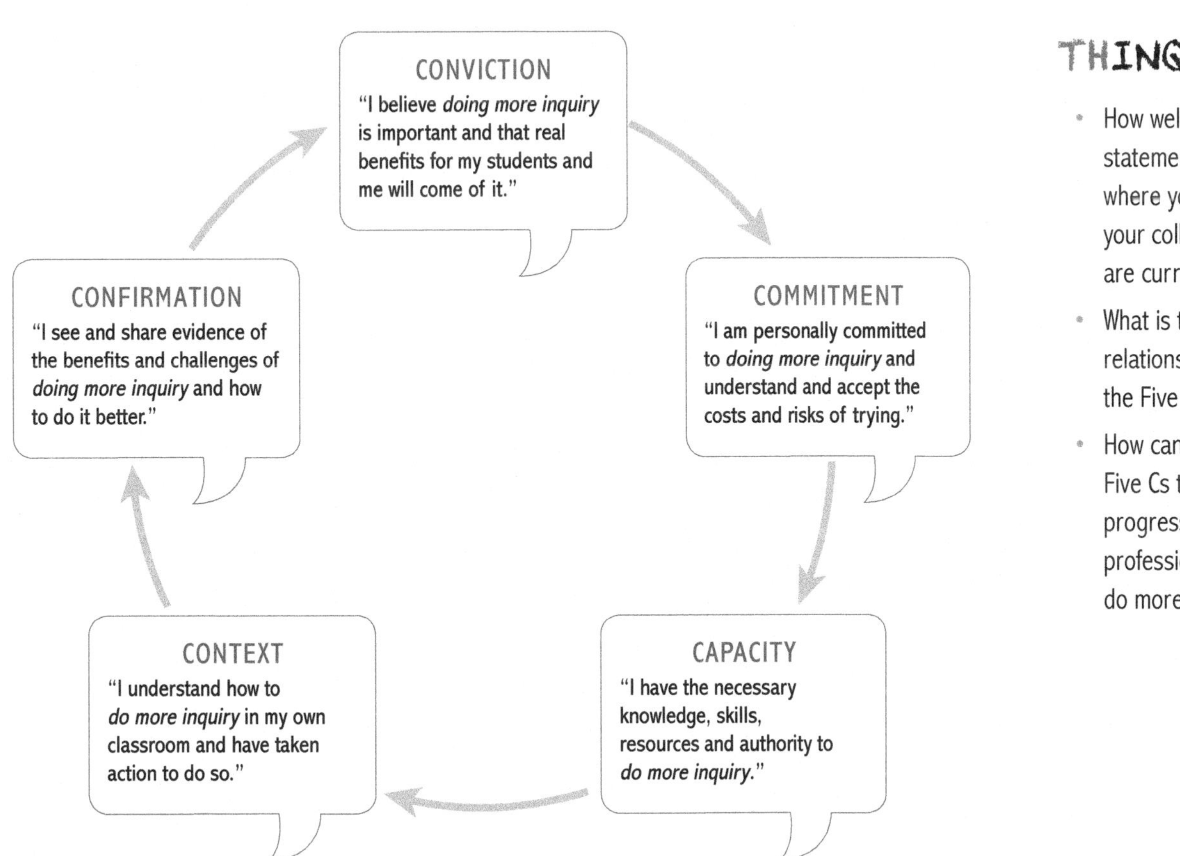

FIGURE I.1 The Five Cs of THINQ.

THINQ

- How well do these statements reflect where you and your colleagues are currently?
- What is the relationship among the Five Cs?
- How can you use the Five Cs to assess progress on your professional quest to do more inquiry?

Book study notes

Many schools and school teams have used the THINQ series for a book study. A book study is a good vehicle for collaborative learning and helps to create a shared language among staff members. Your school may choose to explore a chapter per month at a staff meeting or take a more accelerated approach to the material. Please feel free to reach out to us to participate in your book study via a virtual meeting. You can contact us through LinkedIn at www.linkedin.com/in/jennifer-watt-canada or www.linkedin.com/in/jill-colyer-0046b531 or at www.intersectional-inquiry.ca on the web.

Questions and prompts that may help guide reader discussion include the following.

1. George Couros (2015) talks about effective staff development as moving individual teachers from their own Point A to Point B, rather than moving all teachers to a prescribed line that has been determined by someone else. If you apply this idea to your own learning, what is your current Point A when it comes to inquiry-based learning, and what is your Point B?
2. In many regards, inquiry-based learning seems logical and intuitive: we know that children and adults become highly engaged and perform at their best when questions are at the heart of learning (Alexander, Gonzalez, Vermette, & Di Marco, 2022; Friesen & Lock, 2010; Schwartz, Tsang, & Blair, 2016; Willingham, 2009). If we know this to be true, what is the best way to incorporate more inquiry-based teaching and learning in our school and district?
3. Some teachers in our experience feel strongly that unless student-driven inquiry is at the core of the learning process, then *inquiry* is not really happening. The THINQ series consultants, Colyer and Watt argue that thoughtfully planned, teacher-guided inquiry is the best way to integrate more inquiry into classroom instruction and assessment because directed inquiry increases the chances that students will succeed during inquiry (Hattie, 2023; Kuhlthau, Maniotes, & Caspari, 2007; Perkins, 2022). What are some ways that you can allow for student choice, voice and autonomy within a teacher-directed inquiry?
4. One of the key points we make in this book is that educators shouldn't think about inquiry-based learning as an all-or-nothing proposition. Instead, the goal is for educators to integrate more inquiry-based instruction and assessment into the work they already do in classrooms. If this is the goal, identify three to five areas of your own practice where you could integrate some aspect of inquiry-based learning.
5. Although some educators have larger blocks of time available within their timetables to facilitate inquiry-based learning, many do not. As a result, educators across the country have been experimenting with ways to incorporate inquiry into small pockets of time, e.g., 30 minutes of class time. This has turned out to be a good way for some educators to make their first steps into inquiry-based learning. What are some ways that inquiry could be facilitated in your classroom or school in 30 minute blocks, 60 minute blocks, or half days?
6. Our comprehensive review of an extensive body of research has led us to conclude that we are moving from the Knowledge Age to the Age of Creativity, where people must be highly skilled in producing creative opportunities and innovative solutions. If inquiry-based learning is a critical teaching and learning tool and the means to the end — where fostering inquiry-driven creative thinkers is the *end* — how critical is inquiry-based learning to the future of public education?
7. Colyer and Watt argue that assessment for and as learning are critical to the inquiry process. In what ways might including more inquiry-based learning in your instructional practice also improve your assessment protocols?

Chapter 1
GETTING STARTED:
Inquiry-based learning with primary learners

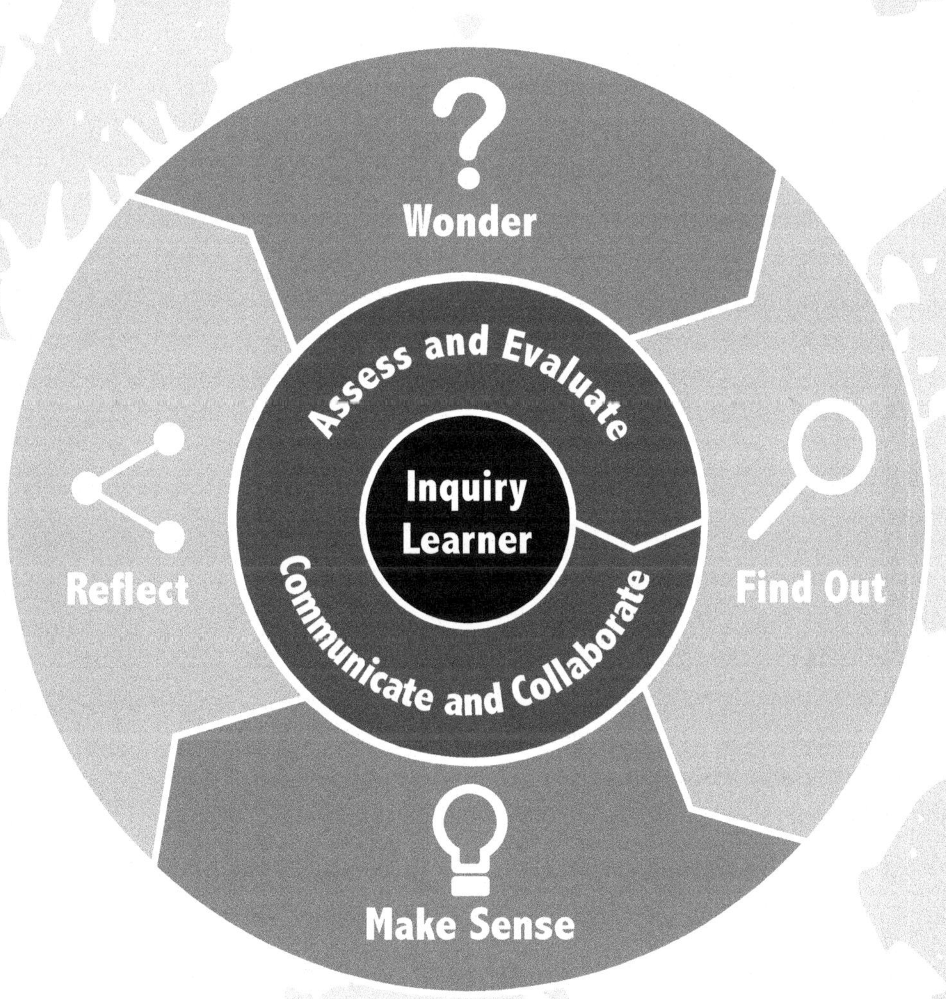

Neither inquiry nor the taking on of a critical perspective is something for the later years. It needs to happen from the very start.

—Jerome Harste

Big Idea
We learn by asking questions (inquiring).

CONVICTION
What are your beliefs about learning and learners?

In this chapter, we delve into the concept of inquiry-based learning and its advantages for primary learners. We focus on the importance of cultivating inquiry dispositions in children and practical ideas for teachers that include creating a classroom environment that supports the development of inquiry skills.

1.1 What is inquiry learning?

Inquiry learning is anchored in curiosity and our innate desire to make sense of the world around us (see figure 1.1). When we ask questions, wonder about something and use our heads and our hearts to investigate both what fascinates us and confuses us, we are engaged in inquiry. An inquiry-based classroom is organized around the deliberate use of questions to stimulate learning. In classrooms that are inquiry-based:

- teachers use carefully developed questions to provoke and guide students through their learning;
- there is less teacher-to-student talk and more student-to-student talk;
- students spend large amounts of time uncovering the curriculum through carefully planned inquiries;
- students learn how to learn as opposed to just what to learn in the form of isolated and fragmented content;
- students spend more time working collaboratively, rather than individually; and
- students share their learning with each other to push learning to a deeper level.

FIGURE 1.1 In an inquiry-based classroom, curiosity and wonder infuse all aspects of classroom work.

Inquiry learning, therefore, is more than just a process. In an inquiry-based classroom, teachers adopt an inquiry stance and explicitly guide their students to learn how to think outside the box, consider multiple perspectives, and reflect on their learning. Teachers use students' questions to develop units of study that connect the interests of students to curriculum expectations. When teachers adopt an inquiry stance, they allow for significant student choice, try to facilitate more student voice and attempt to remain open and flexible in the classroom.

THINQ

- How would you describe the nature of an inquiry-based classroom?
- How infused with the spirit of inquiry is your classroom?

Inquiry in Action

A grade 1 inquiry into slugs

One day in October, while out on the property for a nature walk, Jane's grade 1 students found a snail. The students were thrilled and Jane decided to let them bring the snail inside and also had them collect materials to create a habitat for the snail (see figure 1.2). Once everything was assembled and the snail was in its new home, Jane determined what the students already knew about snails:

- "Snails crawl outside in nature."
- "Snails hide in their shells."
- "Snails have slime on the bottom."
- "Snails have antenna."

She also found out that the students had a number of additional questions about the snail:

- "I wonder if the snail is a girl or boy?"
- "I wonder if the snail will eat strawberries?"
- "I wonder if he eats his food in his shell?"
- "I wonder what his antennas are doing?"

Jane decided to develop an inquiry to support a science curriculum unit on the life cycle. Normally, the Life Cycle Unit was done in April, but Jane knew she didn't have to teach it at that time and decided to follow the students' interests and integrate the inquiry even though it was October.

FIGURE 1.2 Every day students observed the snail in its habitat, made notes of any changes, and recorded any new questions they had.

Her inquiry involved a number of components: mapping the life cycle of the snail, learning about habitats and plants, building vocabulary, and developing fine motor skills as the students sketched the life of the snail (see figure 1.3). An unexpected surprise occurred when three tiny snails appeared! At the conclusion of the inquiry, the students reflected on their new learnings:

- "Snails do not like bananas."
- "Snails lay eggs. Baby snails are inside."
- "Snails have orange poo when snails eat carrots."
- "Snails have teeth."

THINQ

- What did the inquiry look like, sound like, and feel like in Jane's classroom?
- In what ways was Jane operating from an inquiry stance in this case study?

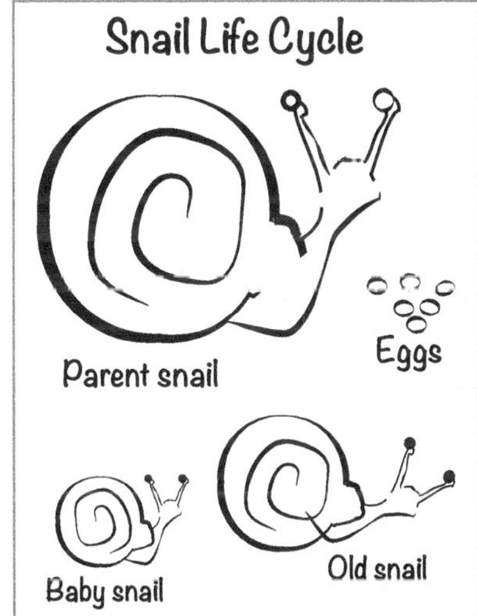

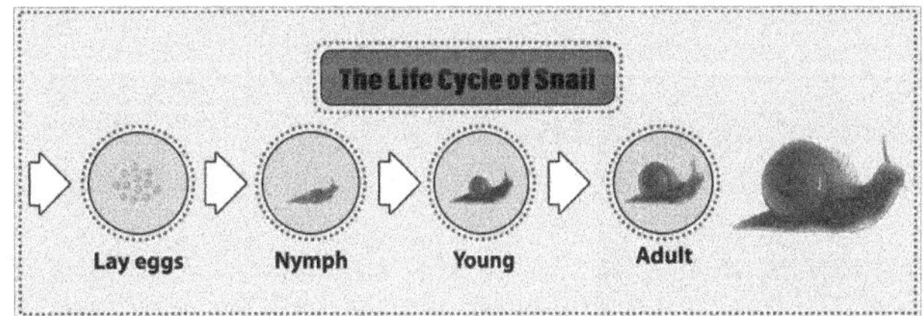

FIGURE 1.3 Students captured the life cycle of a snail in their learning journals. Teachers can offer examples like these as a springboard.

1.2 Is inquiry a better way to learn?

Big Idea
Inquiry results in students learning how to learn.

As educators, we may intuitively feel that inquiry-based learning is a better and more natural way for students to learn. But are our assumptions supported by research? In short, yes. Absolutely! In this section, we'll cover foundational and contemporary thinking, as well as some myths and misconceptions about inquiry.

Foundational research

Inquiry learning is rooted in progressive and constructivist educational philosophies of the early 19th century. Progressive educators, such as John Dewey (1938, 1944), proposed that learners should "do" the discipline by thinking, communicating and verifying knowledge in an authentic manner. He felt that passive, transmission-based pedagogies were flawed since the memorization of facts, discrete procedures and algorithms was quickly forgotten because the learner had no part in working with them or in building relevant new knowledge.

The basis of a social constructivist theory were laid by Lev S. Vygotsky (1962, 1987), who stressed the fundamental role of social interaction in the development of cognition. He emphasized the collaborative nature of learning, the importance of cultural and social context, and that learning is an active, ongoing process that continues throughout life.

Paulo Freire (2017) advocated for an education where learners would critically engage with knowledge by grappling and building upon what is known, and strive to change the world based on creating new knowledge.

Loris Malaguzzi (1996) was the driving force behind the world-renowned Reggio Emilia approach to education. He believed that students learn naturally through inquiry and play, and that it is our job as educators to foster the wonder of learning (see figure 1.4).

Traditional learning	Inquiry learning
Have to learn	**Want to learn**
What to know	**How to know**
Tell and memorize	**Ask and inquire**
Only one right answer	**Many conclusions**
Teacher-directed	**Learner-centered**
One-size-fits-all	**Personalized**
Passive learning	**Active learning**
Assess for marks	**Assess for learning**

FIGURE 1.4 By taking an inquiry stance, many important aspects of best practice teaching, learning and assessment can be advanced.

THINQ

- How familiar are you with the research on inquiry-based learning?
- What concerns you most about inquiry learning pedagogies?

Contemporary thinking about inquiry

While the foundational thinking around inquiry goes back many decades, contemporary educational researchers and thinkers like the ones below continue to advocate passionately for the relevance and necessity of pursuing an inquiry approach to teaching and learning in a digital age.

Helen Timperley, Linda Kaser and Judy Halbert (2014):
"We think that a key requirement for young people today is the development of curiosity. ... [W]e want our learners to leave our settings each year more curious than when they started. We believe this is much more likely to happen if young people are learning in highly engaging and innovative settings where curiosity — for everyone — is a way of life" (p. 23).

Carol Anne Wien (2008):
"If we permit students and teachers to engage with their own questions, their own theories about how things work, and their own processes for making things happen and understanding the world, then we can guarantee interest and motivation. Motivation fuels learning; it is the positive energy that carries the learner through the curriculum" (p. 24).

Carol C. Kuhlthau, Leslie K. Maniotes and Ann K. Caspari (2007):
"Inquiry... requires more than simply answering questions or getting a right answer. It espouses investigation, exploration, search, quest, research, pursuit and study. It is enhanced by involvement with a community of learners, each learning from the other in social interaction.

"An inquiry approach to teaching and learning seeks to develop independent academic competency, career readiness, and life skills, essential in all schools for all students" (p. 2).

Carlina Rinaldi (2004):
"In this attitude to find answers to questions are the roots of philosophy. This why is the only way in which to maintain what is essential in our life ... curiosity. Humanity exists because we have developed our curiosity. In the search for reasons and information lie the roots of ethics" (p. 3).

CONVICTION

How convinced are you that research provides evidence of the benefits of inquiry-based learning? What else would you like to know?

CONFIRMATION

How do your own classroom experiences confirm or contradict the experts?

Educators Ask

Isn't all learning inquiry?

Learning is a broad term that includes any gaining of new knowledge or skill. We learn through experience, practise, study and other means. Inquiry is born out of curiosity. It always begins with a wondering — a problem, a challenge, a question.

Inquiry myths and misconceptions

As with any pedagogy, there are myths and misconceptions that invoke barriers for teachers who are interested in exploring inquiry-based learning (see figure 1.5). Minimizing them means identifying and discussing them together.

COMMITMENT
Do any of these myths and misconceptions limit commitment to inquiry learning in your school?

Inquiry myths and misconceptions	Response
Inquiry is always the best teaching strategy.	A common misconception is that we are advocating that inquiry is the only way to teach. In order for inquiry-based learning to be successful, other strategies need to be in place, including direct instruction and practicing and mastering literacy and numeracy.
Inquiry takes too much time.	We think this misconception exists because educators believe that to "do" inquiry they have to begin and complete all steps of the inquiry process model. This is not true. Focusing on one aspect of the inquiry cycle is a good and valid target. This will allow you to work with students to develop specific inquiry skills.
Inquiry is too unstructured.	Students do not engage in inquiry completely unassisted. In fact, we are big proponents of teacher-directed inquiry. All good teaching involves creating the classroom conditions that increase the chances of student success. With primary-aged learners, teachers will need to plan each stage of an inquiry to support young learners.
Primary students cannot think deeply.	Some people don't believe that primary students can engage in deep learning. We disagree. Inquiry offers an alternative learning situation that gives students choice in their inquiries and allows them to take ownership of their learning, ask relevant questions, explore and investigate using technology, and reflect on what they have learned. The important building blocks for these skills can be established during the primary grades.
Inquiry is difficult to assess.	Inquiry-based learning can and should be assessed the way you assess other learning opportunities. Teachers can assess and evaluate knowledge, thinking, communication and application during an inquiry. You do not need to develop new assessment strategies when your students are engaged in an inquiry; just apply fundamental assessment for, as and of learning strategies. Remember, as well, that you can assess your students on the development of inquiry dispositions. (More on inquiry dispositions on the next page.)
Students need knowledge before they can do an inquiry.	In some cases, this may be true. And it is absolutely good practice for you to teach content and information to your students directly before you launch an inquiry. But you can also launch an inquiry without teaching content first, and then as students generate questions during the inquiry you can stop and teach mini lessons related to the content that is being uncovered.

FIGURE 1.5 There are many myths and misconceptions about what inquiry is and how it works.

1.3 How can we support inquiry dispositions in primary classrooms?

Big Idea

Inquiry dispositions support risk-taking and a sustainable commitment to inquiry learning.

Inquiry dispositions are a person's ability to learn and reason, and they include curiosity, reflection, resiliency, hopefulness and open-mindedness (see figure 1.6). They are what keep the learner on the journey of inquiry because they support wonder and an interest in learning. They make us perseverant and accepting of failure and mistakes as an important part of the journey.

You can begin by modeling these dispositions to your students. What are you curious about? What makes you wonder? What questions have driven and continue to drive your life? Your students benefit from hearing your experiences as an inquiry learner and in seeing first-hand your enthusiasm for aspects of life that they may or may not have considered.

You can also create an inquiry classroom culture that supports both the affective and the cognitive elements of inquiry learning. Students will cycle through a range of emotions while completing an inquiry — from joy and wonder to frustration and sometimes anger. Checking in frequently with your students will help validate their emotions as well as provide information on how you can support their thinking and dispositions.

CONVICTION

How convinced are you that curiosity, reflection, resiliency, hopefulness and open-mindedness are necessary conditions for learning in primary students?

CAPACITY

What do you think you need to learn in order to further engage yourself and your learners in meaningful inquiry-based learning?

THINQ

- Which inquiry dispositions do your primary students already possess?
- What inquiry dispositions do you possess? What do you need to continue exploring?

Some essential considerations for teachers about inquiry dispositions include co-learning and co-creation, patterns of dialogue, provocation, authenticity, tolerance for ambiguity and beliefs about learners.

Open-mindedness
Willingness to consider new ideas

Hopefulness
Feeling or inspiring optimism about the future

Curiosity
Eagerness to learn or know something

Reflection
Ability to think about thinking

Resiliency
Capacity to keep on trying and overcome

FIGURE 1.6 These inquiry dispositions are essential building blocks for creating a sustainable culture of inquiry-based learning.

Co-learning and co-creation

Inquiry-based learning challenges us to be co-learners and co-investigators with our students. A co-learning relationship is established when students and educators pursue significant questions about authentic and relevant ideas together (see figure 1.7). When we talk with educators who are engaged in inquiry learning, we see that they are learning alongside their students and are excited by the prospect of doing so. They are passionate and curious about their world, critical and creative thought, and their own teaching. Throughout this book we look at how educators can be co-learners and creators.

Patterns of dialogue

When educators take an inquiry stance, they need to rethink the patterns of dialogue in their classrooms. Traditional patterns are centered on the educator who does most of the talking. But learning requires talking (Goodwin, 2017). To support inquiry dispositions there needs to be a shift. Communication should be encouraged among all learners (see figure 1.8). When everyone shares ideas, wonderings and discoveries, inquiry dispositions can really take hold.

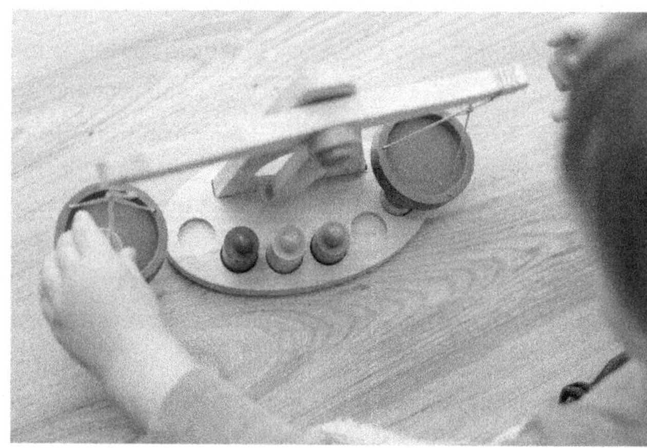

FIGURE 1.7 This student is working with classmates to respond to the question: "How many ways can you balance a scale?" What inquiry dispositions will help them to succeed in this task?

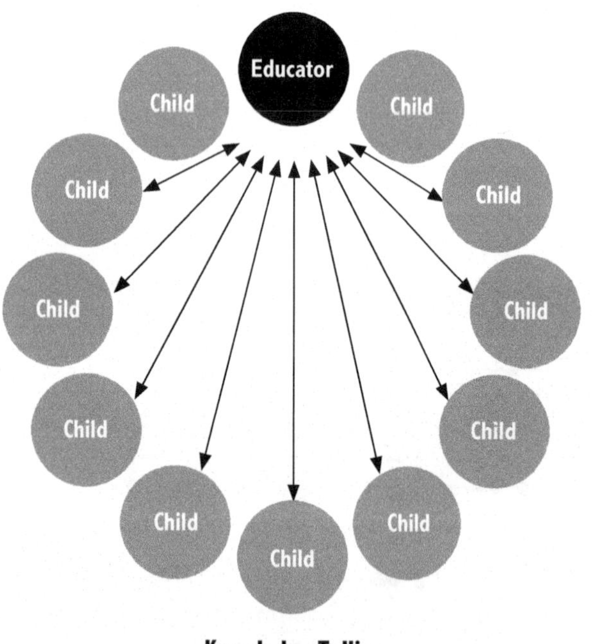

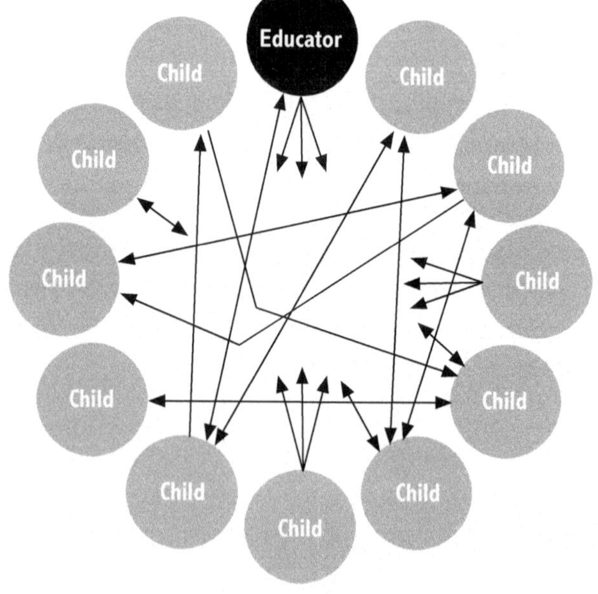

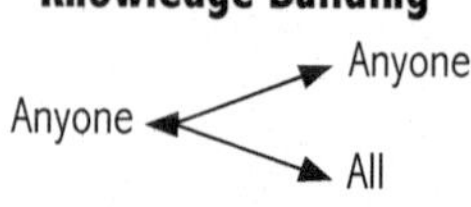

FIGURE 1.8 Traditional patterns of dialogue involve educators "knowledge telling." To foster inquiry dispositions, patterns need to shift to collective "knowledge building."

Provocation

Our job is to help young learners see the world — to notice and explore what is interesting, amusing, different, confusing, conflicting and contradictory. When we rethink our role as being provocateurs rather than just facilitators, we come to understand that facilitators simplify and expedite experiences, while provocateurs provoke, point out dissonance and generate additional questions for further learning. These actions nurture the natural inquiry dispositions that young learners have.

Words Matter

Provocation
A deliberate action or occurrence that causes someone to begin to do something.

CAPACITY

What is your tolerance for the uncertainty and ambiguity of inquiry?

Authenticity

To nurture and grow inquiry dispositions, learning experiences must be authentic. Authenticity derives from the genuine wonder and curiosity of learners. Learning begins with questions and problems that are real, important and essential for learners. Authenticity also means honest reflection, sharing and the candid admission, especially by educators to students, of the possibility of difficulty or challenges during an inquiry.

Tolerance for ambiguity

Inquiry educators also talk about overcoming their own fear and trepidation when conducting inquiry, which comes from never knowing for sure what may happen. This initial fear changes to excitement as they see the benefits to student learning and engagement. These educators have tried and stumbled and tried again to create and hone strategies to make their students, and themselves, better inquiry learners.

Educators Ask

Am I already doing inquiry-based learning?

Educators frequently wonder: Am I doing inquiry? If you are engaging students in asking their own questions, exploring their wonderings, asking them open-ended questions, provoking their curiosity and supporting them to think deeply about their own learning and the world around them, then you are "doing inquiry."

So typically, the issue is not if we are "doing inquiry," but determining:

- How can we offer more opportunities for inquiry in our classrooms?
- How can we deepen opportunities for thinking throughout an inquiry?
- How can we foster inquiry dispositions through all aspects of learning?
- How can we gather evidence of learning during inquiry?

That's where this book comes in. We hope to offer practical examples to deepen and support you and your students' inquiry-based learning journey.

Beliefs about learners

Perhaps more than anything else, sustaining and nurturing inquiry dispositions must be deeply rooted in positive beliefs about the potential of all learners — that they are competent, capable of complex thinking, curious and rich in potential.

Inquiry-based learning encourages human curiosity. It demands rigorous thought. It involves knowledge building and it pushes the learner to repeatedly explore ideas from new perspectives and viewpoints. Students are in control and are active, rather than passive, participants in the learning process.

Therefore, successful inquiry educators have confidence in their students' abilities and are responsive to their interests. These educators take appropriate risks in their teaching by following the curiosity of their students and by challenging them to question, explore and conclude, and to stretch beyond the obvious and easy-to-answer questions.

THINQ

- Would you add any other ways to nurture inquiry dispositions beyond the ones described here?
- Which ones do you think would yield the best results in the context of your own classroom?
- Which of the reflective questions could you answer most positively and which ones were more challenging?

Inquiry in Action

Reflective questions for primary educators

An inquiry stance to learning means being reflective of one's own practice. How would you answer the following questions?

- Am I curious?
- Do I think out loud about my wonderings?
- Am I a co-learner?
- Am I flexible and spontaneous?
- Am I willing to yield the plan I currently have for an opportunity that arises in the moment?
- Am I open to act on opportunities for learning?
- Do I offer multiple ways for students to demonstrate skills and knowledge?
- Do I provide materials and resources that allow for inquiries to grow?
- Do I reflect on student wonderings and use these as next steps?
- Do I engage learners in frequent discussions about learning?
- Have I created a safe environment that allows students to take risks?
- Do I know and focus on big ideas and conceptual understandings?
- Do I support and encourage students to investigate their wonderings?

1.4 Is there a standard model or method of inquiry?

Big Idea
Inquiry learning, regardless of grade or subject area, has three common and essential traits.

In the previous section we looked at inquiry dispositions and why we believe inquiry learning is a powerful way for primary students to learn. There are many pedagogies that encompass inquiry-based learning in their purpose and match it in quality. There are also specific types of inquiry that teachers can choose from. These include problem-based, project-based and play-based learning, to name a few. Your district or school may have a preferred type, or you may begin by trying out a form of inquiry that relates most to your students' needs and interests.

There are many different versions of inquiry learning, and it is easy to feel overwhelmed by the complexity of so many variations. Some focus on the creation and innovation of an object. Others focus on technology and the creation and sharing to a larger world audience. Still others are used with particular age groups. Regardless of the many types, we find it useful to focus on three essential traits that are present in all types of inquiry learning (Colyer & Watt, 2016). We will first identify and explain these three traits and then present an inquiry model for grades 1–3 students.

Essential traits of inquiry

All inquiry is rooted in three traits (see figure 1.9), which include, first, an essential question that invites the learner to wonder, think deeply and solve. Answering a question or solving a problem involves the second trait, which is a method of discrete steps or stages of a cycle. The cycle helps learners engage in critical and creative thinking, which is the third trait. This method may be particular to a discipline. In answering the question or solving the problem, the student experiences a developmentally-appropriate version of the way professional or expert learners in a field engage in their work. Like professionals, they think critically, self-reflect, contribute, communicate and share findings. New knowledge is created.

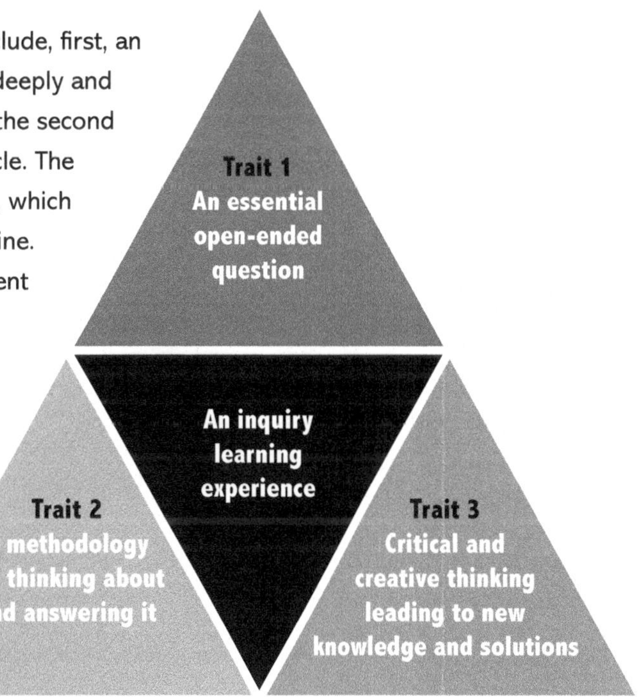

FIGURE 1.9 All inquiry learning experiences share three essential traits.

An inquiry model for primary learners

An inquiry model for primary learners sparks wonder and develops foundational skills in thinking and research (see figure 1.10). Inquiry at the primary level also establishes norms for learning that involve collaboration, communication of new learning and reflection. Primary students are at varied literacy levels and some will still be emergent readers. It is necessary, therefore, that teachers create the conditions for success by providing research materials that are age appropriate, at a variety of reading levels and in a variety of forms (e.g., photos and video clips as well as print). Primary students have great enthusiasm for learning, and with its focus on open-ended questions and exploration, inquiry-based learning is a natural fit for this age level.

THINQ

- Which part of the inquiry process do you think will come most easily to your primary students?
- What is the one area where you may have to provide the greatest support?

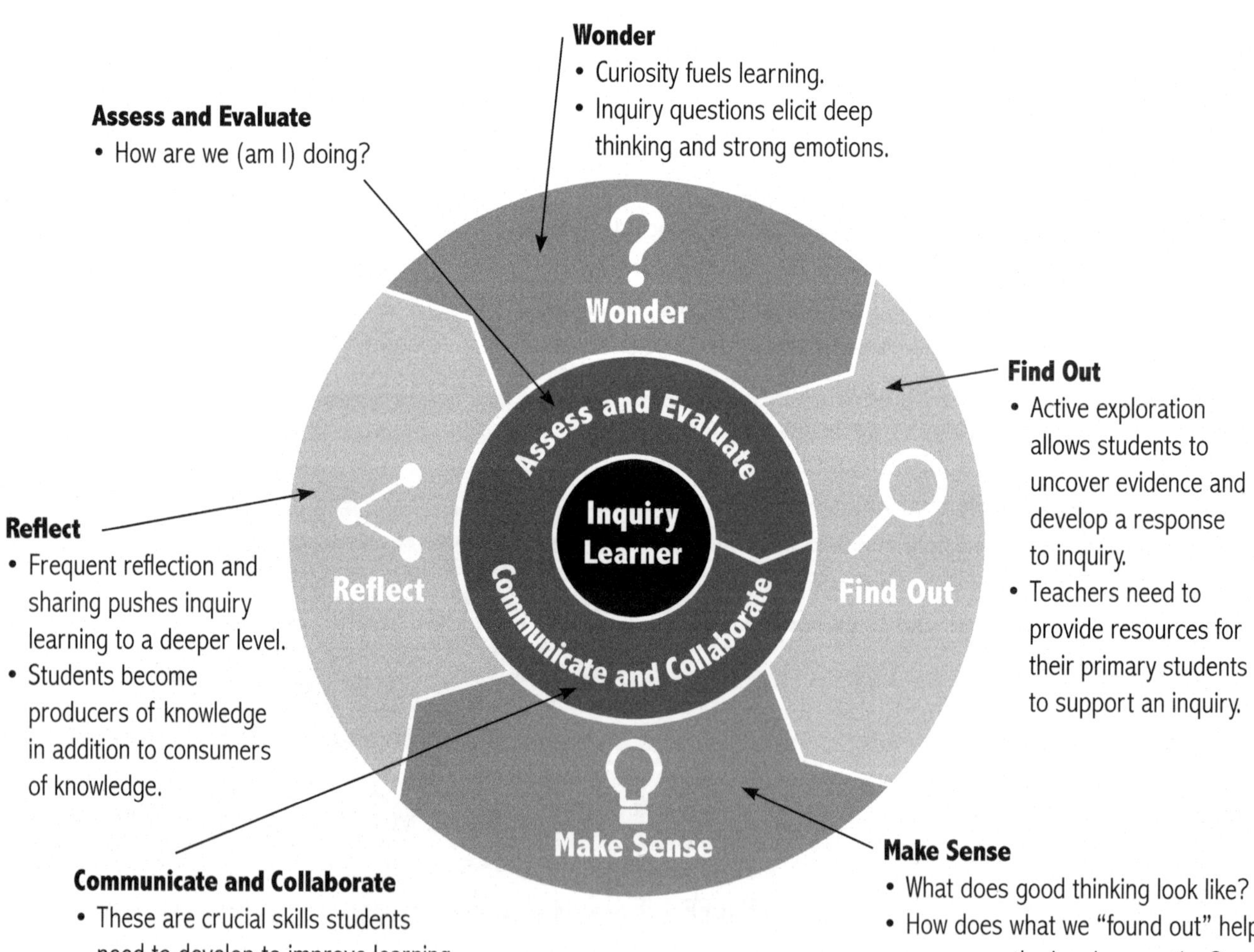

FIGURE 1.10 This is a model that we feel is both accessible and informative for primary learners and educators.

1.5 What is the primary teacher's role in inquiry learning?

When we look into inquiry-based classrooms, educators are employing many different strategies that allow for authentic questioning and learning to occur (see figure 1.11, page 14).

Talk less and listen more

According to Alfie Kohn (2006), in outstanding classrooms, teachers do more listening than talking, and students do more talking than listening. Terrific teachers often have teeth marks on their tongues. Simply put, let the learners do the talking and if you are going to respond, try and make your response a question.

Be open to student questions

Encourage, welcome and invite students' questions and use the questions to drive inquiry. Let your students know that you are interested and want to hear their questions. This gives voice to learners' ideas.

Ask open questions

Think about the questions you ask — do they allow an entry point for all learners? Ask questions that open up thinking, not close it down. Allow for wait time, both when you ask questions and when students do so, and revisit their questions often. When in doubt, say, "Tell me about..."

Notice and name

Make thinking visible by noticing and naming the learning. This allows learners to know why they are doing what they are doing. It also sets the stage for them to be able to notice and name their own learning and that of their peers.

Know and honor student interests

When we know our students, we can assist them in making connections to prior knowledge and experiences and support them with their personal inquiries.

Establish a culture that supports wondering

An environment that encourages questions and thinking by both learners and educators means that all thoughts and wonderings are acknowledged and honored.

Big Idea

Educators should be co-learners who model their wonder and thinking with students.

CAPACITY

Which of these strategies do you use now and which ones would you like to try to do more often?

Think aloud

Let your students hear you thinking out loud about what you are doing and thinking, especially about your wonderings and misconceptions. Think aloud about how you are going to find out about your wondering as well. Modeling is a powerful way to engage students in thinking out loud themselves. Educators' wonderings can spark inquiries as well.

CAPACITY

What do you think you need to do to embrace the effective practices of inquiry-based educators? Do you require additional information?

Use the power of "co"

Co-create, collaborate and co-negotiate. Knowing that your students are proficient, talented and intelligent allows you to be a co-learner alongside them, and lets them realize that there are times when they will be leading the learning.

Be responsive, adaptive and flexible

Be open to "going with the flow" of an inquiry. Understand that some inquiries will take off while others will not — and that is okay. Enjoy the surprise and unpredictability of authentic learning.

Use authentic, thought-provoking materials

Offer texts, artifacts, natural and found objects, people, learning experiences and places that instill a sense of wonder and cultivate more questions. Allow students to provide these materials as well, and let them be the "knowledgeable other" when they have expertise.

Take a broad view

Have a deep, working knowledge of conceptual understandings, program expectations, skills, knowledge and student development. This enables educators to support inquiry broadly, scaffold learning, use intentional materials and resources, and ask provoking questions that promote thinking and learning in all areas.

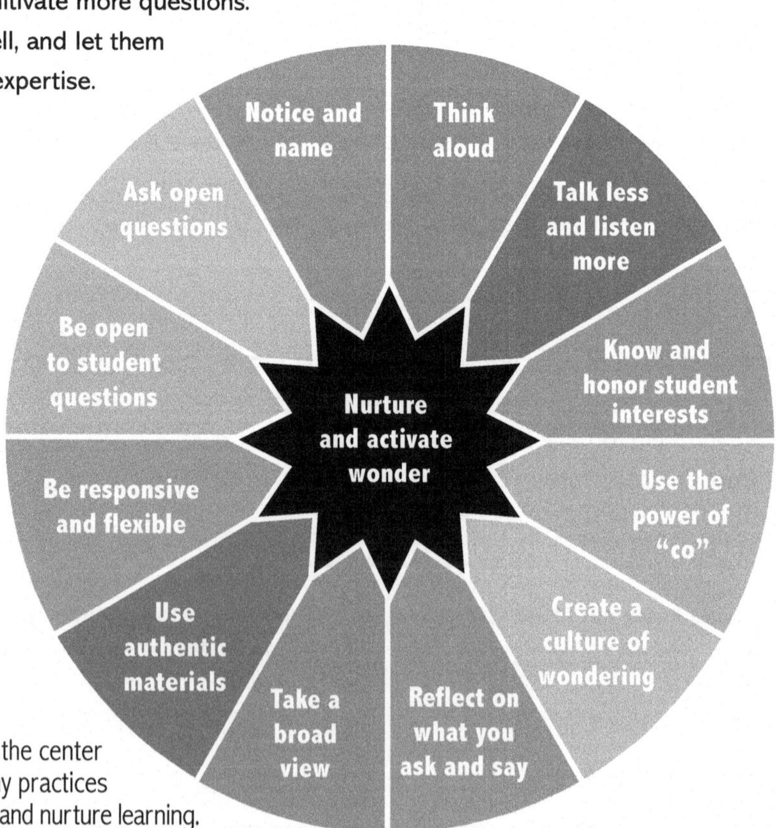

FIGURE 1.11 Wonder is at the center of inquiry, but there are many practices educators can use to activate and nurture learning.

1.6 Is inquiry appropriate for primary learners?

> **Big Idea**
> Inquiry develops important learning dispositions that make primary students better and more confident learners.

Inquiry involves the most natural ways primary students learn at early stages of cognitive development. They can ask questions, seek answers and share their discoveries (see figure 1.12). The primary grades are the foundation for inquiry at a later level when students can think more abstractly.

Primary learners are developing the skills and knowledge that inquiry-based learning allows them to practice. An inquiry-based environment also allows students to be self-directed, learn through their interests, demonstrate knowledge in multiple ways, exercise choice and use their voice. It supports their capacity to develop self-regulatory behavior, which includes responding to stressful situations and being able to deal with new challenges (Jacobs, 2022).

Through purposeful inquiry-based learning, students practice and develop conceptual understandings and skills in all areas. The integrated nature of inquiry enhances social, mental and physical well-being for primary learners. Inquiry allows for the development of new learning in many realms.

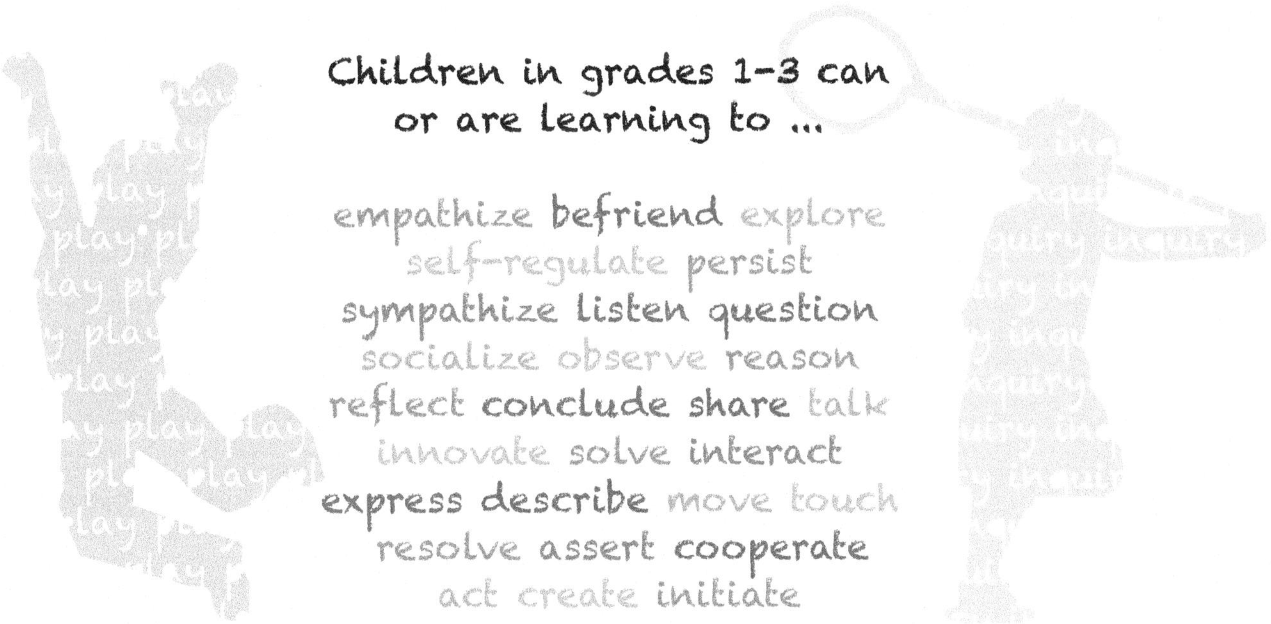

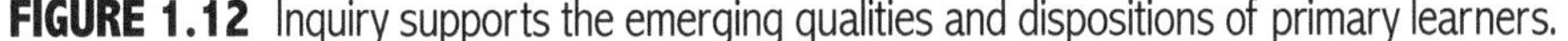

FIGURE 1.12 Inquiry supports the emerging qualities and dispositions of primary learners.

1.7 How does inquiry differ from a traditional program?

Big Idea
Inquiry classrooms focus on big ideas and transferable skills.

Inquiry-based learning gives all learners opportunities to build knowledge and helps develop effective and independent learners. We believe that students learn best when they are fully invested in the process of knowledge building, rather than when an educator always decides how knowledge will be dispersed. This means moving away from thinking of educators as all-knowing to seeing them as co-learners who are skilled at asking questions and provoking wonder in their students (see figure 1.13).

This also means refocusing our learning goals from the completion of tasks and activities to genuine thinking and learning. As inquiry educators we need to be continually asking ourselves whether we are asking for rote learning and recall or intentionally developing critical and creative thinking through inquiry. Are we creating learning experiences that are based on student interest and need? Are our students focused on big ideas and essential skills or facts and details? Are we knowledge telling or knowledge building?

Figure 1.14 illustrates how inquiry-based learning may differ from more traditional notions of teaching and learning. It suggests that inquiry-based classrooms are focused on big ideas and transferable skills as opposed to the coverage of predetermined content or the completion of tasks.

THINQ

- How would you evaluate your teaching relative to the categories in figure 1.13?
- How would you evaluate your classroom relative to the categories in figure 1.14?

Traditional teaching	Inquiry teaching
Educator is the expert	Educator is a **co-learner**
Educator tells	Educator **models**
Educator controls	Educator **activates**
Educator corrects mistakes	Educator **gives feedback**
Educator gives answers	Educator **asks questions**
Educator is a manager	Educator is a **provocateur**
Educator assesses task completion	Educator **assesses learning**

FIGURE 1.13 In an inquiry-based classroom, students benefit when educators participate as co-learners who model and activate learning.

Comparing a traditional program with an inquiry-based approach		
Elements	**Traditional**	**Inquiry-based**
Duration	Length of the learning experience is fixed and predetermined.	Within limits, length of the learning experience is determined by the inquiry progression.
Topics	Determined by educator and curriculum, and may or may not be of interest to students.	Negotiated by educator and student, with integrated curriculum goals; student interest is the inquiry focus.
Planning	Educator plans topics and designs learning experiences in advance.	Educator listens to student wonderings, observes students and uses student interest to determine the next steps.
Objectives	Educator decides based on curriculum goals and may or may not include inquiry experiences.	Educator assesses students' prior knowledge to determine where inquiry and learning could go next.
Knowledge building	Knowledge is gained through educator-designed experiences, activities and events.	Knowledge is gained through exploration, investigation and communication in flexible groupings.
Resources	Resources are provided by the educator.	Resources are brought in by students, educators and experts.
Time	Topics are often taught at educator-determined times of the calendar year.	Topics are uncovered when students indicate interest and engagement. Inquiries involve many different curriculum areas and skills.
Focus	Activities are planned by the educator to focus on specific concepts.	Learning focuses on exploration, investigation and communication. Educator notices and names the learning.
Assessment	Typically of products and completed tasks from predetermined activities.	Includes a balance of observations, conversations and products generated through the inquiry.
Evidence of learning	Usually one method of representation selected by the educator (e.g., paper and pencil).	Students demonstrate learning in a meaningful manner (e.g., drawing, writing, building, constructing, videoing, drama and dance).

FIGURE 1.14 There are significant differences between a traditional primary program and one that takes an inquiry-based approach.

Revisit and reflect

This introductory chapter explored what inquiry-based learning is and how it benefits the primary learner. Inquiry is a dynamic process that is more important today than ever because to succeed in the future, students need to be able to do more than just memorize content. We explored why nurturing inquiry dispositions is important for young learners and what teachers can do to operate within an inquiry stance. And finally, we explored the capacity of primary learners to engage in inquiry and how inquiry-based learning environments strengthen their emerging qualities and skills.

THINQ

- What interests you most about inquiry-based learning?
- What are the opportunities and challenges you face in "going deeper" with inquiry learning?
- With your colleagues, consider Reproducible 1A, *An inquiry process model* (page 23). How does this compare to your current practice and capacity for inquiry?
- Consider Reproducible 1B, *Teacher inquiry readiness checklist* (page 24). How ready are you?
- How does inquiry learning align with the goals of your school and your school board or district?

Big Ideas

1.1 We learn by asking questions (inquiring).

1.2 Inquiry results in students learning how to learn.

1.3 Inquiry dispositions support risk-taking and a sustainable commitment to inquiry learning.

1.4 Inquiry learning, regardless of grade or subject area, has three common essential traits.

1.5 Educators should be co-learners who model their wonder and thinking with students.

1.6 Inquiry develops important learning dispositions that make primary students better, and more confident, learners.

1.7 Inquiry classrooms focus on big ideas and transferable skills.

See page 25 for a reproducible version of these big ideas.

Reproducible 1A

An inquiry process model

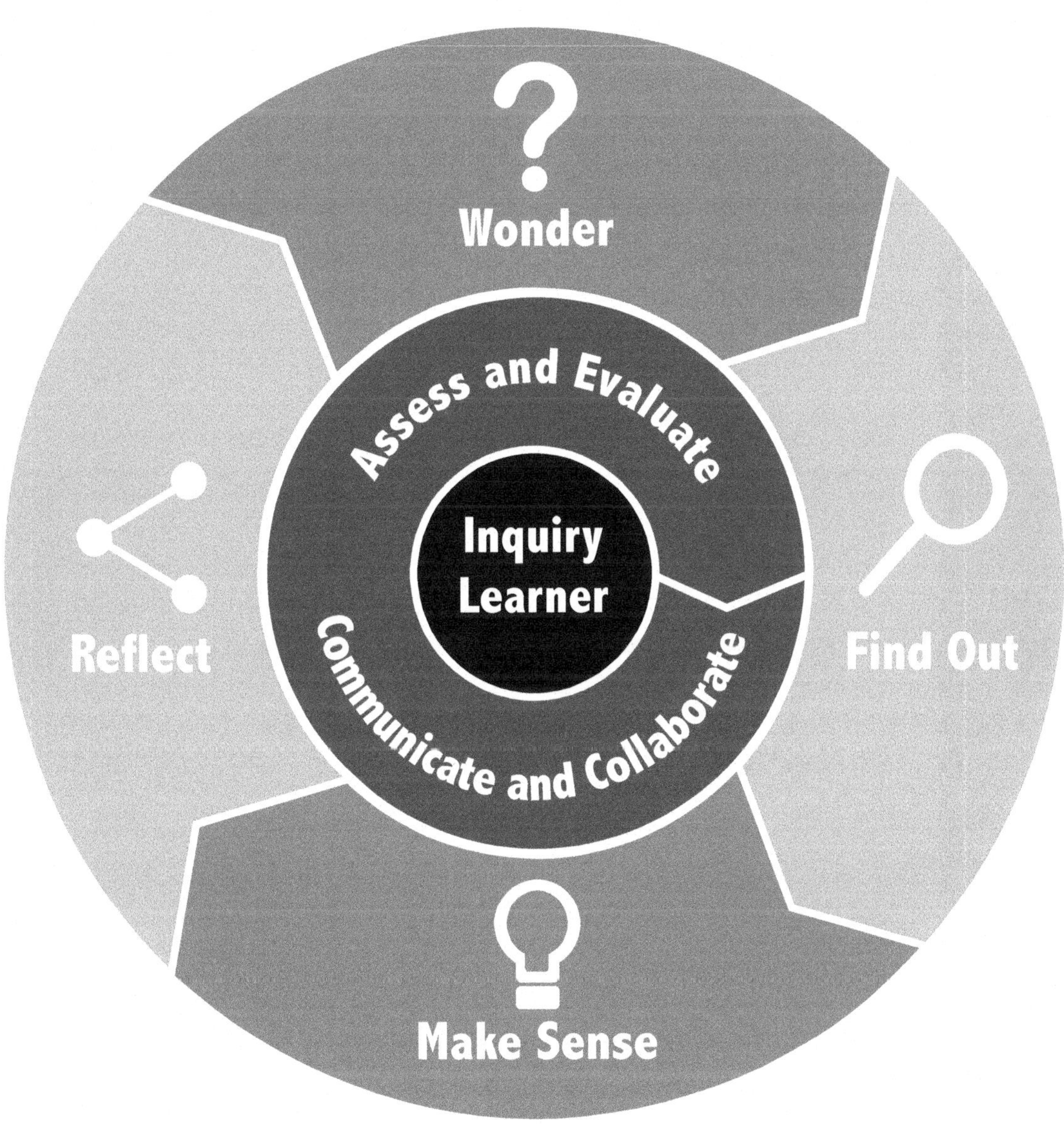

Reproducible 1B

Teacher inquiry readiness checklist

Check which of the following statements represent your knowledge, beliefs and understanding of inquiry learning. Use this checklist for self-reflection, for planning and sharing with colleagues, and to determine next steps in deepening your inquiry practice.

Conviction

- I believe in the main assumptions of inquiry-based learning: that learning is constructivist, learner-centered and demands critical and creative thinking.
- I am convinced by the research that advocates for taking an inquiry stance to learning in a play-based context.
- I believe that learners are competent, capable, curious and full of potential.

Commitment

- I am committed to bringing more inquiry-based learning to my classroom and have reflected on not only what makes me excited but also what makes me uncertain.
- I am connected to other committed educators who are interested in and supportive of inquiry education.

Capacity

- I understand that inquiry is an ongoing, open-ended process driven by the curiosity and wonderings of students.
- I understand what the role of a primary educator is in an inquiry-driven classroom.

Context

- I have thought about my strengths as an inquiry educator and the areas in which I need to make improvements.
- I accept that inquiry learning in my classroom should be a recursive, iterative and non-linear experience.
- I have thought about my students' individual readiness and know where to start.

Confirmation

- I know what my professional goals are with respect to doing more inquiry.
- I understand how I will assess my progress, what is working and how to improve.

Reproducible 1C

7 big ideas about inquiry-based learning at the primary level

1
We learn by asking questions (inquiring).

2
Inquiry results in children learning how to learn.

3
Inquiry dispositions support risk-taking and a sustainable commitment to inquiry learning.

4
Inquiry learning, regardless of grade or subject area, has three common essential traits.

5
Educators should be co-learners who model their wonder and thinking with children.

6
Inquiry develops important learning dispositions that make primary students better, and more confident, learners.

7
Inquiry classrooms focus on big ideas and transferable skills.

Chapter 2
ASSESSMENT AND EVALUATION:
Understanding how our primary learners are doing

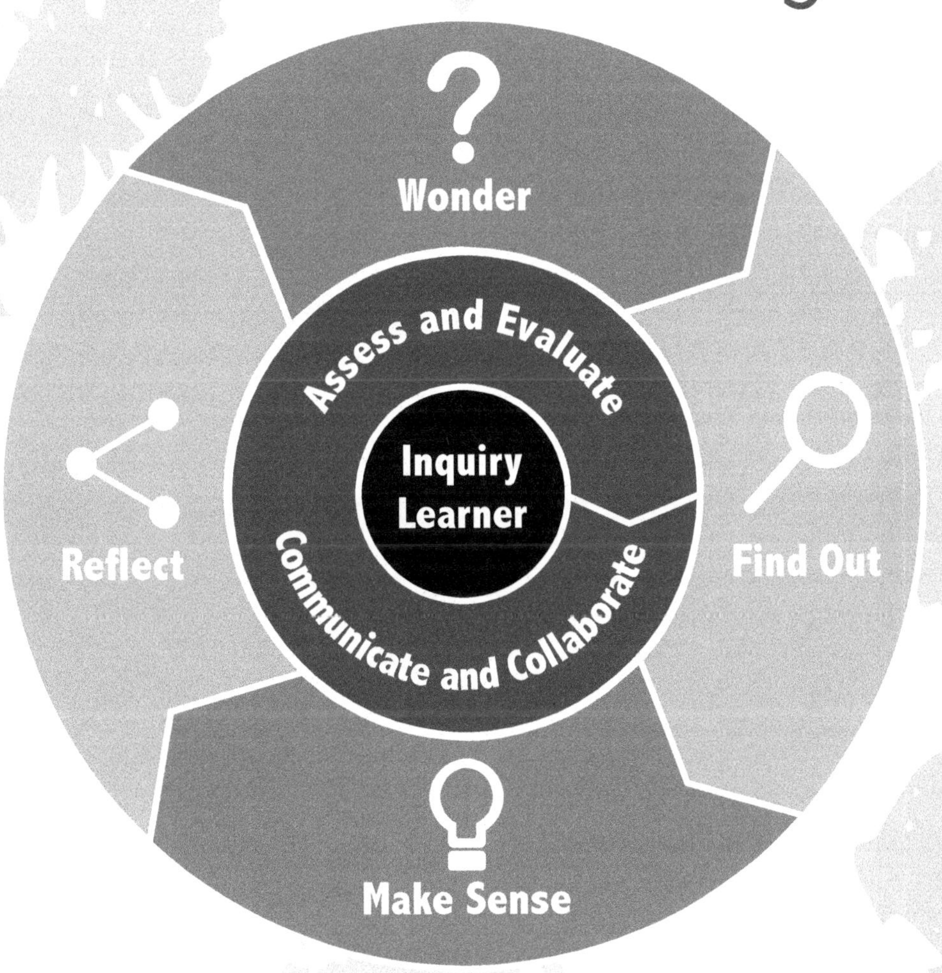

In relation to assessment the teacher positions themselves as an inquirer into the student's learning . . . . In an inquiry classroom instruction and assessment are kind of two sides of the same coin.

—Kath Murdoch

Big Idea
At the heart of assessment, teachers and students are asking, "How are we doing?"

This chapter examines key considerations in assessing inquiry-based learning. We explore six essential inquiry abilities that can anchor assessment planning, the role of students as partners in the assessment process, the important role of feedback and practical ways to document and support balanced assessment that moves learning forward.

2.1 How do we assess inquiry?

We begin our assessment discussion by acknowledging that traditional notions of assessment focused on correct and incorrect answers (passing and failing) do not resonate in an inquiry-based primary classroom. Grades 1 to 3 are important years for establishing literacy and numeracy foundations and to support students in becoming autonomous, self-regulated learners. So it is best to see assessment as a way to improve student learning, rather than a way to determine what is "right" or "wrong" (see figure 2.1).

Assessment is useful, constructive and positive for both educators and young learners because it sheds light on what a student knows and can do. Students and teachers should regularly and intentionally make time to reflect on how they are doing with their inquiry learning journey by asking independently, "How am I doing?" and collectively, "How are we doing?" These questions are relevant to both academic and social-emotional learning. They allow students to develop an understanding of their needs as individual learners, and they allow educators to reflect on whether or not we are operating a supportive learning community.

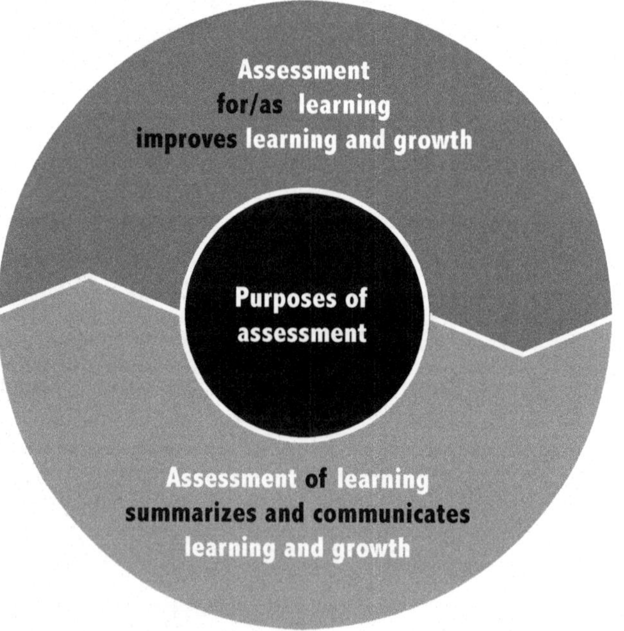

Source: Ontario Ministry of Education, 2010.

FIGURE 2.1 Teachers can apply the sound assessment practices they already possess to the inquiry-based learning that happens in their classrooms.

The simple answer to the opening question is that you will assess inquiry in your classroom the same way you assess other types of learning: by looking for evidence of knowledge, thinking, communication and application. You will use many of the same assessment skills that you currently possess, but you will likely tweak and use them in a slightly different way when you are approaching your classroom through an inquiry lens. In this chapter, we will discuss how to do that.

2.2 What exactly do we assess during inquiry learning?

Big Idea
Inquiry skills and abilities can, and should, be assessed.

CONVICTION
Are you convinced that primary learners can and should be developing their inquiry abilities and that you can help them do it?

The processes and skills of an inquiry stance are the core of inquiry and assessment. Inquiry should be as varied and unique as each classroom and learner, but the processes and skills should remain constant. We have identified six essential inquiry abilities that can help you and, equally important, your students, understand what inquiry is all about (see figure 2.2).

Before we discuss these in detail, we want to share that primary-aged students can indeed develop these inquiry skills and abilities. We have seen it with our own eyes! Just as you establish classroom routines and behavior protocols with your students, you can also help your students develop inquiry skills and abilities.

Ask questions

The first essential ability of inquiry learners is to ask questions. Young learners are natural questioners, and it is the job of primary educators to encourage, welcome and invite their questions and use them to drive inquiries. Students will ask questions based on wondering, observations and experimentation, and they are a key element of "understanding what is currently known" and also of "thinking together" as we clarify meaning, stretch our thinking, uncover beliefs, and innovate or create something new.

We know that learning happens best when students are engaged in their learning; when students' own questions drive the learning, not only may they be more invested but they are also building lifelong skills of agency (Edutopia, 2015; Hough, 2022; Organisation for Economic Co-operation and Development, 2019; Rothstein & Santana, 2011). Asking questions is an essential skill and supports all other essential abilities. Chapter 3, *Wondering and questioning: The heart of inquiry* (page 59), provides more information on questioning and assessing this essential inquiry skill.

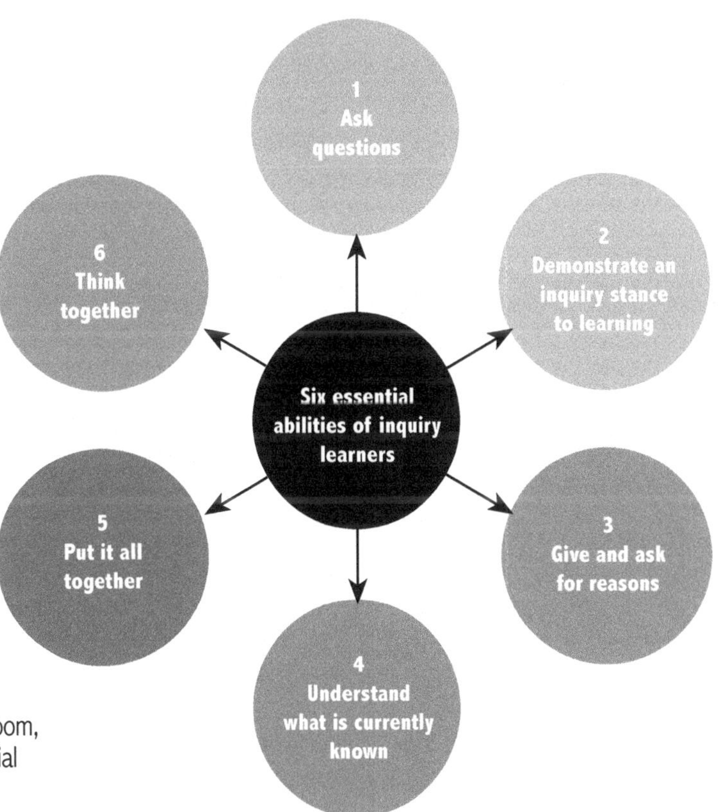

FIGURE 2.2 In an inquiry-based classroom, teachers assess and evaluate the essential abilities of students as inquiry learners.

Demonstrate an inquiry stance to learning

When students and teachers demonstrate an inquiry stance to learning, they are embracing curiosity and wonder, resiliency, reflection, hopefulness and open-mindedness. In chapter 1 (page 5) we called these concepts "inquiry dispositions." Although we have highlighted five inquiry learning dispositions, it is often best to choose one at a time to focus on. Inquiry dispositions should have meaning to your students and be selected based upon the specific focus within your classroom, or in connection to your school, board, or district priorities.

> **CONTEXT**
> Where are the inquiry abilities of learners in your classroom? What can they do and what could be developed further?

To support your thinking around inquiry dispositions, we have included Reproducible 2A, *How to model and assess inquiry dispositions* (page 51). This reproducible defines the dispositions and offers suggestions on what they may look like in your classroom. It also outlines how inquiry-based learning supports these dispositions and provides prompts for student reflection which could be used for student self-assessment. It is especially important for students to have time to reflect on their inquiry dispositions while in the process of an inquiry, and not just at the end. In a primary classroom, technology can help capture student responses to reflection prompts (see figure 2.3).

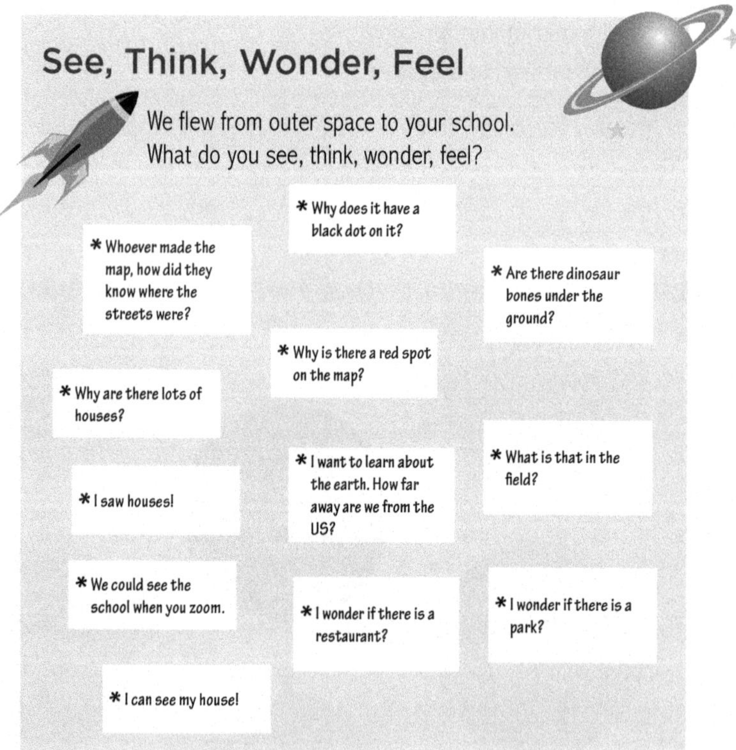

FIGURE 2.3 A digital tool such as Padlet can capture questions asked by grade 2 students in response to being introduced to an aerial map of their community on Google Maps.

It is our position that when an inquiry stance is fostered in a classroom, it contributes to a student's positive attitudes toward learning and toward themselves as a learner. Strengthening this inquiry disposition supports student agency and plays a key role in preparing our learners to be active and responsible citizens in the 21st century world.

Give and ask for reasons

When students give and ask for reasons, they are engaging in high level critical and creative thinking processes. These include conceptualizing, analyzing, synthesizing and evaluating. Students benefit when the development of this inquiry ability is made explicit and supported through a structure or methodology. For example, students may apply a visible thinking routine such Harvard's Project Zero (n.d.): "What makes you say that?" These higher level critical thinking skills could be focused upon in greater detail within a particular unit or throughout the inquiry process.

Understand what is currently known

This fourth essential ability, understand what is currently known, homes in on students' understanding of content knowledge and the processes used to find a response to an inquiry. Although teachers can find out what students know by asking questions, allowing for preliminary experimentation and exploration will help primary students to understand what they know and will keep your classroom positioned in an inquiry stance.

Inquiry in Action

Initial ideas + exploration = new knowledge

Providing opportunities for exploration helps students and teachers challenge initially held ideas and formulate new knowledge. Jacob's grade 2 Health and Physical Education curriculum includes a unit on sending and receiving. His goal was for the student to learn the best way to send and receive an object. He decided to surface their original ideas, allow for exploration and then help students to synthesize their new knowledge.

Key question

What is the best way to send and receive something?

Initial ideas

Shared by grade 2 students:

- small things go farther
- light objects are easier to catch
- heavy things go farther
- round things are easier to catch

Exploration

Jacob had the students explore throwing and catching a variety of objects including small hard balls, large soft balls, large hard balls, rubber chickens, foam pieces, pieces of cloth, markers, and baseball mitts. Students investigated how variables such as weight and size can affect distance and accuracy, as well as their own comfort level.

New knowledge

- light things don't actually go very far
- small things are easier to catch than big things
- soft things are easier to catch but harder to throw
- depends how good you are at throwing and catching

Chapter 4, *Finding out* (page 85), provides more detail on assessing the essential ability of understanding what is known and explores the ways students gather and use information at this stage of the inquiry process.

Putting it all together

Our fifth essential ability, putting it all together, asks students to apply what is known and draw and communicate conclusions. At this stage, students work toward making sense or synthesizing all of the information they have collected and begin looking for patterns or trends. For example, students may be communicating through mathematical processes such as graphs or charts, or they may be looking for patterns or trends on a digital map they have created collaboratively.

Chapter 5, *Making sense* (page 111), takes a deeper look at assessing the essential ability of putting it all together.

Inquiry for ALL

Some students may find it difficult to express their understanding through writing. They could be multilingual learners or have a learning exceptionality. Teachers can use illustrations and other visuals such as graphic organizers to collect evidence of student learning.

Think together

The sixth essential inquiry ability connects to the reflect and share stage of the inquiry process and is an opportunity for students to share their new knowledge and push the thinking even deeper by reflecting on their ideas or conclusions. It asks students to listen to each other with respect, to think together to build on each other's new ideas, to assist in drawing inferences and to identify their own assumptions and beliefs. Thinking together allows for idea improvement and the creation of new knowledge. Underlying this ability is the belief that ideas and knowledge are strengthened when shared.

You may find Reproducible 2B, *The six essential inquiry abilities for assessment* (page 52), and Reproducible 2C, *An inquiry rubric* (page 53), helpful in your thinking about and planning for inquiry assessment. Chapter 6, *Reflecting and sharing* (page 139), provides more detail on the essential ability of thinking together.

THINQ

- Which of the six essential abilities of an inquiry learner do you feel that primary-aged students naturally possess? What might be the hardest to develop, if any?
- How do the six essential abilities of an inquiry learner connect to your mandated curriculum?
- How could you use the six essential abilities of an inquiry learner to support planning of formative and summative assessments?

Inquiry in Action

Bubble Mania: What does a STEAM inquiry look like in grade 2?

Students in a grade 2 class participated in an inquiry exploring science, technology, engineering, the arts and math (STEAM). The inquiry addressed some key expectations from the teacher's grade 2 curriculum and also supported the development of literacy, numeracy and essential inquiry skills.

The inquiry began with a provocation where students were shown a video clip of giant bubbles — without showing how they were made — and students blowing lots of tiny bubbles. Students were curious about many things and had lots of questions about the best way to create a bubble-maker that could produce different kinds of bubbles, especially big bubbles. Students brainstormed ideas and looked at potential building materials. They shared their ideas and concepts with peers. Students investigated what could make the biggest bubble through experimentation. They created, tested, tweaked, tested again and observed what worked and what didn't work, gathering valuable knowledge about how best to design a bubble-maker (see figure 2.4).

At this point the teacher stopped the experimentation — which was hard because the students were having so much fun — and brought the students back together to share what they observed, what seemed to work and their ideas for design improvement. They reported what they had learned through the process this far. Then they had a chance to apply it again.

Through this inquiry, students were able to develop their essential inquiry abilities as well as deepen their understanding of the math and science behind their designs. They had a chance to reflect on their learning and what they might try differently next time, and they considered the advice they would give to someone trying to build a bubble-maker. In the end, they were left still wanting to learn more, like how they could build a bubble-maker that creates a bubble that isn't a sphere.

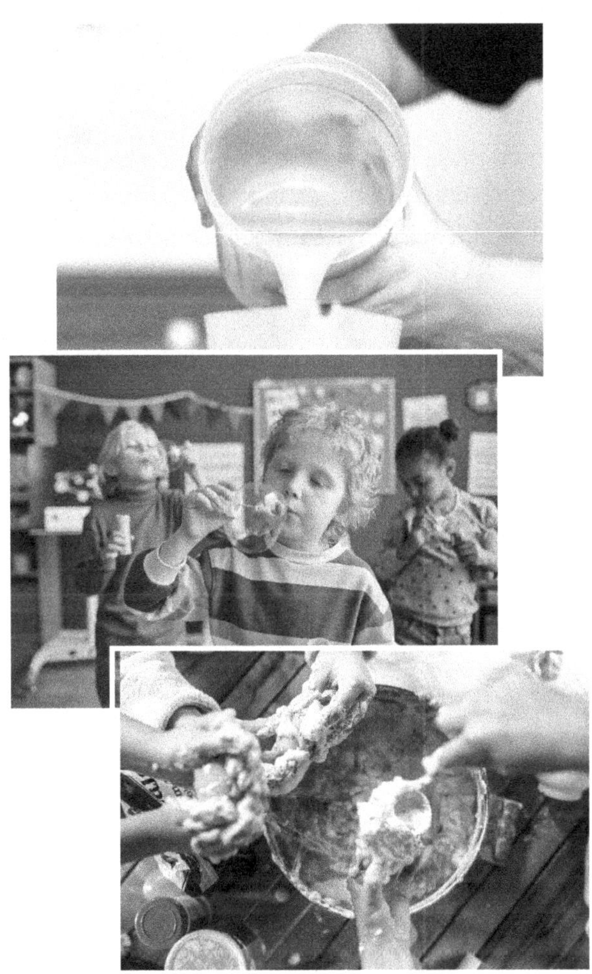

FIGURE 2.4 Students engage in hands-on, fun activities to further STEAM inquiry.

THINQ

- How did this teacher provoke her students' thinking? What other provocations could she have used?
- How did this teacher give students an opportunity to stretch their thinking?
- What opportunities for assessment and evaluation would be available in this example?
- What inquiry dispositions have the students demonstrated?

2.3 How can we become partners with our students in assessment?

Big Idea
Assessment should be welcomed, not dreaded, by students.

Learning activities and assessment should be as seamless as possible, so that students understand that assessment is how teachers determine what students know and can do at a particular point during a learning period. The more that we can involve students in the assessment process, the better chance we have of teaching students that assessment is a helpful and natural part of improving as a learner. In this section, we discuss noticing and naming the learning as well as co-creating learning goals and success criteria.

CONTEXT
How do students in your classroom feel about assessment?

CAPACITY
As a co-learner, how do you currently model and reflect on your inquiry abilities with your learners? How could you be more effective or intentional?

Noticing and naming the learning

One way to build assessment partnerships with our students is for educators to "notice and name the learning." Noticing and naming the learning is a form of descriptive feedback intended to make learning visible to the learner. As students participate in and reflect on inquiry experiences, noticing and naming the learning helps them develop and deepen their understanding of what learning looks like (see figure 2.5).

When students are given the opportunity to notice and name the learning with other learners, they begin to share in the learning, reflect on their own learning and consider the learning of their peers. This supports and fosters students' growth and helps them learn the language and skills of assessment. This also allows young learners to practice metacognition.

As a form of feedback, noticing and naming the learning offers educators many opportunities to: (1) make thinking and learning visible, (2) consolidate learning, (3) build metacognitive skills, (4) show growth in learning, and (5) identify for educators and learners where to go next in the learning. Figure 2.6 provides examples for the different purposes of noticing and naming the learning.

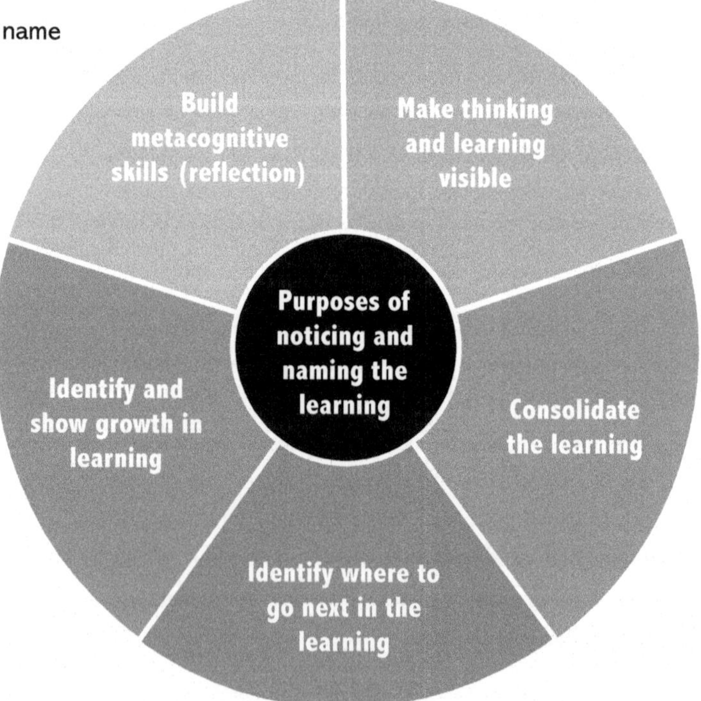

FIGURE 2.5 Noticing and naming the learning makes learning visible for both educators and students and helps to foster assessment partnerships.

Examples of noticing and naming inquiry learning		
Purpose	**Description**	**Inquiry example**
Make inquiry thinking and learning visible	Noticing and naming inquiry learning.	As her grade 3 students were exploring different types of materials to build structures, the teacher approached a pair of students and said: "I noticed that every time your structure collapses, you experiment with a new type of material. This shows that you are being an inquirer and keeping an open mind."
Consolidate the learning from inquiry	Noticing and naming learning from an inquiry to help consolidate and make explicit what knowledge and skills have been constructed.	A teaching team had been facilitating an inquiry on the ways in which humans have an impact upon animals and the places where they live. After a nature walk through a local community forest, students had brainstormed various human factors that may be having an impact. Students had been placed into small groups and each group was learning more about one of these factors. After each group shared with the class, the teachers asked each individual student to draw a conclusion about the top three factors having the greatest impact on animals and their habitats. In different small groups, the students compared their top three factors and were surprised at the various choices that had been made.
Build metacognitive skills through reflection	Noticing and naming the learning in order to make inquiry thinking visible and to help students reflect on what was done and why.	In grade 1, the teacher had spent time teaching his students about inquiry vocabulary as part of his language arts curriculum, which mandated that students use different speaking strategies for a variety of purposes. He then introduced a variety of loose materials to the students and gave them time to "muck about." Some students sorted the loose parts, some used them to build, some created jewelry, etc. At the end of the mucking about time the teacher asked students to reflect on how they were being inquirers. He prompted them to look at some of the inquiry vocabulary he had posted in the room. The students were confidently able to state that they had *investigated, made sense, persevered, wondered* and been *curious.*
Show growth in learning through the inquiry	Noticing and naming the learning to help with application of learning from the inquiry.	In a grade 3 inquiry into structures, the teacher had her students make careful notes in their inquiry journal to share their thinking at the beginning, middle, and end of the inquiry. The teacher had the students explain their growth in learning, as evidenced by the journal notes, and students shared their inquiry journal with their parents at parent-teacher conferences.
Identify where the inquiry should go next	Noticing and naming the learning in order to focus on new opportunities to extend the inquiry and the learning.	A grade 1 teacher observed a group of his students writing words in puddles with sticks. After recess, the teacher asked his students if they could find the words they were writing in the puddles inside the classroom. The teacher used that information to make a decision about where to go next in the learning and co-created a word wall with his students so that they could start to build a common vocabulary. He also introduced the students to online dictionaries on their tablets to build their technology skills and understanding.

FIGURE 2.6 Educators and learners can both notice and name learning, use it to make learning visible, and then extend and improve it.

Co-creating learning goals and success criteria

Another way we can become partners with our students in assessment is to involve them in the co-creation of learning goals and success criteria (see figure 2.7). This may seem counterintuitive when we are working with very young learners; after all, teachers know more about curriculum expectations and subject matter than their students. But learning goals provide a clear target for learning and ensure that students understand where they need to go and what they need to do. When students know what they're learning, they are empowered to play a greater role in their own learning (Coulombe & Causarano, 2018; McDowell, 2020).

Success criteria should be a work in progress in the classroom, a growing document where students have the opportunity to change, add or drop criteria as they deepen their understanding of what quality looks like. Whether teacher created or co-created, criteria for quality in an inquiry should focus on the learning happening through the inquiry, not on task completion. Completing a task does not always mean learning has occurred. Using student friendly language is also important, as is avoiding a long list of criteria for quality. Success criteria will play a crucial role in helping build capacity both peer and self evaluation.

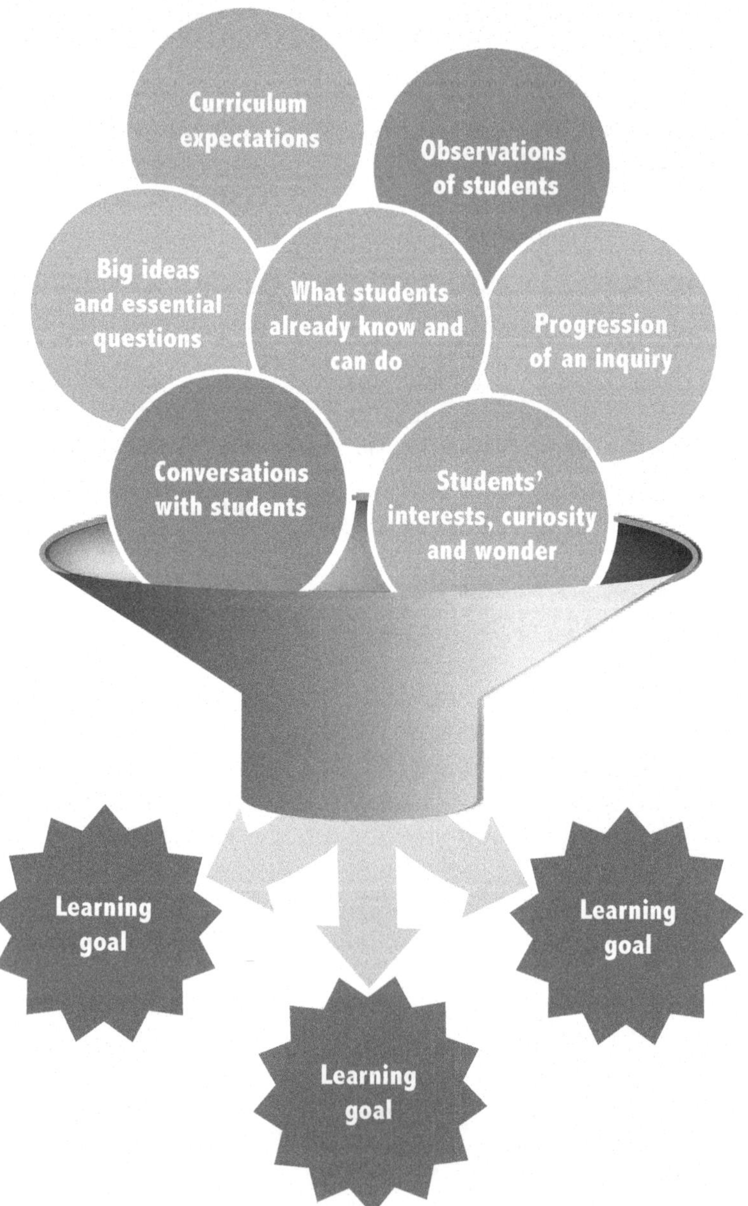

FIGURE 2.7 Learning goals are shaped by many factors. They represent the knowledge, skills, abilities and dispositions that students develop based on curriculum expectations.

THINQ

- Have you had success with using noticing and naming as an assessment strategy?
- How could you make noticing and naming a greater part of your everyday practice?
- What other strategies do you employ to make students assessment partners in your classroom?

2.4 How can I use feedback to improve learning during an inquiry?

Big Idea
Feedback plays a critical role in increasing student learning.

Research suggests that effective feedback, when accepted and acted upon and used in conjunction with clear learning goals, has the capacity to motivate and empower learners, as well as improve student achievement (Frey, Hattie, & Fisher, 2018; Hattie & Clarke, 2019). This applies to inquiry-based learning classrooms, just as it does in other classroom situations.

In order for feedback to be effective, students must see a purpose for the feedback. Effective feedback is dependent on clearly established learning goals and criteria for quality (Brookhart, 2012). There must be a clear connection between what students are learning and what they are doing. In order to support students in inquiry learning, feedback should be specific to inquiry abilities, skills or dispositions.

Feedback is not merely advice or praise, nor is it highlighting mistakes or deficiencies. Feedback should be task specific. It should clearly describe student strengths or where a student is going and offer steps or suggestions that can help the learner decide what's next in their learning journey. Feedback must be timely, and primary learners will benefit from on-the-spot oral feedback throughout the inquiry process (Chappuis, 2012; Wiggins, 2012). Students must also be provided with an opportunity to immediately act on feedback they receive.

CONVICTION
Are you convinced by the research that feedback is a critical strategy for improving student learning?

CONFIRMATION
Do your own classroom experiences validate the research about the positive impact of feedback on learning?

Inquiry in Action

A feedback protocol

Feedback is a skill that needs to be taught explicitly and practiced. It is likely that most of your primary students will be new to giving effective feedback. The following protocol can be used with primary students.

First target

In pairs, have students practice listening to one another without interruption while making eye contact.

Second target

Have each student listen carefully and then repeat what the other student has said. Not word for word, but the main idea or a point or two.

Example: "I heard you say you think that police officers are good role models."

Third target

Have each student listen carefully, repeat what the other student has said, and then make one suggestion.

Example: "I heard you say you think police officers are good role models. Why?" or "You think police officers are good role models. Can you give a reason why?"

Once students feel they have become good at giving feedback they can come and demonstrate for you. Then you can rotate each student to a new partner and repeat the process.

Effective feedback needs to be modeled and explicitly taught. Our learners need to know that feedback should be focused on the work, not the person. Feedback is specific and provides a suggested action to take. Students may benefit from feedback stems or prompts such as:

- one strength is...
- and next time...
- I noticed that...
- your idea is...
- I wonder if...

To support students in providing effective feedback to their peers, invite them to look at feedback samples and deconstruct what makes useful feedback. In addition to being taught how to give feedback, students should also learn how to receive feedback, as well as how to question or disagree with feedback when appropriate (e.g., "You said I needed more pictures as examples, but I have included four pictures."). Feedback involves hard work from all involved but ultimately, the person giving the feedback should not be working harder than the person receiving the feedback. Figure 2.8 provides a list of suggestions on how to use feedback effectively during inquiry learning.

Student, teacher and peers all play a role in creating a feedback rich classroom. It is a relationship of reciprocity: if students receive the opportunity to provide other learners with feedback, they have the chance to share in the learning of others as well as reflect on their own. Learners benefit from being a part of the feedback cycle, from having more "eyes on their work," from giving feedback, and from participating in conversations centered around what quality work looks like. These mutually beneficial relationships are especially important to establish with primary learners who are just beginning to adopt this open learning stance. Reproducible 2D *Student exploration: Can you identify an argument?* (page 54) helps students consider how to offer constructive responses supported by reasons.

Strategies for effective feedback

1. Use technology (audio, video, photos and document sharing) to facilitate "real time" self and peer feedback.
2. Take advantage of opportunities to provide on-the-spot feedback to students based on evidence of learning gathered as you observe and converse with students in the midst of learning.
3. When posting the criteria of quality work for a particular inquiry, be sure to return to the list throughout the inquiry process to allow students to revise the list based on new learning in the class.
4. Provide students with exemplars of student work and ask them to provide oral feedback based on one or two criteria. Take samples of the feedback and use it for a class discussion on the qualities of effective feedback.
5. Highlight (do not annotate) a student's written work and return it to them, asking them to determine what criteria of quality was highlighted and how it can be improved.
6. Ask students to highlight in their written work their arguments and supporting evidence in different colors as a way to see at a glance if they are meeting important overall criteria.
7. When students submit work to you, ask them to identify one criterion that they would like you to provide feedback on (this feedback could differ from criteria used in self or peer assessment).
8. Provide students with (or post in class) checklists of basic requirements that they must complete before work is assessed. Return work that does not meet the checklist requirements (do not assess it).
9. Avoid or postpone, for as long as possible, putting marks, levels or grades on assessment pieces. Descriptive feedback is what is most helpful for the learner at this stage.
10. Ask yourself before you provide extensive feedback to students whether the learner has had opportunities to self-assess based on criteria for quality they understood.

FIGURE 2.8 There are many ways to provide effective feedback. What strategies work best for you and your students?

THINQ

- What methods of feedback do you feel most confident with? Which new strategies would you like to try and why?
- How do you create classroom conditions where students are effective, comfortable and confident in giving, accepting and questioning feedback?

Educators Ask

How can we provide opportunities for students to act on feedback in a meaningful way?

One effective way to provide useful feedback to students is through the use of tablets. We saw this in action when students in a grade 1 class began an inquiry focused on community.

Although focused largely on some big ideas in their social studies curriculum, it also incorporated other curricular expectations and provided an opportunity for students to strengthen their inquiry skills and dispositions. After some initial exploration of the concept, they began trying to answer the question "What makes a community great?"

One task they completed was to explore their classroom as a community (see figure 2.9). With partners, they created short videos highlighting what made their class a community and what made it great. The students made their initial videos in a short period of time, immediately shared their work and asked for feedback from peers, which was provided using a "stars and stairs" model.

Students were then given the opportunity to explore the idea of their school as a community. Acting on feedback they had received, they then took their learning deeper, this time creating videos of their school as a community and highlighting what made it great. They shared their work and again invited feedback. Finally, they explored their neighborhood as a community, including visits to a local fire station and a grocery store, and shared their learning in another series of videos highlighting what made their community great.

FIGURE 2.9 Students can explore their community.

2.5 Why is balanced assessment important in primary classrooms?

Big Idea
Balanced assessment is essential for equity, reliability and validity.

Inquiry assessment is a three-stage, iterative process that entails gathering, evaluating and responding to evidence of the quality of a student's inquiry skills and dispositions (see figure 2.10). When we gather evidence of each student's thinking and learning, evaluate their understanding and skill in a fair and accurate manner, and respond appropriately to their needs, we can feel confident in our inquiry assessment. But how do we ensure we are gathering evidence of each student achieving their best, interpreting it in an unbiased and honest manner, and responding to the needs of each unique learner in our class?

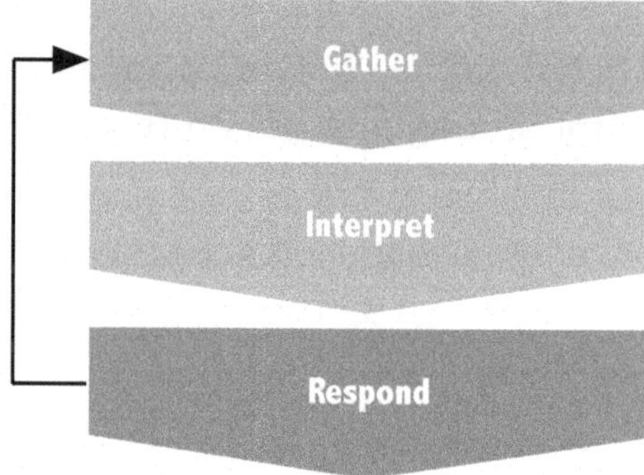

FIGURE 2.10 There are three stages to the inquiry assessment process.

Given the emergent and diverse nature of literacy development among primary students, it is essential to triangulate assessment data in order to make assessment fair for, and reflective of, all learners. This means collecting evidence through a balance of conversations, observations and products (see figure 2.11). Another way of thinking of this is gathering evidence of what learners say, what learners do and what learners create.

Do you ever suspect that a student knows or understands more than what they have shared on a test or project? Is this really an issue of their not understanding, or is it about the types of opportunities they have been given to communicate their learning? That same student may be able to better share their understanding through conversation or some other demonstration of learning. Conversations and observations can give us a clearer and more equitable insight into student learning. They can also help us provide more timely and practical feedback. Gathering evidence of student learning by listening to and observing what students are saying and doing, in addition to what they create, can help give a more accurate assessment of student learning (Ontario Ministry of Education, 2010, 2016a).

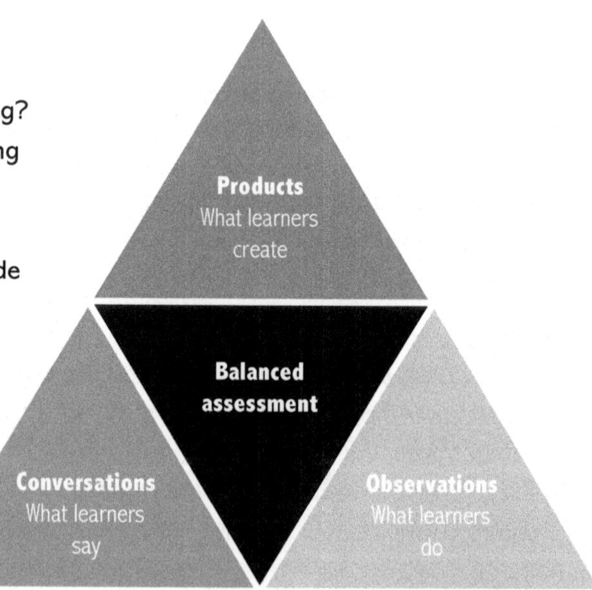

FIGURE 2.11 We can feel confident in our assessment of primary students when we have captured evidence of learning in a variety of ways.

Observations and conversations are not only powerful formative assessment tools but also can be used as evaluative assessment. For example, if a student is able to demonstrate logical thinking during a small group discussion or if in your conversation with the student they articulate their logic, then this evidence is absolutely valid. If they are unable to demonstrate their logic for a similar problem during a written task, it may be that they require support with word choice, organizing their thinking or writing it down.

> **CONVICTION**
> How convinced are you that for primary learners a balanced approach to gathering evidence is essential for fairness, reliability and validity?

As we move into the second stage of the iterative inquiry assessment process we begin interpreting the evidence we have gathered. In order to increase the validity of our interpretation, we must make sure that the criteria of quality are understood by the learner in advance. Co-creating the criteria and providing timely feedback based on the criteria will ensure that our assessment is more valid.

During the third stage of the inquiry assessment process, we respond to the evidence of learning we have gathered and interpreted. You should consider whether to carry on with the next task confident in the student's abilities or, alternatively, provide additional feedback or redesign your teaching next steps.

Throughout these three stages of inquiry assessment, our decisions will have an impact on our goal of gathering evidence of students achieving their best work at a given point in time, positively or negatively (see figure 2.12). This is an exciting, creative aspect of teaching — deciding what pedagogical moves you will make to provide the best instructional and assessment methods for your students. The beauty of inquiry learning is that you have the time and opportunity to observe students learning, engage the learner in conversations and provide feedback that moves their learning forward as you proceed through an inquiry.

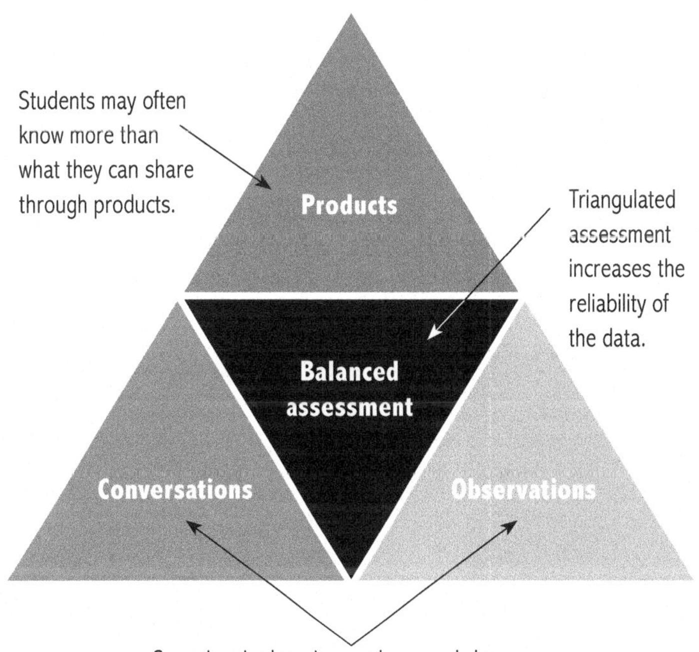

FIGURE 2.12 There are three important reasons why a balanced approach to inquiry assessment is essential to gathering reliable and valid evidence of student learning.

2.6 How can we use evidence and documentation to improve learning?

Big Idea
There are as many ways to document as there are to learn.

Capturing evidence of student learning is critical to fair and balanced assessment. As you can see in figure 2.13, there are many ways to capture student learning in an inquiry-based classroom, and primary learners can play a key role in documenting their own learning, Reproducible 2E, *28 ways to document learning* (page 55), is also available. This evidence of student thinking and learning, or documentation, can be used in the process of pedagogical documentation. Pedagogical documentation encourages us to listen to student voice, understand more about how students think, and reflect on how best to deepen and extend learning. So what makes documentation pedagogical? *Pedagogical* refers to the process of deconstructing and analyzing documentation to make thinking and learning visible to educators, students and parents.

CONTEXT
How much of your documentation is pedagogical? How do you know?

FIGURE 2.13 Choosing how best to document learning depends on the unique characteristics of you and your learners.

It is not enough just to gather evidence. Our goal is always to use documentation to improve learning, and in this regard, less may be more. Large quantities of documentation, without analysis and understanding of what it means, may overwhelm educators and defeat the purpose of doing it. Pedagogical documentation should facilitate a deeper analysis of the student learning experience through the three phases of inquiry assessment. The process of pedagogical documentation can be framed into three stages and aligns nicely with our inquiry assessment process (see figure 2.14):

- observing and capturing
- collaborative analysis
- responding and sharing

Documentation through the stages of inquiry assessment

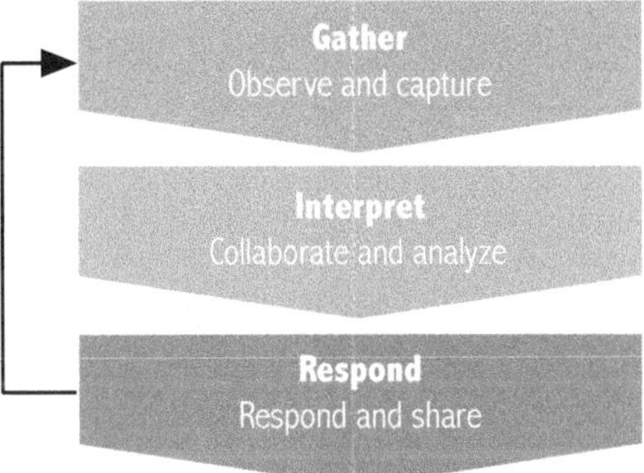

FIGURE 2.14 The process of pedagogical documentation can be framed into three stages and aligns nicely with our inquiry assessment process.

Teachers observe, and documentation is captured and gathered during the initial stage of inquiry assessment. Once multiple examples of what individual students are saying, doing and creating has been gathered, you can begin the analysis and interpretation. During the interpretation stage, we consider what the documentation is telling us about the learner, our instructional practice and what our next move is to best support that student. We consider how the information can support our assessment of inquiry, as well as our own professional learning. If possible, interpretation should be completed collaboratively with colleagues who can offer multiple perspectives on the documentation and response.

Primary learners should be invited to be partners in the process of pedagogical documentation and be provided opportunities to capture, select, interpret, respond, reflect upon and share their learning. Documentation can be planned or spontaneous. This is assessment as learning in action and is a powerful tool for developing important metacognitive skills, ownership of learning, and inquiry skills and dispositions. The following sections cover the relationship between documentation and assessment, managing the data, using technology for documentation, documentation and evaluation, and planning assessment.

THINQ

- How might you make your documentation more pedagogical?
- How might you make your interpretation more collaborative?
- How might you make your students more active partners?

The relationship between documentation and assessment

Pedagogical documentation is the journey that educators, students and parents take when they revisit evidence or artifacts of student inquiry in order to analyze and interpret ongoing thinking and learning, and guide next steps. Documentation provides an authentic account of a student's learning, and it shows accountability when planning and communicating each student's progress.

Documentation serves different assessment purposes in the inquiry classroom (see figure 2.15). When educators as researchers reflect on the documentation, they have an opportunity to determine whether their pedagogy has been effective and where to go next in instruction. Documentation also allows educators to determine what students are learning and whether they have demonstrated growth in relation to goals and expectations.

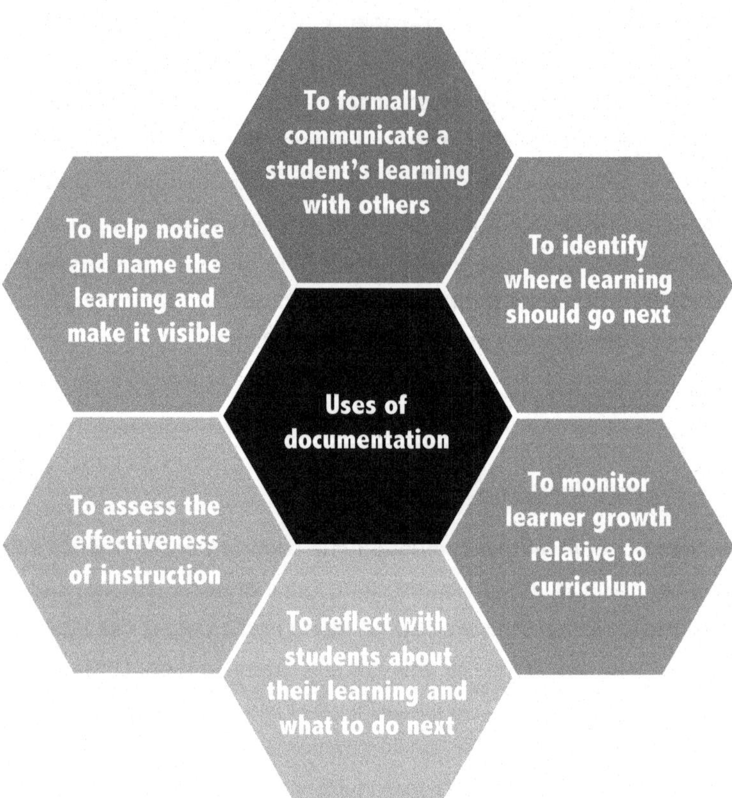

FIGURE 2.15 The value of documentation should be measured not by how much evidence is collected but by the degree to which it helps improve, summarize and communicate students' learning.

Managing the data

It is recommended that you develop a system to collect and manage documentation. Create a plan to ensure you capture evidence of all students over a period of learning and that no one has been missed. You may choose to simply use class list recording sheets to record observations or to use technology to support the gathering and storing of assessment data. The sheer amount of evidence you can collect can become overwhelming. Being clear and intentional about the purpose for your documentation (e.g., helping students to develop deep inquiry questions and supporting students in being able to "think together") may also help you to better focus your collection efforts. Students should also play a part in capturing, collecting and systematically sharing their learning with you. To build upon the assessment partnership, you may also consider digital student portfolios that help educators and students store, organize and share learning. Figure 2.16 outlines some important tips to remember when documenting.

CAPACITY

What are the greatest challenges you face in gathering, interpreting, responding to and managing documentation? What else do you need to know?

Documentation tips	
Take detailed notes	Record the date, time of day and context in which the image or video was taken. Your notes can be kept in a specific notebook or file, or you can simply jot down who you documented into your day plan book. This attention to detail will help you down the road when you engage in the analysis.
Keep your videos short	Try to keep your video recordings around 30 seconds to one minute in length. If you are capturing in the moment of learning, stop and start recording again. This will give you smaller videos to work with when you are reviewing your documentation. Long recordings can result in large digital files that are more difficult to upload and will quickly use up your storage.
Organize your data	Plan your organization strategy in advance. Will you be uploading images and storing them under the date, or will you be saving them under student names? How will students share or upload their documentation?
Keep it anonymous	Privacy is a concern when capturing images of students learning. Try to avoid identifiable features or names of students. Refer to your board or district's policy on capturing images of students.

FIGURE 2.16 The more documentation and analysis you do, the easier it will become.

Using technology for documentation

Today, in our pockets and knapsacks, we carry the most amazing information and communication technologies. Handheld devices offer primary educators powerful tools to make documentation and assessment more effective and efficient (see figure 2.17).

When educators share with Emma's family that "Emma's inquiry skills are much improved," they are now able to give tangible evidence through photos or videos of Emma's learning, which have been gathered over time. This use of technology makes the learning real to families. The capacity of these devices to capture in-the-moment learning brings practical meaning to the concept of making learning visible. Not only is gathering evidence more effective, but pedagogical analysis and sharing can be enhanced as well. We can now review, reflect more deeply upon and share moments in learning.

CAPACITY

How can you use technology to make your documentation more effective and efficient? What can you learn from your colleagues in this regard?

Using technology for documentation and assessment

Stages	Key questions	Issues
Planning	• What learning can I best document with technology? • What learning might I be unable to document unless I use technology?	• Learner wonderings and interests • Curriculum expectations • Family needs and expectations
Gathering	• What devices and applications should we use, and how and when will we use them? • What level of skill and understanding will I need, and whose advice could I seek? • What role might students play?	• Accessibility and reliability of devices • Educator expertise • Learner participation
Reflecting on learning	• How can I give in-the-moment feedback to learners? • How can technology allow me to better reflect on a student's learning? • Can technology help me to reflect upon my own practice? • How can students use it to reflect on their own learning?	• Printing, posting and sharing • Classroom display • Learner access • Professional reflection
Communicating learning	• How can I use it to create a record of a student's learning? • How can I use it to better share a student's learning with their families?	• ePortfolios and storage • Sharing with colleagues • Family access

FIGURE 2.17 Getting the most out of using technology for documentation requires forethought, collaboration and professional judgment.

Tech-Enabled Inquiry

Apps to support documentation

There are many digital tools that can be used to support documentation and make student thinking visible. When choosing a platform or tool, consider the purpose — are you using it to engage parents in the inquiry process and assessment, for your own professional learning, or as an opportunity to capture student voice? Also consider the ease of student use and whether the tool captures student thinking and learning, or also manages and stores information. Determining your purpose and audience will assist you in selecting the best tool or platform for your needs.

Google Workspace to Education Fundamentals (also known as *G Suite*; http://bit.ly/3vzXM2F) offers many features that support documentation. Many school boards are connected with Google Workspace and offer large digital storage. Google Drive allows you to create a folder system to organize your data. Google Docs, Google Maps, and Google Slides give you a platform to work collaboratively online, and Google Classroom offers a virtual classroom where you can have students collaborate.

Seesaw (http://seesaw.com) provides a way to display student work as well as link the images to the students so you can maintain a chronological record of your documentation. This platform also allows you to share with parents and have them comment on images.

Evernote (https://evernote.com) allows you to save notes and insert images into the notes. Notes can be saved in an online portfolio format that can be shared with students or parents.

The learning management system that your school district has purchased to use is likely to offer many built-in tools to help store and share student work and give access to parents so they can follow their student's progress. You can upload documentation, store it in a portfolio and share via students' portfolios. One example of this is *Brightspace Portfolio* (https://community.d2l.com/brightspace).

Numerous other apps support documentation by capturing student learning and helping to make student thinking visible. Some examples include *Adobe Spark Video* (https://express.adobe.com/page/9bPqZ), *Thinglink* (www.thinglink.com), *Padlet* (www.padlet.com), Explain Everything (https://explaineverything.com), *Educreations* (www.educreations.com) and *Book Creator* (https://bookcreator.com). Many of these apps work seamlessly in uploading files to other documentation platforms or sharing tools.

Technology is always changing. It is important to note that you should always check with the privacy policy of your board or district as there may be conditions regarding the ownership of material on different apps. For each digital tool, consider where information is stored and other licensing agreement details or restrictions such as the age of user. When in doubt, consult with your administrator or IT specialist.

THINQ

- How do you currently use technology to facilitate student learning?
- What technology do you use to capture evidence of learning for assessment purposes?
- What technologies does your district license or use?

Documentation and evaluation

Assessment of learning, where evidence of student learning is summarized, takes place at some endpoint in student learning. What that endpoint is and when it has been reached involves judgment; it may be determined by the curriculum, the end of an inquiry or unit, or in preparation for a reporting period.

Evaluations should only be given after students have had multiple opportunities to explore and make sense of an inquiry and practice, receive and act on feedback. It should not involve new skills or understandings, new tasks or additional success criteria. It should not introduce added layers of complexity that are new to learners.

A teacher who regularly documents and triangulates evidence of student learning will have plenty of data and a clear idea of how a student is doing before having to quantify the evidence into a mark. Likewise, when students are partners in the assessment process, they have a much better understanding of where they are in their learning. Although the demands of report cards and external pressures for marks may make you feel pressured to specifically quantify student learning against a mandated standard, we advise holding off as long as possible. The upcoming chapters provide specific and practical ideas to support assessment and evaluation at different stages of the inquiry process.

Educators Ask

I take lots of images of student work; aren't I already doing pedagogical documentation?

Capturing documents, images or videos of student work is a component of pedagogical documentation; however, it is just the first step in the process.

Pedagogical documentation is the process educators use to capture, gather, interpret, reflect and make instructional changes to support student learning. This shifts documentation beyond the act of simply capturing student learning to a situation where the educator becomes a co-learner with students and colleagues. When we engage in pedagogical documentation, we are engaging in the process of examining and responding to the learning.

If you are capturing images of student work and are interested in exploring pedagogical documentation, consider spending some time analyzing your triangulated evidence of learning. These guiding questions can help you begin to analyze your documentation.

- How might this evidence be useful?
- What patterns or items of interest do we notice from this evidence?
- What are the limitations of this evidence and what further questions emerge?
- Based on this documentation, what are the implications for future learning for this student or for our teaching?

Share your documentation with students to hear their perspectives. Having a colleague offer their opinion will also give you an alternative perspective of the learner and their learning. We have included Reproducible 2F, *A protocol for documentation* (page 56), to support your analysis of student work.

Planning assessment

An inquiry assessment plan is an outline of your learning intentions based upon your key questions (see figure 2.18) and learning goals. We encourage you to work collaboratively with colleagues as you will find the assessment planning process is the same regardless of grade level or subject area.

Key questions when creating an inquiry assessment plan

- How will I get to know my students so that inquiry activities will be purposeful and meaningful to them?
- How can I stretch and extend my students' curiosity and interests in terms of curricular topics and subjects?
- What is the real question or fundamental problem of the inquiry?
- What is the goal of this inquiry (e.g., consider key concepts, inquiry skills, inquiry dispositions, supporting content or corresponding curriculum expectations)?
- How will I sustain student curiosity and interest, voice and choice, diversity and originality?
- What opportunities will I provide for practice and feedback?
- What do I predict may be the areas of greatest student support?
- What are key misconceptions and preconceptions about this concept, topic, phenomenon or process?
- What are the criteria of quality for this inquiry?
- How will I support each student's learning during this inquiry?
- What quality evidence will I gather of student learning for this inquiry?
- How (and when) will I judge student achievement of this inquiry?

FIGURE 2.18 You can use these questions as a starting point for planning an inquiry unit.

THINQ

- Do you feel you have balanced evidence from triangulated sources? How might you address an imbalance, if there is one?
- In what ways could you incorporate pedagogical documentation into your daily practice? How could you engage students to help you in this process?

Educators Ask

Shouldn't students know the content and have the skills before beginning an inquiry?

At times we are asked to weigh in with an opinion on whether the "how," or the process with which a student applies inquiry skills and dispositions, is more important that the "what," or the specific content knowledge that is required in the inquiry.

This age-old "content versus skills" debate is unhelpful. Inquiry learning is a critical assessment and application of what is already known about a topic, synthesized in new ways to build new knowledge to answer a question or problem. Teachers who claim they must wait until students "know the content" before conducting an inquiry are confused about what inquiry learning is. Teachers who claim that content knowledge is not important to an inquiry are also confused about what inquiry learning is.

Another sticking point for teachers in inquiry learning is the desire to have students master inquiry skills before entering into an inquiry learning unit. This is an impossible aim because the development of inquiry skills is ongoing. Moreover, all learners continue to further develop their inquiry skills despite their years of experience and expertise.

The final sticking point of inquiry assessment involves the timing of assessment. Assessment practices of the past were typically "add-ons" at certain points, usually the "end" of a unit of study. Now we view assessment not as events but as everyday classroom experiences where learners show what they know, what they can do, look for advice and feedback, and provide the same for themselves and their peers.

Revisit and reflect

This chapter emphasizes the six essential inquiry abilities that we present as a way to anchor your assessment planning and communication with students. Key assumptions of the chapter were:

- assessment improves both teaching and learning
- inquiry is a dynamic process where learners build capacity to assess themselves and each other on an ongoing basis
- the phases of inquiry assessment (gather, interpret and respond) are dynamic and multifaceted
- pedagogical documentation can engage the learner and inform the teacher by supporting inquiry assessment

We explored how to engage students as partners in inquiry assessment, the critical role of feedback and how pedagogical documentation can support and enhance student voice, learning and experience within inquiry learning. Student learning is improved when both teacher and students can recognize and respond to the learning while it is taking place during an inquiry (Clarke & Hattie, 2019, OER4Schools, 2013).

Big Ideas

2.1 At the heart of assessment, teachers and students are asking, "How are we doing?"

2.2 Inquiry skills and abilities can, and should, be assessed.

2.3 Assessment should be welcomed, not dreaded, by students.

2.4 Feedback plays a critical role in improving student learning.

2.5 Balanced assessment is essential for equity, reliability and validity.

2.6 There are as many ways to document as there are to learn.

THINQ

- How might you use Reproducible 2G, *6 big ideas about assessment and inquiry* (page 57) to explain to family members why inquiry-based learning is important in today's world and how it can be meaningfully assessed and evaluated?
- How might the six essential abilities of inquiry learners support or enhance assessment?
- How might you help to scaffold student self and peer assessment of inquiry dispositions?
- In what ways could you make your students partners in inquiry assessment?
- What are the possibilities of inquiry assessment in your classroom? What are the challenges? How might you address head-on or work around these challenges?
- Complete Reproducible 2H, *Teacher checklist: Purposeful planning for inquiry* (page 58) to further your thinking on effective assessment planning.

Reproducible 2A

How to model and assess inquiry dispositions

Inquiry Disposition	What it looks like in a classroom	How inquiry-based learning supports this disposition	Student reflection prompts
Curiosity and wonder	Teachers and students are eager to learn or know more about the world and its people. They ask important, deep, relevant questions. These questions are not answered easily — nor does the teacher or student have the correct answer in mind at the outset. They are honestly perplexed by an issue/question/problem/challenge and have the motivation to uncover a possible answer/solution.	Inquiry-based learning begins with a question, a curiosity or a wondering.	An important question that I find interesting is . . . I really want to know . . . I think it is important to answer this question because . . . The question is hard because . . . I feel I'm becoming a better questioner because . . .
Resiliency	Teacher and students have a capacity to keep on trying and overcome. They enjoy the challenge of thinking deeply and persevering when faced with challenges. Teacher and students trust that they can figure out difficult problems by using their reason and intelligence.	An inquiry-based learning environment can provide a safe and inclusive environment to foster resilience. Students have opportunities to strengthen their adaptive skills and bounce back from mistakes.	I overcame a challenge by . . . What I learned from my mistake was . . . Next time I will . . .
Reflection	Teacher and students intentionally take time to think, wonder about and reflect on their thinking and learning. Student thinking is made visible throughout the inquiry process.	Inquiry-based learning supports metacognition. Students reflect on their thinking, their choices, further courses of action and unanswered questions.	I solved the problem by . . . I changed my thinking because . . . I improved my idea by . . . My biggest challenge was . . . A question I still have is . . . I am still confused by . . . My next step is . . .
Hopefulness	Teacher and students see the world as it is and like to think about how it can be improved. They care about and have a sense of purpose and commitment in their inquiries.	Inquiry-based learning is future oriented and involves problem-solving. It encourages students to create and share new knowledge and to be change agents.	I think solving this problem is important because . . . I feel . . . I think my ideas could make a difference because . . . We created new knowledge by . . .
Open-Mindedness	Teacher and students are genuinely interested in other perspectives and attitudes. They are open to possibilities and are willing to consider new ideas and view learning as a continual process.	Inquiry-based learning is an adventure. It is typically not a linear process but one with twists and turns. This gives students a feeling of what a true expert might feel when attempting to solve a problem.	My thinking is different than before because . . . A different way to think about this is . . . My prediction was right/not right because . . . A different way to do this might be . . .

Reproducible 2B

The six essential inquiry abilities for assessment

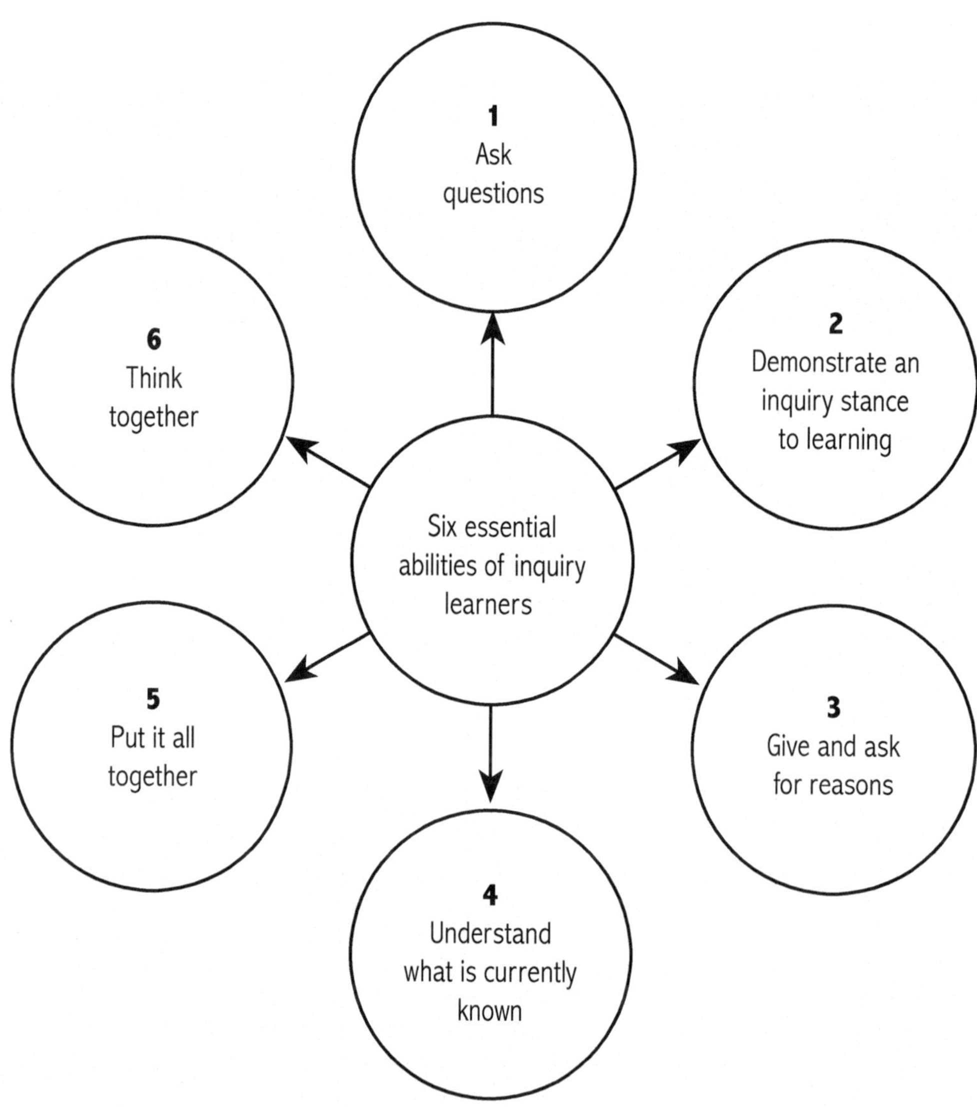

Reproducible 2C

An inquiry rubric

Areas that need work	Success Criteria Categories	How work exceeds
	Learn what is currently known about the question/problem The student will: • Demonstrate knowledge (e.g., facts, structures, principles) and understanding of content (e.g., concepts, ideas, relationships, safe procedures) important to the inquiry	
	Apply inquiry skills and processes The student will: • Apply inquiry skills to extend the inquiry, push thinking deeper, offer solutions and ideas not yet considered and reflect on learning • Make learning connections (e.g., between ideas, relating subject specific learning to a larger context, interdisciplinary connections)	
	Application of thinking skills The student will: • Use critical and creative thinking skills in order to engage in problem solving or provide an answer or course of action. • Use planning skills and strategies (e.g., brainstorming, formulating questions, generating ideas) • Use processing skills (e.g., observing, revising, interpreting, evaluating, justifying a conclusion based on evidence)	
	Communicate new understandings The student will: • Communicate clearly and purposefully for an audience • Express and organize ideas and information • Use appropriate and relevant vocabulary and terminology	

Reproducible 2D

Student exploration: Can you identify an argument?

Arguments are the ways in which we try to present our thinking to the world and convince others that our view is correct. Arguments do not have to involve anger and telling. Creating an argument is simply the way we reason or think through a question or problem.

Arguments have two main components: a belief followed by the reasons we believe. Arguments are different than explanations, opinions or descriptions.

Take a look at the statements below and decide which ones are arguments.

Statement	Is this an argument? If so, write the number 1 beside the belief and 2 beside the reasons for the belief.	Is this an explanation, opinion or description?
1. The rule about playing mini sticks at lunch is not fair. I want it to be changed.		
2. It is very muddy today. I better wear boots since I have to walk to school.		
3. Our lunch hour is too short. We only have 15 minutes which is not enough time to open and eat all of your food.		
4. Our class uses computers and tablets.		
5. We should paint in class because it is fun.		
6. All kids should get to have a pet. Pets help teach you to be responsible. Pets can also help to keep you active because they may need to get out and walk or play.		

You may notice that some arguments are stronger than others. Try to think why that is. Which argument do you think is the strongest? Why?

Reproducible 2E

28 ways to document learning

Reproducible 2F

A protocol for analysis of pedagogical documentation

Part 1: Studying the documentation

- Individually study the work of the learner.
- Make notes of what you see and hear to gather as much information as possible from the documentation:
  - What do you see?
  - What do you hear?

Part 2: Interpreting the documentation

- What does the documentation suggest about the learner's thinking?
- What are some questions I have?
- What are some assumptions I might be making about students and the learning?
- What ideas and questions are learners exploring?
- How did my words/actions influence the experience?
- Were there other influencing factors? What do I notice in different contexts?
- How might this information be used to plan for learning?

Part 3: Implications for practice

- What are the implications of this documentation for assessment for learning?
  - What further evidence of learning or information do I still need?
  - What might be the next action for the learner?
  - What does the evidence suggest to inform my pedagogical moves?

Source: Adapted from Kahlon, R. (n.d.). Pedagogical documentation. *Accessed at https://sites.google.com/tdsb.on.ca/robkahlon/best-practices/pedagogical-documentation on February 29, 2024; Ontario Teachers' Federation. (n.d.).* Protocol for analysis of pedagogical documentation. *Accessed at https://www.otffeo.on.ca/en/wp-content/uploads/sites/2/2018/05/Protocol-for-Analysis-of-Pedagogical-Documentation.pdf on November 29, 2023.*

Reproducible 2G

6 big ideas about inquiry assessment

1
At the heart of assessment teachers and students are asking, "How are we doing?"

2
Inquiry skills and abilities can, and should, be assessed.

3
Assessment should be welcomed, not dreaded, by students.

4
Feedback plays a critical role in improving student learning.

5
Balanced assessment is essential for equity, reliability and validity.

6
There are as many ways to document as there are to learn.

Reproducible 2H

Teacher checklist: Purposeful planning for inquiry

Check which of the following statements represent how you plan for inquiry learning. Use this checklist for self-reflection, planning and sharing with colleagues, and to determine your next steps in deepening inquiry practice.

- I design learning tasks connected to essential questions in students' lives and subject disciplines as well as to the world while focusing on clear and achievable learning targets.
- I design inquiry tasks that allow for optimal student autonomy and appropriate cognitive demand.
- I establish classroom conditions that support inquiry (e.g., purposeful student talk, individual reflective thinking, honoring student interests and experiences).
- My learning tasks and assessment plan detail inquiry learning opportunities based on the distinct stages of an inquiry process.
- My learning tasks and assessment plan promote growth in inquiry dispositions (e.g., curiosity, perseverance, risk-taking, hopefulness, open-mindedness).
- My learning tasks and assessment plan balance inquiry learning in addition to other learning opportunities.
- I have opportunities to co-plan, co-teach and co-assess inquiry learning activities and products with colleagues.
- I have resources that support my learning in inquiry-based pedagogies.
- Parents and community members will be apprised of and included in inquiry learning.

Chapter 3
WONDERING AND QUESTIONING:
The heart of inquiry

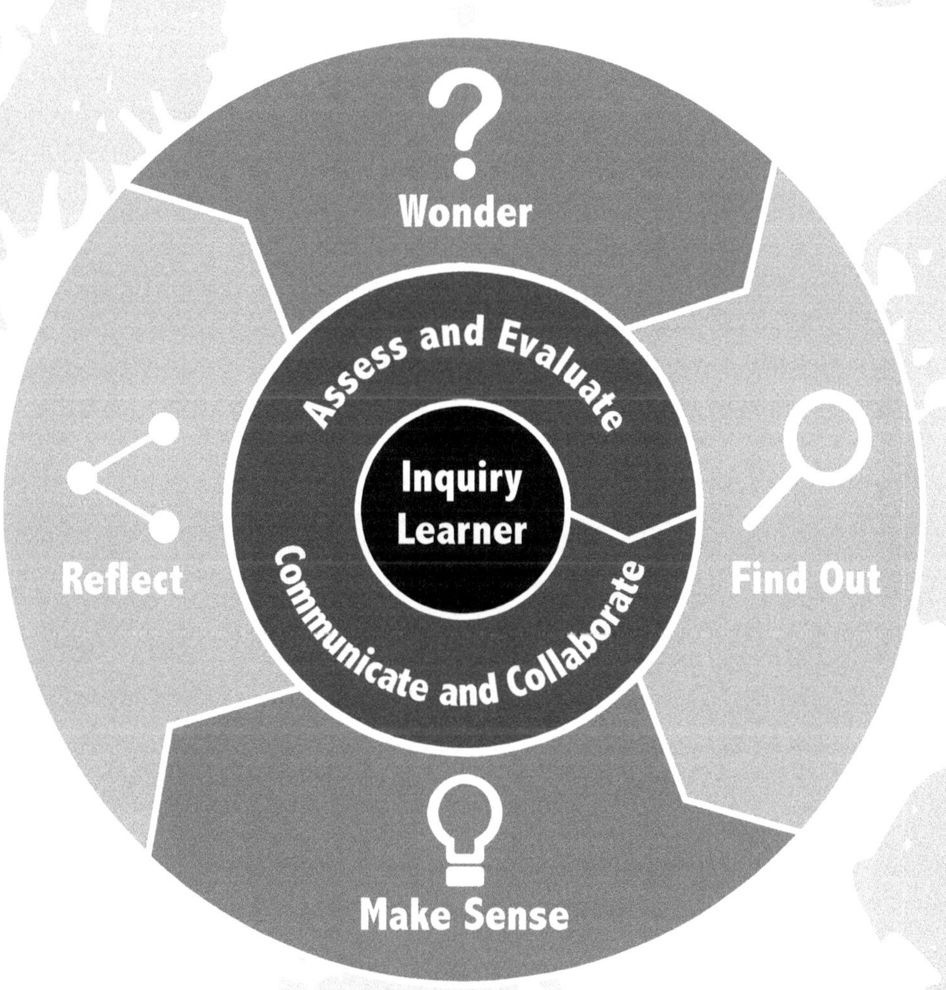

Thinking is not driven by answers. It is driven by questions.

—Richard Paul and Linda Elder

Big Idea
Our curiosity fuels our learning.

This chapter invites you to think about how you can help foster curiosity, risk taking and persistence in your students. We explore the importance of classroom culture that encourages wonder and inquiry and discuss the pivotal role of powerful inquiry questions in capturing and sustaining student interest. We also offer practical ideas on how to enhance young children's skills at asking questions and how to assess those skills.

3.1 How can I nurture wonder in my classroom?

Inquiry begins with wondering. Learning begins with questions. We are all curious about the way the world works. Our curiosity fuels our learning. Our curiosity provides purpose to our learning.

We can sense when wonder is at work in our students. They are both fascinated and focused. Questions arise. Imagination and critical thought transpire. At these moments, the learner feels excited and determined to dive deeper into their learning. How can we plan and prepare our classroom activities to allow students to become skilled questioners? How can we honor questions and position questions at the forefront of learning? Teachers should consider how to help students move from wonder to questioning and then from questioning to inquiry; the following sections discuss these shifts in more detail.

From wonder to questioning

Teachers have to feel confident in their co-learning stance with students in order to welcome questions to the fullest. Students need to know that in a caring and supportive inquiry community, questions should not be used to distract, belittle, bully or embarrass others. Instead, questions should be used to reflect our curiosities and drive learning. Similarly, teachers shouldn't ignore, deflect or discourage students' questions but encourage, stimulate and respect them. Student questions reveal three very important things to teachers: what students know, what students don't know and who they are (see figure 3.1). Questions reveal interests, fears, hopes, concerns, likes and dislikes.

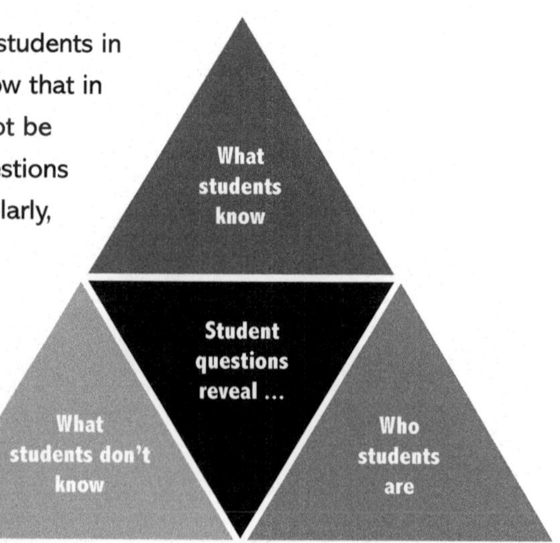

FIGURE 3.1 We can learn a lot about our students by listening carefully to the questions they ask.

Questioning plays center stage in an inquiry classroom (see figure 3.2). It is the one of the six essential abilities of inquiry learners. Questioning also intersects and supports the other five essential abilities. You cannot show curiosity without questions. Using questions for different purposes and different perspectives demonstrates open-mindedness. Asking for reasons complements the skill of giving reasons. Understanding what is currently known and putting it all together involves questioning authority, being skeptical and assessing sources. And lastly, there is no thinking together without questioning together.

FIGURE 3.2 In this classroom, the teacher engaged students with the thought-provoking question: What is learning? The students will add to their initial responses throughout the school year.

From questioning to inquiry

Authentic inquiry is launched with questions or problems that learners want answers to or want to learn more about. There is a common misunderstanding that educators must wait for the right question for an inquiry to start. Anything that sparks students' interest can be the right question (see figure 3.3). There are times when questions may not lead to deep inquiries, or there may be provocations that we think will spark an engaging investigation but do not. Don't be discouraged! Questions, shared events or problems will arise, and meaningful inquiry will happen. Don't wait for it — be engaged, maintain an inquiry stance and develop a pedagogy of listening, and your learners will lead you there.

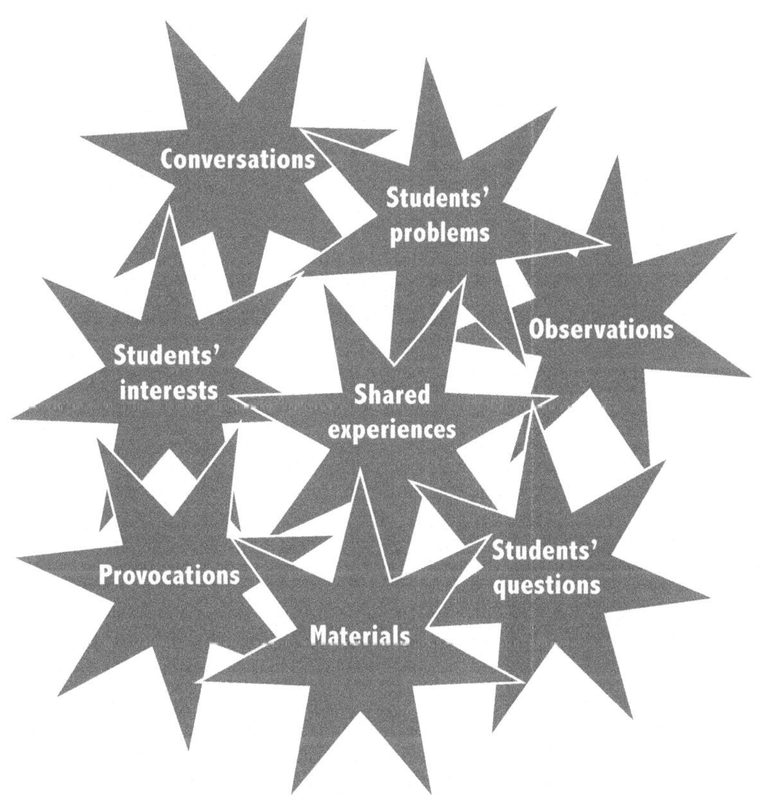

FIGURE 3.3 The spark for an inquiry can come from many different sources.

3.2 How do inquiry questions drive learning?

Big Idea
The purpose of an inquiry question is to get your students to think deeply about a topic being studied.

CAPACITY
How confident are you in your understanding of the qualities of a good inquiry question? What else would you like to know?

Our primary students love questions. As any teacher of a primary grade knows, if we allowed it, our students would ask questions all day long! (Is that a new shirt? Does it hurt to get your ears pierced? Why can't I bring my dog to class?)

This steady stream of questions, although sometimes exhausting, points to the fundamental truth that primary learners are overflowing with wonder. They are curious about everything around them. But these questions are different from inquiry questions.

An inquiry question is a special type of question that helps drive units of learning. The purpose of an inquiry question is to entice your students to think deeply about the mysteries of life. In his book *A More Beautiful Question*, Warren Berger (2014) argues that in a more complex and dynamic world, questions become more valuable than answers. These mysteries can be categorized by subject disciplines but are often interdisciplinary in nature (see figure 3.4). As you read the sample inquiry questions, identify the core concepts and consider possible supporting content that you would use to plan an inquiry based on an inquiry question.

We hope that as you read through these sample questions, your curiosity and inquisitiveness are sparked. Inquiry questions are helpful to learners because they stimulate thinking and feeling, and they drive learning by signaling what is truly essential and fascinating. They can often be deceptively simple, but they cannot be simply answered.

In their book *Essential Questions*, Jay McTighe and Grant Wiggins (2013) make the case for teachers to collaboratively create inquiry (or essential) questions. The use of questions signals to students that inquiry is the goal of learning in your class and makes it more likely that a unit of study will be intellectually engaging. The use of questions also forces us to clarify and prioritize what is truly important in terms of learning for our students.

Questions to drive learning

Social Studies

- Who am I?
- What makes a good friend?
- What is fair?
- What makes a good community?
- Should we have rules?

Language Arts/Literacy

- How can stories change the world?
- How do words help and heal?
- Should there be rules in writing?
- Why does reading give you power?
- Why do people read?

Mathematics

- What kinds of problems can we solve by measuring?
- Where is the math in this room and school?
- How can there be different answers to the same question?
- How do fractions help us in real life?
- How is math just like a puzzle?

Health and Wellness

- How long will I live?
- What are all the ways I can move my body?
- How safe are my food choices?
- How can friends have an impact on my health?
- How are my mind and body connected?

Science

- How are humans the same as and different from other animals?
- What is the impact of machines on the world?
- How can something be both liquid and solid?
- How much have air and water changed?
- Are humans or plants more fragile?

FIGURE 3.4 Although at first glance inquiry questions may look "simple" they are actually complex and designed to stimulate much thought and discussion.

CONVICTION

What are your beliefs about the relationship among wondering, questioning and learning in your classroom?

Inquiry for all

Questioning games

Questioning games help build the skills of the primary learner and allow them to take risks while having fun.

1. **Mystery Bag:** Create a modified "show and tell" by bringing something to school that can be put in a bag. Other students must guess what's inside.
2. **Why/What If/How Game:** Introduce an interesting and relevant problem. Have students use the Why/What if/How? format to ask as many questions they can in a two minute time frame.
3. **Dice Game:** Assign each digit on a dice a topic (e.g., friends, science, sports). Also assign each digit a question starter (e.g., what, when, why, how, who, where). Students roll the dice and create questions. How many questions can be created in one minute with multiple rolls of the dice?
4. **Ask an Intelligent Assistant:** Students create humorous and serious questions for artificial intelligence interfaces (e.g., "Siri" for Apple).

The qualities of an effective inquiry question are detailed in John Barell's (2003) book *Developing More Curious Minds* (see figure 3.5). A good inquiry question is an invitation to think (not recall, summarize or detail); comes from genuine curiosity and confusion about the world; makes you think about something in a way you may have never considered before; invites both deep thinking and deep feelings; leads to more good questions; and asks you to think critically, creatively, ethically, purposefully and reflectively about essential ideas in a discipline. Also consider Reproducible 3A, *8 characteristics of effective inquiry questions* (page 79).

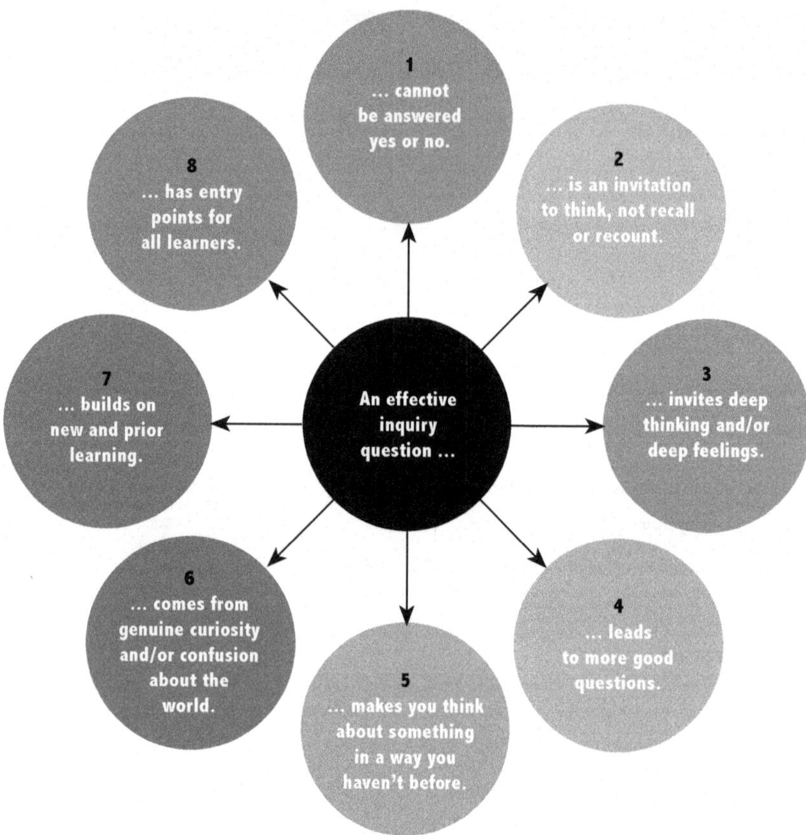

Source: Barell, 2003.

FIGURE 3.5 The most effective inquiry questions share common qualities that make them exciting, provocative and intellectually challenging.

There are many places to find great inquiry questions: in curriculum documents, board documents and in teacher resources. Great inquiry questions are sometimes difficult to create from scratch, so we suggest looking to your colleagues, board, school and online sources to generate inquiry questions that can anchor and drive learning for the school year, an entire subject area or a particular unit of study. We suggest that groups of educators take time to find, develop, revise and choose inquiry questions that are appropriate for their classrooms. This is the starting place for an inquiry-friendly learning community.

THINQ

- How do you currently use questions in your classroom?
- How can you better use questions to drive learning rather than just pique interest?
- Which of the questions in figure 3.4 (page 63) could you use in your classroom right now?
- How might you modify some of the sample questions to better fit into your classroom?

3.3 What are some ways to provoke and launch an inquiry?

Inquiry questions can be used to generate interest and launch an inquiry, but they are not the only way to begin. Teachers have many creative and novel ideas for stimulating student interest. We will refer to these creative ideas as provocations because they provoke student interest in learning. Since these provocations can be used to spark and motivate learning, they can also be used to launch an inquiry. In this section, we discuss some considerations to remember when selecting a provocation and then the finer points of provoking inquiry in the primary classroom.

Considerations when selecting a provocation

Provocations are intended to accomplish three things. First, provocations allow students to see how other learners respond with different levels of emotion, curiosity and open-mindedness to a problem or issue. Second, students note how other learners have distinct knowledge to share and that collaboration is an effective way to learn. Lastly, provocations help to fuel student interest, wonderings and curiosity. After all, we want learners to see school as a place of wonder and curiosity, not a place where they just sit and receive information.

Some provocations, like a scientific experiment, may cause amazement. Others, like stories of real-life injustice, may trigger outrage. Try not to shy away from your students when they share strong feelings, as these emotions are often the best place for learning to begin. Provocations act as a springboard for student questions and provide an opportunity to build on the questions posed by others. All of these question threads are what fuel and sustain inquiry.

Big Idea

Provocations that elicit strong emotions are often the best place to begin an inquiry.

CAPACITY

How confident are you in your ability to provoke and launch an inquiry? What else would you like to know?

Educators Ask

What if students don't respond to a provocation?

There may be a few students who are not inspired by a particular provocation. This may occur if the provocation does not tap into a student's interests or particular learning style or if it requires more English language than a student currently possesses. That is why we should use a wide variety of provocations to launch the inquiries in our classrooms. By differentiating the provocations, we increase the likelihood of reaching all of the students in our classroom across a period of learning.

Inquiry in Action

How a current event sparked a grade 3 inquiry into Syrian refugees

Context

As part of her curriculum, Shawna teaches an immigration unit with a particular focus on immigration to the local area. This unit often includes visits to the local museum and historical society, mapping activities and an exploration of the reasons why people choose to immigrate. As part of her regular balanced literacy protocols her students also complete ongoing current events presentations.

Spark

One year, at the beginning of the unit, one of her students did a current events presentation on a Syrian refugee family that had recently settled in the region. This particular story sparked a great deal of interest among her grade 3 students:

- What is the difference between an immigrant and a refugee?
- How do they figure out where to live if they cannot speak English yet?
- How are they going to be ready for winter if they've only lived in a warm country?
- How do they get used to Canadian food?
- Are they sad because they are so far from home?

Planning

Shawna realized that because of the high student interest in this topic, she could use it to develop a full inquiry and drive the learning for this unit (see figures 3.6–3.10 for examples of the students' learning in action). This meant that she would not teach the unit the same way she had in the past. Shawna taught in an International Baccalaureate (IB) school, so she needed to develop an overarching inquiry question that reflected the initial interest shown by her students, the core components of her provincial curriculum, and the requirements of the IB framework, in this case, that the inquiry result in an action.

FIGURE 3.6 Toy drive so that Syrian children would feel welcome.

FIGURE 3.7 Some of the grade 3 students with items they collected at the toy drive.

How can we best help Syrian refugees?	
Curriculum	Why do people live where they do in our province?
Student interest	Syrian refugees
IB Framework	Students take action in response to an identified need.
Action	Make December the "Month of Giving" and involve the entire school community in helping the new Syrian refugee family in our region.

FIGURE 3.8 Students ready to sell goods they made at the make-and-bake sale. Cash proceeds were given to the settlement center.

Learning more

During this inquiry, students watched videos to learn about the reasons that people settle in a particular place, read case studies about immigration and participated in a Skype interview with a settlement officer who helps new refugees in their region. The students wanted to make sure that the action they were going to take would be truly helpful, so after reflecting on what they learned, they decided on three components to their action plan:

- A warm clothing drive
- A make-and-bake sale to raise money for the refugee center
- A toy drive so that the new Syrian children felt welcome

Collaboration and community support

Shawna's grade 3 students approached the grade 2 class for help because the grade 2s were working on the inquiry question "What makes a good community?" The two classes agreed to collaborate and asked the school administration for its support, making the argument that conducting all three of these action components would require that the entire month of December be devoted to the initiative. The school administration agreed and the entire community got behind their plan of action.

FIGURE 3.9 Students developed a series of posters to advertise the bake sale.

FIGURE 3.10 Students calculated the results of the clothing drive.

Provocations for the primary classroom

There are many different methods, strategies, tools and techniques educators can employ to provoke an inquiry in a primary classroom. In the previous Inquiry in Action feature we shared how a current event presentation acted as a spark to an inquiry into Syrian refugees in a grade 3 class. In this section, we examine some of the approaches and experiences that have worked for other educators. The best ones are those that, on any given day, evoke the most powerful responses from learners. Remember how important it is to differentiate, so try a number of different strategies to ensure you have a better chance of reaching all of the students in your classroom.

CONTEXT

What are your learners most curious about? What kinds of provocations might activate their thinking?

Inquiry in Action

Take a walk... anywhere

Getting out of the classroom and going outdoors, somewhere else in the school or on a trip is an excellent way to provoke wonderings. Traditionally, these types of experiences are done at the end of a theme or unit of study. If we flip our thinking around and use these experiences to launch an inquiry, the avenues are endless.

These wonderings (see figure 3.11) were sparked during a walk outside to collect leaves. Each student collected a number of leaves and shared their wonderings. A community circle was formed to discuss the questions posed. Some of the students had answers to their co-learners' questions. Materials were provided by both the educators and the students to investigate the life of leaves. Stewardship was a focus, as well as the idea that life is a cycle and that humans are often a part of the cycle for other living things.

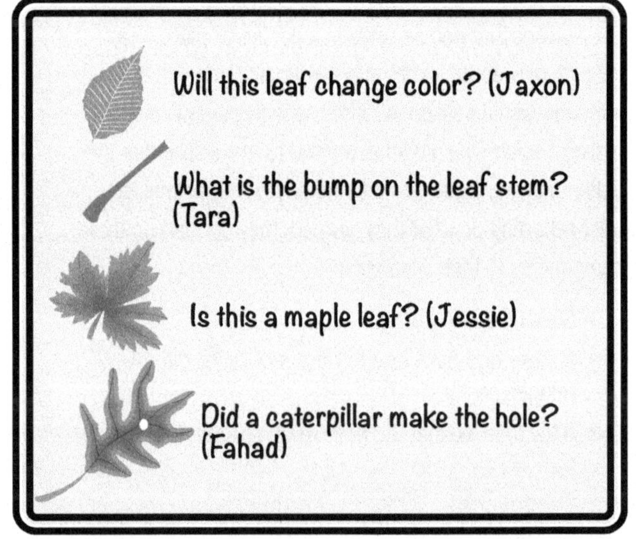

FIGURE 3.11 Students shared their wonderings about leaves.

Inquiry in Action

Question of the week/day/month

The question of the week center could be placed anywhere in the environment. Questions of the week could be taken from the Wonder Wall (a designated space in the classroom where students can pose questions they are curious about) or be a question posed by educators. Primary students love it when their wondering is the question of the week. Time is given each week to share responses to the question and to do some research to discover answers. This experience allows for educators to model where answers to questions can be found.

We have found that when students see the question at the start of the week, they engage their families as well. Experts on topics can be found everywhere.

This was a question of the week that educator Cara posed to her class because it was a wondering that she had after seeing cut tulips in a vase (see figure 3.12). Upon reflection, she realized that her initial question could only be answered with "yes" or "no," so she added a second question that was much more open. In fact, tulips can grow up to an inch after being cut!

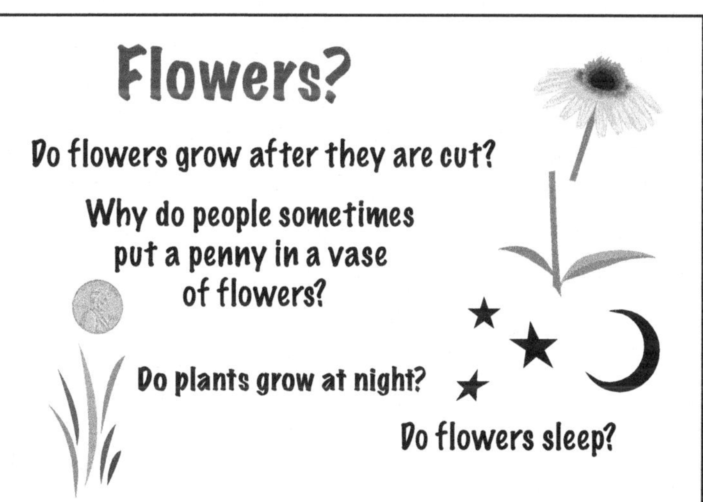

FIGURE 3.12 One teacher used her wonderings about flowers to drive discussion.

Inquiry in Action

Photo a month

This is a good provocation for an inquiry that can start in September and go until June. Choose a spot outside of the school and take a photo of the class in that spot every month of the school year. These photos are a great way to initiate a discussion and ongoing inquiry about seasonal changes and stewardship.

This teacher took a photo of the class under the same tree in the schoolyard each month. It was a great ongoing inquiry that all the learners took part in (see figure 3.13).

FIGURE 3.13 The seasonal changes in a single tree can launch a yearlong inquiry for the entire class.

Inquiry in Action

The Wonder or Observation Window

This idea comes from *A Place for Wonder* by Georgia Heard and Jennifer McDonough (2009). It is simple and inexpensive and provides an ever-changing view for wonderings that can be used as provocations for inquiry.

A Wonder Window is created by taping off a square or any shape on a classroom window and leaving a journal there so that learners can share their thoughts and wonderings. Educators can use these wonderings as provocations for inquiries. If you are lucky enough to have windows that face different directions in your room, then two Wonder Windows allow for comparison. Placing a bird feeder or a plant in the window adds to the experience.

The Wonder Window in Meghan's class had a frequent visitor, which sparked an interest in black-capped chickadees and other winter birds, and what birds do when the weather changes (see figure 3.14).

FIGURE 3.14 A chickadee often visited the classroom Wonder Window.

Inquiry in Action

Where do we find answers?

This is a lesson that can be taught explicitly and revisited later. With wondering comes the question, "How do we find answers?" This is an excellent question to pose to learners. An anchor chart that lists sources for answers can be co-created. The chart is then posted in the classroom and can be added to when new resources are discovered (see figure 3.15). It can be referred to frequently during inquiry experiences by both teachers and students.

How We Explore and Answer Questions

- Google
- iPad
- people
- books
- computer
- TV

FIGURE 3.15 Anchor chart for an inquiry about finding answers.

Inquiry in Action

The wonderings of Do-ists and Do-ers

This idea was created by two teachers who wanted to support their learners in asking a greater variety of questions. This seemed very challenging for their class. Together they talked about what kinds of people ask questions and decided to expand on this idea. They listed "ists": scientists, archaeologists, chemists, biologists, artists, gymnasts, etc. They also listed "ers": dancers, doctors, swimmers, writers, hairdressers, etc. They gathered texts and resources about these roles, read them, and displayed them in the classroom. The educators created a slideshow (see figure 3.16) and asked the learners what kinds of questions these people might ask. It got the juices flowing and when students asked questions, the educators would say, "That is the kind of question an engineer might ask." This modeled language became the language the students would use as well.

FIGURE 3.16 Example slide from the teacher slideshow.

Inquiry in Action

RAN chart (Reading and Analyzing Nonfiction)

This idea comes from Tony Stead's (2005) book *Reality Checks* and is an excellent alternative to the KWL. The RAN chart explores prior knowledge, but it also addresses misconceptions that learners may have. These misconceptions are often a great way to dig deep into an inquiry so that thinking can be challenged and new knowledge can be built. The KWL chart includes the following categories (see figure 3.17).

What we know	What we want to know	What we learned

FIGURE 3.17: Standard know, want to know, learn (KWL) chart.

The RAN chart adds two more elements to the framework, resulting in a chart with space for what we think we know, what we were right about, misconceptions, new information, and what we're still wondering about. Teachers or students can write the facts that they think they know about a topic on sticky notes, and these notes can be moved to other columns as the inquiry grows.

Inquiry in Action

Can... Have... Are...

When a wondering is shared or an idea for study is proposed, a great way to explore prior knowledge is the framework of Can... Have... Are.... This allows both students and teachers to examine what they already know about something and where they might go next in the inquiry. It is also a way that misconceptions can be addressed.

Frances and Vanessa used the Can... Have... Are... framework to lay the foundation for an inquiry about caterpillars and butterflies. All thoughts and ideas are honored as prior knowledge is shared and recorded. In this example the teacher did the recording (see figure 3.18).

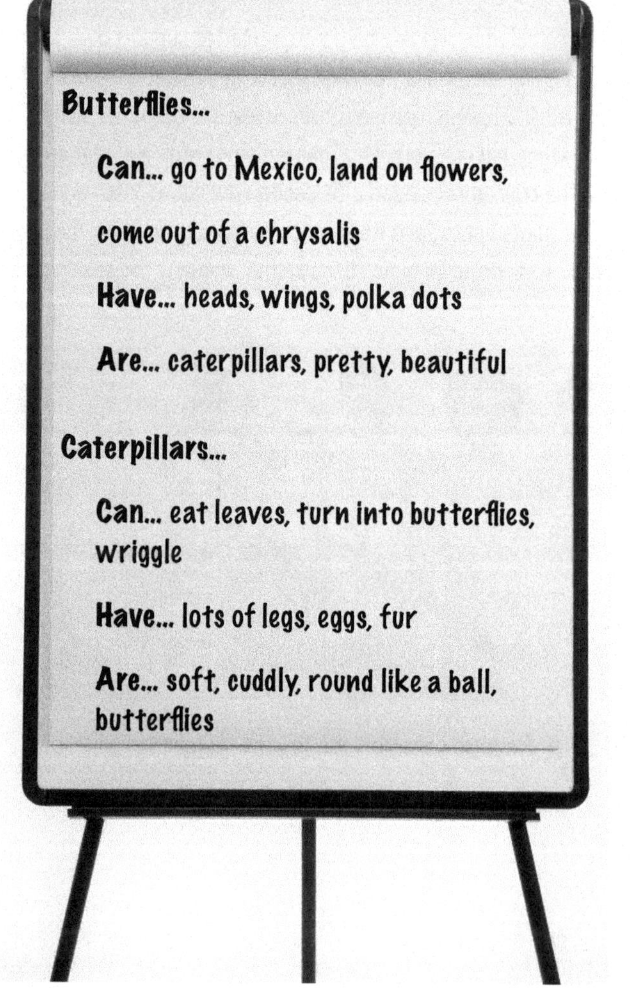

FIGURE 3.18 Teachers recorded student thoughts and ideas about caterpillars and butterflies.

THINQ

- What are your students most curious about? What types of provocations might activate their thinking?
- Which of these provocation strategies have you tried and how successful have they been in tapping into student wonderings?
- Which of these provocation strategies are new to you and might you like to try?

3.4 How can I help students develop their questioning abilities?

Big Idea

The ability of students to develop strong questions during an inquiry comes with time and practice.

CAPACITY

How confident are you in your ability to help primary students develop deep and thoughtful questions?

Inquiry-based learning requires considerable amounts of reasoning which may pose challenges for many primary students. We can't just ask students to "think harder" — we need to describe exactly what good thinking involves and encourage students to be attentive to their own thinking, even when we are not there prompting them to do so. Analytical questions can assist an inquiry learner to "think about their thinking" and to improve thinking.

In their work on critical thinking, Linda Elder and Richard Paul (2010) identify eight universal elements that can be used to analyze and improve thinking:

1. **Purpose:** goals, objectives
2. **Question at issue:** problem, issue
3. **Information:** data, facts, observations, experiences
4. **Interpretation and inference:** conclusions, solutions
5. **Concepts:** theories, definitions, laws, principles, models
6. **Assumptions:** presuppositions, axioms, taking for granted
7. **Implications** and consequences
8. **Point of view:** frames of reference, perspectives, orientations

These elements of thought are the springboard of the analytical questions provided in figure 3.19 (page 74). These analytical questions break down thinking (either a learner's thinking or the thinking inferred from evidence) into discrete parts that can be carefully examined.

This framework may seem very sophisticated for a primary classroom. However, asking analytical questions based on the eight elements of thought and phrasing them in ways that are appropriate for your primary learners will be helpful to your students during an inquiry. Even in primary classrooms, focusing on different ways of thinking can assist an inquiry learner to "think about their thinking" and to improve it. These kinds of questions can guide students, model thinking and generate important assessment information to help students improve their thinking. You could consider using some of these analytical questions in students' portfolio work and conferencing.

Questions to unpack an inquiry	
Questions to begin and unpack an inquiry	• Why do we/you care about this issue? • What do we hope to find out? • How can we/you answer the question/solve the problem? • What questions do you have?
Questions that unpack concepts (concepts are an idea of what something is or how it works)	• What is the main idea you are using in your thinking? • Can you explain that to me? • Are there other ideas or ways of solving this problem?
Questions that unpack working with "what is currently known"	• Where did we/you find this information? • Is this good quality information? • What does this information tell us? • What does the author or speaker take for granted? • Are there other sources or people we/you should listen to? • What is your point of view? • Can you explain your thinking? • What are you finding difficult?
Questions that unpack reaching a conclusion or "putting it all together"	• Do you have all the information you need? • How did you reach your conclusion or solve the problem? • Are there other possible conclusions/solutions? • Why is what we/you learned important or helpful? • What will happen now?

FIGURE 3.19 Asking questions is a powerful way to guide students toward a successful conclusion to their inquiry.

THINQ

- Which of the eight elements of thought do your students typically use?
- Which of the eight elements of thought do you need to introduce to your students?
- Thinking back to the importance of triangulated assessment evidence, what evidence of student learning could you use to assess student responses to the questions above?

3.5 Does every interest, wondering and question become an inquiry?

Big Idea

When launching an inquiry, ask yourself, "What?" "So what?" and "Now what?"

This question is often asked by educators trying to create an inquiry-based environment. In fact, it is a common misconception about inquiry: that we choose from the constantly changing and fleeting interests of students. It would be wonderful if we could follow each student's wondering, but we know this is not realistic. So how do we decide? We like the way Tiziana Ciccone (2016) has used the reflection model of "What? So What? Now What?" to consider if an interest or theory could become an inquiry (see figure 3.20).

This reflection model can also address the question of how long an inquiry should last. Since inquiry is an in-and-out process, more questions and wonderings constantly arise. We can use the reflection model to help determine if the inquiry is continuing to lead to new learning. Most teachers we have worked with say they know when a learning activity has come to an end, but also keep in mind that when documentation is revisited, the spark may ignite again. If the inquiry was initiated by a problem, the solving of the problem could mark the close of an inquiry, unless another problem arises.

Educators know their students and can tell when they are engaged and interested. But ask your learners! In a community meeting, knowledge circle, or during a discussion about an ongoing inquiry, ask if all questions about the topic have been answered or whether more needs to be uncovered. Remember that some inquiries may last just a day or two. Sometimes it may involve the whole class, a small group or an individual student. Therefore, when something is "done," it will look different in each classroom, within groupings or with individuals.

What?

- What is the student's theory or wondering?
- Is it fleeting or momentary?
- Based on your knowledge of the student, is it something they seem truly curious about?

So what?

- Is this an important question?
- What is the most substantial aspect?
- Can it be linked to prior knowledge?
- Are there connections to curriculum?
- Can new knowledge be built?
- Could learners make their thinking visible?
- Can it be connected to something in real life?

Now what?

- What do those interested already know or think about the wondering?
- Where do we hope to go?
- How will we co-plan and co-negotiate?
- What materials/resources are needed?
- Who will provide them?
- How will we capture students' thinking and learning?
- How will we revisit this thinking and learning?

Source for questions: Ciccone, 2016.

FIGURE 3.20 This reflection model can help decide when to initiate, pursue or conclude an inquiry.

3.6 How do I assess students as they ask questions?

Big Idea
Primary students can begin to learn the importance of metacognition and self-assessment.

In chapter 2 (page 27), we suggested that the six essential abilities of inquiry learners are central to all inquiry and inquiry assessment. Questioning is one of these essential inquiry skills and is critical to every facet of the inquiry process. For example, a student cannot "understand what is currently known" if they do not ask questions of sources and ideas. "Thinking together" cannot happen without students respectfully asking each other, and themselves, to identify beliefs and explain reasoning. Students really cannot express their curiosity and wonder without asking questions.

We have included three tools to assist you and your students with assessment of questioning skills in the primary grades. Reproducible 3B, *Assessment planning template: Asks questions* (page 80) can be used to plan and capture assessment evidence you acquire through conversations, observations or products. Reproducible 3C, *Inquiry rubric and self-check: Asks questions* (page 81) allows either you, your students or you in partnership with your students to assess each student's abilities and skills related to questioning. Reproducible 3D, *Student exploration: What I see, what I think, what I wonder, what I feel* (page 82) is a self-assessment, self-reflection tool for students. This template can be used at any time during an inquiry, or at the end of an inquiry.

Although some teachers feel that widely divergent literacy levels make it very difficult for young primary students to become involved in the assessment process, we believe that it is important to establish good assessment and metacognition protocols in the primary grades. After all, even if they aren't great at self-assessment, the fact that we ask them to self-assess sends the message that they are part of the assessment process. This is a very important way to create a culture of inquiry and questioning in our classrooms.

Educators Ask

Can or should I level student questions?

It may be tempting to level or assess students' questions based on charts showing various combinations of the parts of speech such as the one in figure 3.21, but we advise against this practice. Students should create questions for various purposes and recognize the purpose of questions. For example, "How big is Mars?" is an excellent question aimed at gathering information. The question, "Why would we want to go to Mars?" is another excellent question that asks for evaluation of information. Students require practice and modeling to extend their repertoire of questions based on different purposes.

Learners need to ask all types of questions during an inquiry, yet many of them would be considered "low level" by some questioning assessment tools. But it is very difficult to interpret the complexity of many questions based on parts of speech. What we need to consider instead is the learner's purpose and the thinking behind their question. For example, the question, "When is it acceptable to fight?" or "Is war wrong?" may be scored as a low questions when in fact these questions meet all the criteria of a deep inquiry question. It is important to keep in mind that all questions that move the inquiry along are important; from information gathering "factual" questions to synthesis, application and evaluative questions as in figure 3.22.

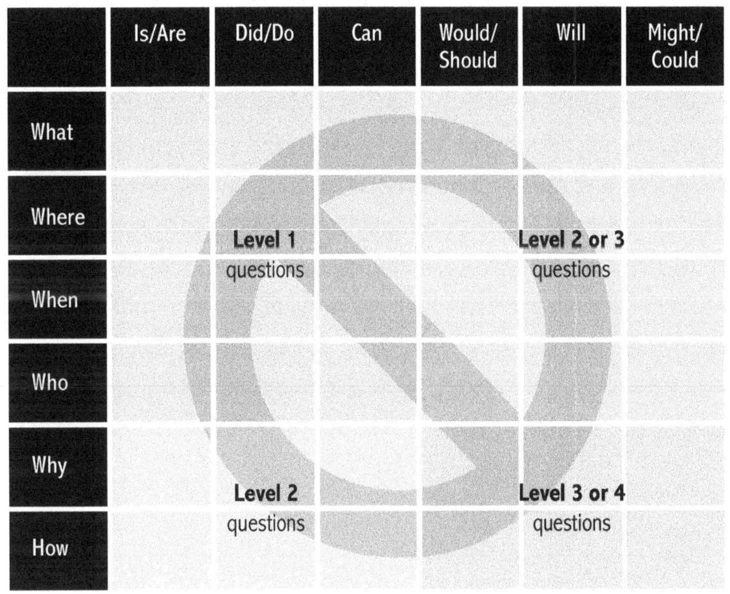

FIGURE 3.21 It may be tempting to assess questions using a table such as this one. However, it's quite possible a student could generate a Level 4 "Who is" question as well as a Level 1 "How might" question.

	Is/Are	Did/Do	Can	Would/ Should	Will	Might/ Could
What						
Where		**Factual** questions			**Predictive** questions	
When						
Who						
Why		**Analytical** questions			**Application Synthesis** questions	
How						

FIGURE 3.22 Questioning charts provide a visual anchor for students who need support in extending the types of questions they are asking. Avoid placing a value on or judging students' questions prematurely.

Revisit and reflect

This chapter looked closely at the importance of wondering and questioning in an inquiry-driven classroom. A classroom culture that encourages curiosity, risk-taking, open-mindedness and persistence fosters wonder and inquiry.

We outlined the importance of creating and using powerful inquiry questions to capture and hold student interest and propel their learning. We also explored the use of a variety of engaging provocations to spark student interest, launch an inquiry and generate ongoing questions during an inquiry. We discussed how teachers can help students to improve their questioning abilities, as well as how to manage the wide variety of questions raised in a primary classroom. And finally, we focused specifically on how educators can assess questioning skills and how to establish important self-assessment protocols with primary-aged students.

Big Ideas

3.1 Our curiosity fuels our learning.

3.2 The purpose of an inquiry question is to get your students to think deeply about a topic being studied.

3.3 Provocations that elicit strong emotions are often the best place to begin an inquiry.

3.4 The ability of students to develop strong questions during an inquiry comes with time and practice.

3.5 When launching an inquiry, ask yourself, "What?" "So what?" and "Now what?"

3.6 Primary students can begin to learn the importance of metacognition and self-assessment.

THINQ

- Where could you place Reproducible 3A, *8 characteristics of effective Inquiry questions* (page 79) as a reminder for you and your colleagues of what makes a good inquiry question?
- How could you use Reproducible 3E, *6 big ideas about wondering and questioning in primary* (page 83) with colleagues or parents to help your school move forward toward being more of an inquiry-based learning environment?
- To conclude your exploration of this chapter, take some time to complete Reproducible 3F, *Teacher checklist: Wonder and questioning in my classroom* (page 84).

Reproducible 3A

8 characteristics of effective inquiry questions

Source: Barell, J. (2003). Developing more curious minds. *Alexandria, VA: ASCD.*

Reproducible 3B

Assessment planning template: Asks questions

Name: ______________________ Date: ______________

Essential inquiry ability — Asking questions	Evidence gathered		
	Conversations	Observations	Products
Asks questions • Asks and refines relevant questions for different purposes (to get information, to clarify, to dispute, to drive an inquiry) and from different perspectives.			
Demonstrates curiosity • Actively asks many questions that demonstrate eagerness to learn. • Understands the importance of questioning to learning.			
(Gives and) asks for reasons • Asks for justification of beliefs, proposals and solutions. • Thinks together. • Listens to, builds on, considers and assists with the questions of others. • Asks relevant questions of other people to further an inquiry (to get an opinion or some advice, to debate, to dispute, to inquire, to brainstorm).			
Understands what is currently known • Asks critical questions of "what is already known" (i.e., sources, data, strategies, theories).			
Puts it all together • Asks and understands the importance of analytical questions to improve their thinking at each stage of an inquiry.			

Reproducible 3C

Inquiry rubric and self-check: Asks questions

Name: ______________________________ Date: ____________________

Areas that need work	Standard for this criterion	How work exceeds expectations
	Asks questions • Asks and refines relevant questions for different purposes (to get information, to clarify, to dispute, to drive an inquiry) and from different perspectives.	
	Demonstrates curiosity • Actively asks questions that demonstrate eagerness to learn.	
	(Gives and) asks for reasons • Asks for justification of beliefs, proposals and solutions.	
	Thinks together • Listens to, builds on, considers and assists with the questions of others. • Asks relevant questions of other people to further an inquiry (to get an opinion or some advice, to debate, to dispute, to inquire, to brainstorm).	
	Understands what is currently known • Asks critical questions of "what is already known" (i.e., sources, data, strategies, theories).	
	Puts it all together • Asks and understands the importance of analytical questions to improve their thinking at each stage of an inquiry.	

Source: Rubric based on ideas from Dietz, M. (2000). Single point rubric idea. *INTASC Academy, Milwaukee, WI, as cited by Gonzalez, J. (2015, February 4).* Meet the single point rubric. *Accessed at www.cultofpedagogy.com/single-point-rubric/ on February 29, 2024.*

Reproducible 3D

Student exploration: What I see, what I think, what I wonder, what I feel

Name: ______________________________ Date: ______________

Inquiry focus: ______________________________

In each of the spaces record what you see, think, wonder and feel about your inquiry.

What do I see?

What do I think?

What do I wonder?

What do I feel?

Reproducible 3E

6 big ideas about wondering and questioning in primary

1
Our curiosity fuels our learning.

2
The purpose of an inquiry question is to get your students to think deeply about a topic being studied.

3
Provocations that elicit strong emotions are often the best place to begin an inquiry.

4
The ability of students to develop strong questions during an inquiry comes with time and practice.

5
When launching an inquiry, ask yourself, "What" "So what?" and "Now what?"

6
Primary students can begin to learn the importance of metacognition and self-assessment.

Reproducible 3F

Teacher checklist: Wonder and questioning in my classroom

Check which of the following statements represent your teaching practice. The focus of this checklist is questioning, an essential quality of inquiry thinking. Use this checklist for self-reflection, planning and sharing with colleagues, and to determine next steps in deepening inquiry practice.

- Students' questions are addressed in meaningful ways in my classroom.
- Students get to practice asking different types of questions in my classroom.
- Students understand why asking questions is important to learning in general, and inquiry learning in particular.
- Students in my classroom know there are different types of questions with different purposes and apply this knowledge.
- Students pose questions (including inquiry questions) and real world problems that relate to their lives and the "real world."
- Students ask analytical questions of their thinking during an inquiry.
- Students understand the criteria for effective questioning and can effectively self- and peer-assess questions.
- I use a variety of provocations to pique and sustain student curiosity, wonder and questioning.
- I pose questions and/or real world problems that relate to students' lives and the "real world."
- I pose questions and/or real world problems to provoke student curiosity and accelerate students' desire to learn.
- I organize factual knowledge around conceptual frameworks and open-ended inquiry questions to facilitate knowledge retrieval and application.
- I pose analytical questions to help students improve their thinking.
- I pose instructional questions to reveal students' prior knowledge, including preconceptions and misconceptions regarding important concepts.
- I assess students' questioning abilities through conversations, observations and products.

Chapter 4

FINDING OUT:

The investigation and exploration phase of an inquiry

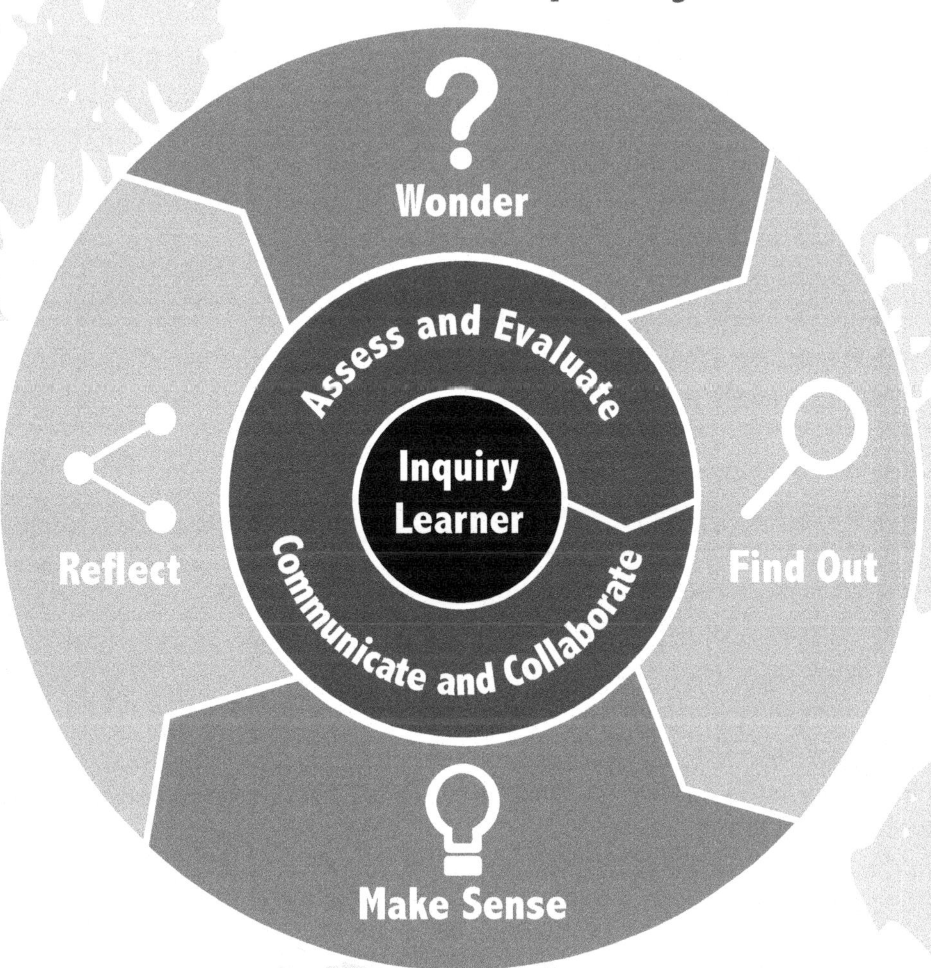

It is the mark of an educated mind to be able to entertain a thought without accepting it.

—Aristotle

In this chapter, we equip educators with tools and strategies to support student research. Some young learners are just beginning to *learn to read*, yet they can be empowered to *read (and view, listen or explore) to learn*. In a structured literacy program, students working through a scope and sequence of reading instruction may not have been exposed yet to specific skills that enable them to decode and comprehend relevant text. This chapter also helps educators support students in learning how to work with information as they investigate and explore through inquiry.

4.1 How do I get my students interested in finding answers to their questions?

We have deliberately called this stage of inquiry "finding out" because we want to signal the fact that this is an active, interesting and exciting phase. However, our inquiry work with teachers often uncovers a common concern: teachers feel they are pretty good at working with inquiry questions in their classroom but they do not feel they have the ability to sustain an inquiry. In other words, they aren't sure how to support students in finding answers to their questions. We are confident that teachers already have the skills and abilities to sustain an inquiry in their classrooms. After you have read and reflected on this chapter, we believe you will feel confident as well. Getting students interested in inquiry and sustaining that interest begins with creating an investigative mindset and developing investigate skills.

Creating an investigative mindset

The key to making this stage engaging for your primary students is to treat it as an exploration, mystery or puzzle. Since this stage is important, we think it's worth trying to make it fun and engaging. Primary learners love to solve puzzles and mysteries, just like everyone else. By putting students in the role of knowledge seekers and problem solvers and giving them some control of their learning, student interest and engagement increases.

> **Big Idea**
>
> Students are naturally curious and their interests will drive them to want answers to their questions.

> **Educators Ask**
>
> **What do I do when students always expect ME to answer their questions?**
>
> Many teachers tell us that they want to create a classroom rooted in investigation and exploration, but that they "get stuck" when their students look to them — the teacher — to answer their questions for them. It's true that students are used to teachers always answering their questions. Many know if they wait long enough, the teacher will provide an answer.
>
> Teachers who are confident in an inquiry-based classroom do not rescue students when they initially request an answer. Data show that more often than not, the student actually understands more than they initially demonstrate (Greene, 2016). When given the encouragement to think in a safe learning environment students actually develop the skills to persevere and trust their thinking abilities (Handelsman, 2012). It's important to resist the temptation to always respond, even if you know the answer. If we want students to think for themselves, then we need to let them think for themselves.
>
> If you want to foster an investigative mindset the next time your students push you for an answer, try responding with a question:
>
> - "That's an interesting question! Where might you find the answer to that?"
> - "I've never thought about that! Let's find out together. Where should we look first?"
> - "This is a new topic for me and I don't know the answer. Please come and share with me when you find something about that."

There are many ways we can signal to our students that our classroom is a place of investigation and exploration, such as the examples in figure 4.1. These ideas communicate the message that your classroom is an active learning environment where exploration and discovery are the norm.

Activities to create an investigative classroom

Place an "Open for Learning" sign on your door with the word "business" crossed out and replaced with the word "learning."

Hand out props and nametags to students, such as lab coats or "Mad Scientist" labels so that they can be "scientists" for the day. If you are doing history, you could print up "explorer" labels.

Create mystery boxes by placing large question marks on shoe boxes, or an assortment of boxes in different sizes. Inside put photos, objects or art that will act as clues or provocations for the day's lesson.

Make predictions posters to place around your room. These posters could contain images where something is about to happen (e.g., a person climbing a tall ladder), with three possible outcomes listed below. Students can guess which one they believe will occur.

Do a countdown to the moment when you send students off to find solutions and answers, to create a sense of anticipation. You can ring a bell, wave a flag or simply count down from five.

FIGURE 4.1 You can send a message that your classroom is an active learning environment: one where exploration and discovery are the norm.

Words Matter

You may want to explain and post these inquiry action words around your classroom.

Analyze
Examine something in detail.

Assess
Evaluate the quality of something.

Clarify
Make something clearer.

Explore
Look at something in a careful way to learn more about it.

Investigate
Discover and examine facts to discover the truth.

Question
Request information.

Solve
Find an answer to or explanation of a mystery or problem.

Developing investigative skills

Teachers tell us that they worry that their primary students simply do not have the skills to investigate and find answers to their questions, but these skills are teachable even with emergent readers.

Model for students that this is an active and interesting phase of inquiry where students get to explore and examine information in their search for answers to their questions. This process of investigation occurs whether teachers provide the information for students, students conduct research and locate the information themselves, or some combination of both.

Using intentional language to build the confidence of students also helps to maintain their interest. Teachers can address students as investigators, researchers and problem-solvers as they work to expand what they know about a topic under investigation. We need to put them at the center of their learning. Shining a light on the process of inquiry, with the purpose of helping students to see it as a puzzle to solve or a mystery to unlock, will engage students and captivate their interest (see figure 4.2).

FIGURE 4.2 It can be more interesting and engaging for primary students if they see an inquiry question as a mystery waiting to be solved.

4.2 Where does literacy fit into inquiry?

Big Idea
Literacy protocols fit naturally into inquiry-based learning.

CONVICTION
How convinced are you that developing both inquiry and literacy skills and abilities are compatible and mutually supporting?

When the initial excitement about a question turns into the challenge of investigation, primary educators need to be able to give just the right level of support. There is a wide range of abilities and skills when considering learners who enter and exit the primary grades. Grade 1 students may have just left a play-based classroom in which inquiry has been a foundation. Gradually, through grades 2 and 3, students gain the confidence, skills and experience required for the upper elementary grades, where they will be invited to take greater ownership of inquiry and research.

We need to empower our students as they move through this progression to see the excitement in becoming a "researcher" seeking answers. Educators must be intentional about setting up an environment that supports a high level of respect for ideas to be shared, explored and even respectfully challenged. We must cultivate strong skills in speaking and listening so that students are able to hear others' perspectives and then gain a better grasp of their own ideas and strategies for approaching a question or problem. Literacy is an important consideration to keep in mind. In this section, we discuss moving from guided to open inquiry, levels of support and how to incorporate literacy into inquiry.

From guided to open inquiry

Some of the nervousness many teachers feel when investigating and exploring is due to a misconception about the degree of student autonomy involved. With the wide range of available multimedia resources, strategies for differentiating, and an emphasis on scaffolding, students do not need to be independent, proficient readers and writers in order to do research. As illustrated in figure 4.3, inquiry learning is a continuum that, at one end, has a large degree of teacher direction and a small degree of student autonomy. The continuum continues to the point of minimal teacher direction and maximum student autonomy.

Primary teachers will want to work on the left side of the continuum. The level of teacher direction will need to remain high, especially in the early stages of familiarizing students with inquiry. So a guided inquiry approach is absolutely necessary in the primary grades. How far individual classes and students move along the continuum through grades 1 to 3 will depend on many variables, and teachers will need to have flexible goals and expectations. There is no specific point along this continuum where primary learners should be at the end of grade 3 in regard to "finding out." What matters most is that students "do inquiry." We are confident that when learners increase their independence and skills as literate learners, they can also acquire greater skill, familiarity and independence as inquiry learners.

FIGURE 4.3 As you move from guided to open inquiry, teacher direction decreases and student autonomy increases. Primary educators will want to work on the left side of this continuum.

Levels of support

In order to get just the right balance of support for our students, we need to know them well. Levels of support, to be effective, should be highly contextualized and differentiated. Determining when and how to support individual students requires teachers to have a clear understanding of their strengths and challenges. As figure 4.4 suggests, literacy levels, research experience, access to resources and available time are some of the things to consider when deciding how much support might be needed.

More teacher support	Determining your role during the Finding Out stage of an inquiry	Less teacher support
Very little	Do my students have experience locating, gathering and organizing evidence?	Quite a lot
Not yet	Are my students independent readers?	Pretty much
Not much	Do my students have experience finding out and doing research?	Quite a lot
Not really	Do my students have convenient and reliable access to resources, the internet or a library?	Yes absolutely
Very little	How much time do I have for this stage of the inquiry?	Quite a lot

FIGURE 4.4 The level of support you provide when investigating will depend on the skills and experiences of your students and the conditions in your classroom.

Literacy and inquiry

During an inquiry with primary students, literacy levels will be a significant factor in determining the type and level of support you provide. It is important to refer to the diagnostic assessments that you have already conducted so that you can provide students with appropriate reading materials. Knowing your students' ability to decode, comprehend, speak and write will help you to determine where extra support may be helpful.

CONTEXT

How might incorporating literacy protocols into an inquiry "free up" space for inquiry-based learning in your timetable?

Sometimes, primary educators view inquiry-based learning as a discrete component of their daily programming, separate from their literacy block. We encourage teachers to incorporate their literacy protocols into the inquiry process itself (see figure 4.5). The National Reading Panel (2013) outlines five areas of focus for teachers to explicitly and systematically teach their students:

1. Phonemic awareness 2. Phonics 3. Fluency 4. Vocabulary 5. Comprehension

In order to do justice to their literacy program, teachers must designate a large portion of their daily schedule to addressing these five pillars. With a few small tweaks, these instructional priorities can be customized to include inquiry topics.

When developing an inquiry, you can integrate these practices directly into the plan. You can explicitly develop phonemic awareness during the Wonder stage of an inquiry. In the Find Out stage, you can help students focus on specific phonics skills, support fluency, help to expand their vocabulary and ensure comprehension. During the Making Sense phase of the inquiry, students will need to build their vocabulary related to the topic. They will benefit from strengthening their fluency in order to ensure comprehension as they acquire knowledge. Students will also work on applying phonics skills to their writing or sharing their thoughts with a partner or teacher who can scribe for the student. And because all inquiries involve reflection, collaboration, and communication, your students' literacy skills are being developed throughout the process.

Because of this, many teachers use their literacy block as well as their science, social studies or project block for inquiry-based learning.

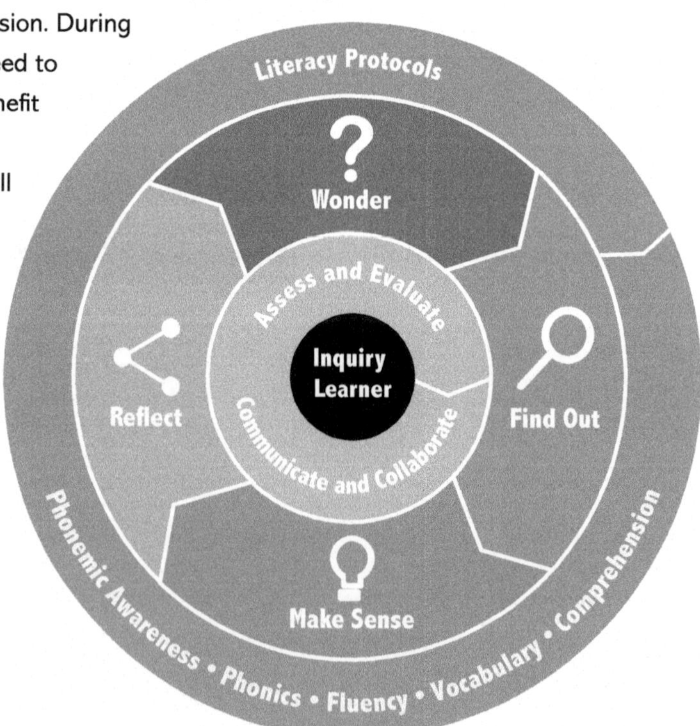

FIGURE 4.5 Literacy protocols can and should be integrated throughout the inquiry process and provide important supports for primary learners as they investigate and find out.

Inquiry in Action

Co-planning + subject integration = successful inquiry

Taking an inquiry approach can seem daunting at first. One of the greatest fears of teachers new to inquiry is not having time to fit everything in. If you are new to inquiry-based learning, integrating disciplines and collaborating with a colleague can make the process easier and more practical.

Collaboration

Kimberlee and Jenn are grade 3 teachers. They decided to collaborate on planning and launching an inquiry. Since they were relatively new to inquiry, they chose to take a guided approach. They selected the inquiry question themselves and intended to lead their students, who were also new to inquiry, through the process step-by-step. They knew that focusing on "big ideas" would keep their question open (no right answer) and accessible to all of their students. They chose a cross-curricular inquiry centered on a social studies topic, Early Settlers in the late 1700s and early 1800s. The question they used was "How would you survive if you were a settler?" which had been shared by a colleague at another school.

Planning

They knew they wanted to take a cross-curricular approach which integrated language arts, math (measurement), science (structures) and art (design) outcomes into the inquiry. Their assessment plan included gathering evidence of learning and providing feedback and support in each of these areas in addition to social studies. They also discussed how and when to intentionally gather observational and conversational evidence of their students' learning. To keep things manageable, they elected to ask all students to design and build the home they would want to have if they were a settler (see figures 4.6–4.8). This was to be the primary means of assessing what their students understood about the challenges and realities of a settler's life. They also intended to ask students to document their thinking and problem solving by recording (written, audio and/or images) the steps they took during the design and construction of their homes.

FIGURE 4.6 An example of a student cabin design sketch.

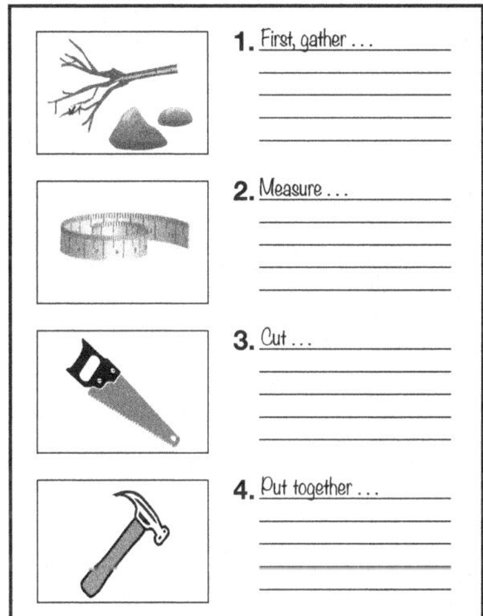

1. First, gather . . .
2. Measure . . .
3. Cut . . .
4. Put together . . .

FIGURE 4.7 Procedural writing template with prompts.

FIGURE 4.8 Students worked together to plan their model.

Support

They reflected on what support their students might need in order to accomplish this task. They were prepared to review linear measurement in math, structural concepts from science, and procedural writing in literacy, anticipating that many students would likely need this kind of support at some point in order to successfully complete the inquiry. Because it had not been introduced, they did a whole class lesson on the design process from the art curriculum. They also assembled a collection of print and digital paintings and photos of settlers' homesteads as source material.

Launch

They launched the inquiry with a read aloud of a novel depicting life in North America in this time period. They also used paintings and images of settlers and their homesteads to generate further discussion. These provocations led to a good deal of student interest and questions that revealed what interested them and what they already knew and didn't know. They shared in groups what they thought a settler's challenges would be and what they wanted to learn more about in this regard. The librarian had prepared a resource bank of sources about this topic. As the inquiry progressed, Kimberlee and Jenn constantly watched and listened to what their students were thinking and doing and reflected together on what feedback they might offer, questions they could ask, and support and resources that might be needed to keep the inquiry moving along.

Getting together to plan in advance can sometimes be a challenge, but Kimberlee and Jenn benefited from sharing ideas, addressing various areas of the curriculum in an efficient way and supporting each other to provide optimal learning experiences for their students.

THINQ

- How could you form a similar collaboration that would allow your students to engage in an integrated inquiry involving more than one subject?
- What kind of support will your students need in order find out, answer the question or solve the problem?
- What are some of the big ideas in the various subject areas for your grade level(s) that would lend themselves to an integrated curriculum inquiry?

Inquiry in Action

Subject integration

Inquiries that integrate across subject areas tend to spark interest and result in very deep learning and high levels of understanding. Fatima, a grade 3 teacher in a rural community, wanted her students engaged in an inquiry on immigration. She had found that in previous years students simply were not interested in the lives of Canadians who sailed to Canada from Europe in the late 1700s. This was part of her curriculum so she did not feel she could "skip it."

She approached both the physical education and performing arts teachers at her school for assistance. After exploring the curriculum expectations together, they helped Fatima with her inquiry by integrating across subject areas. On the day that Fatima's students were timetabled for both physical education and performing arts, the three teachers used the equipment in the school yard to help students imagine that they were sailing to Canada on a ship from Europe in the late 1700s. The students dressed in costumes and, through role playing, felt more connected to the inquiry. Many interesting and thoughtful questions were generated.

4.3 How can I support primary students in working with information, data and evidence?

Big Idea
Teachers need to model how to find answers to ensure student success.

COMMITMENT
Does the need to find and possibly adapt age-appropriate, multi-perspective source materials shake your commitment to do more inquiry?

In a guided inquiry with primary students, the responsibility for collecting research and gathering information is focused more on the teacher than the student. In no way does this mean that students don't take responsibility for the thinking. On the contrary. Each time the teacher provides more information, students should be invited to revisit their initial understanding around the topic, as well as their list of inquiry questions. Even our youngest learners can be invited to participate in metacognition by thinking about their initial thinking and how it has changed based on new information. This may involve the teacher creating charts or webs for, or with, students to be displayed in the classroom or in a digital format to be saved and revisited online. To support teachers in what may seem like the daunting task of helping younger students work with information and evidence, we discuss the following considerations in this section: identifying what is already known, locating appropriate content, websites that support elementary students, video sources, picture book sources, primary sources, and ensuring success for early elementary learners.

Identifying what is already known

Our young students arrive in our classrooms with a wide range of prior knowledge and experiences. By helping students identify their currently held beliefs at each stage of an inquiry, we can reduce the impact that any misconceptions might have on their learning.

Many teachers like to use a framework to provide a foundation for student inquiry. One such model, which places an emphasis on the process of inquiry, is a visible thinking routine called Think-Puzzle-Explore (Ritchhart, Church, & Morrison, 2011; see figure 4.9). Through a gradual release of responsibility approach, the teacher would guide students to reflect, in various ways, on the following questions:

- What do you **think** you know about the topic?
- What questions or **puzzles** do you have about this topic?
- How might you **explore** the puzzles we have around this topic?

Learners can continually update their findings by revisiting the framework.

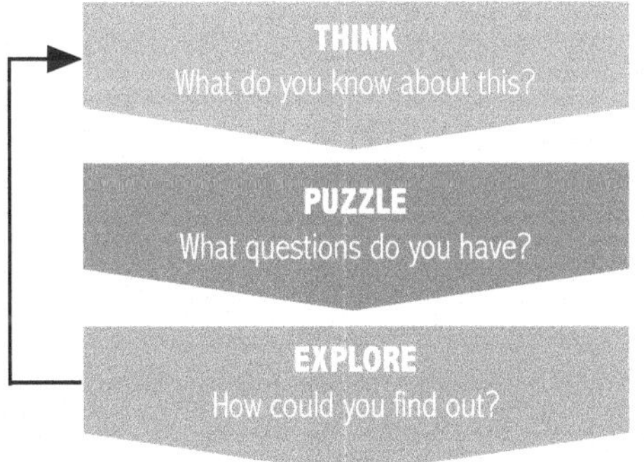

Source: Ritchhart et al., 2011.

FIGURE 4.9 You can use thinking frameworks like Think-Puzzle-Explore to help students reflect on what they know or would like to know.

Locating content that is grade- and age-appropriate

One of the biggest challenges for primary educators is finding information commensurate with literacy abilities. This is an even greater challenge if you are working with multilingual learners or in a language immersion classroom. If you are fortunate to have a teacher-librarian in your school, they can be a key partner in helping to "find out." School libraries are usually well stocked with a wide variety of resources at all different reading and interest levels.

Many online resources have advanced search features that enable users to specify the type of resource as well as the intended audience. When you model research on the internet, it is helpful to choose a search engine that is specifically designed for kids. *Kiddle* (www.kiddle.co), *KidzSearch* (www.kidzsearch.com), and *Junior* (www.juniorsafesearch) are examples of tools that provide an uncluttered interface (see figure 4.10). Results are filtered, providing a safer searching experience for, or with, students. After entering a search term or phrase, the results consist of sites written specifically for kids with easier to understand content. *Kiddle* provides a larger font and bigger thumbnails when generating a list of suggested sites providing specific types of resources (web, images, news, videos). *KidzSearch* even gives students "training" on how to do advanced searches.

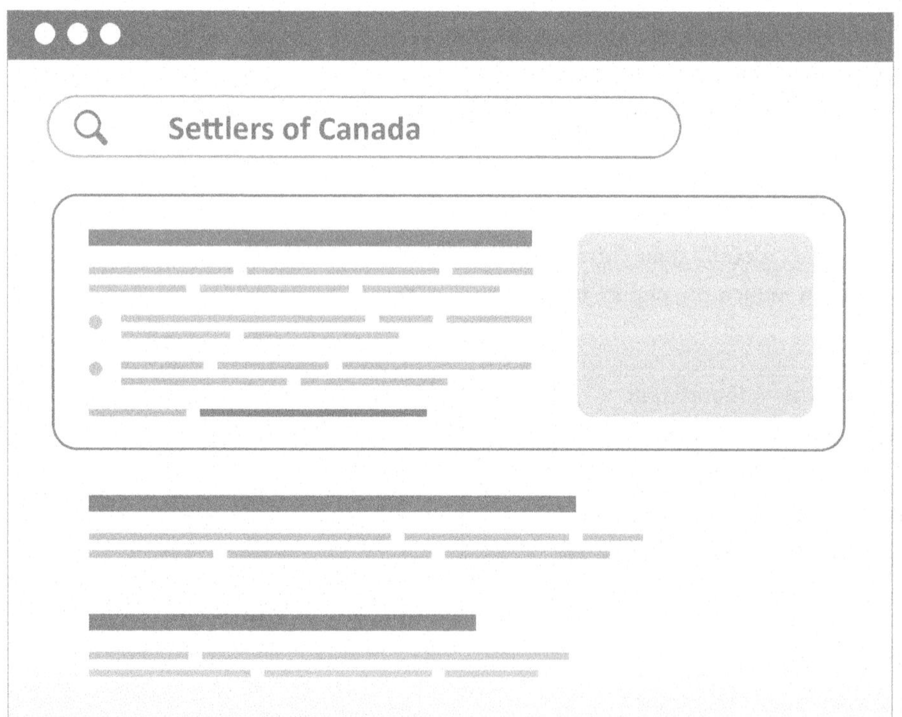

FIGURE 4.10 When you model research on the internet, it is helpful to choose a search engine that is specifically designed for kids.

Inquiry for ALL

Communication tools for primary learners

There are many tools that level the playing field for students with learning exceptionalities. These tools enable students to communicate in ways that wouldn't be possible without technology. Here are just a few:

Speech-to-text – Speaking is converted into typed words on a document.

Text-to-speech – Highlighted text is read aloud in a computerized voice. Advances in this technology have made the voices sound much more "human." In some cases, the words are highlighted as they are read.

Virtual meeting – A meeting is held using a free online program such as Zoom, Skype or Google Meet, in which classes and a visitor can see and hear each other using a laptop or tablet with a built-in webcam.

QR code – QR is short for Quick Response code. It is a square image that when "scanned" using the camera and a special app on a tablet or smartphone will take the user to a specific online resource or website.

Websites that support primary students

There are many websites specifically geared toward inquisitive students. *Pebble Go* (www.pebblego.com) is commonly available at local library websites. It's a kindergarten to grade 3 database for reading and research through games with audio/video support. *Wonderopolis* (https://wonderopolis.org) is a website that is full of questions! Visitors are encouraged to express what they are wondering or to investigate articles, images and videos that give answers to the questions that others are pondering. *Simple English Wikipedia* (https://simple.wikipedia.org) is a variation of the main site where the content has been written at a lower reading level. *Encyclopedia Britannica Online School Edition* (http://school.eb.com) is available in many school districts. There are various types of content, including articles, images, videos, a dictionary and magazines. In most cases, topics are offered at different levels of difficulty. Level 1 is geared for elementary students and Level 2 is aimed at middle school students. Users are able to browse content and then organize favorites into small collections. There are built-in features in some sections that will read content to users. Many videos are also available. Newsela (https://newsela.com) features many free current events articles on a variety of topics as well as a premium subscription with many more offerings. Each article is presented with different versions for several levels of reading difficulty. Accessibility options include a read-aloud feature and video content to meet the needs of young learners.

Video sources

Chances are that your primary students have already watched many videos in their young lives. To enhance understanding while viewing, enrich vocabulary and increase multi-sensory input, use closed captioning when possible. Each video on *YouTube* has a transcript that is automatically generated. Some content creators aren't aware of this option and, as a result, the text for the closed captioning may not be accurate or appropriate. Be sure to check first. *Vimeo* is another popular video-sharing website without ads. Many teachers have created resources to share online.

Learn 360 (https://learn360.infobase.com), a digital streaming service for K–12 students, is widely available to educators, offering videos (most with the option of closed captioning), audio, images, worksheets and more. Advanced searches will provide users with content geared to a specific grade level on a particular topic. Always preview videos to ensure they suit your learning goals and to determine the portion of the video that you will show students. After inserting a video into *Google Slides*, for example, you can right click on the image and choose "video options." You can customize the start and end time to highlight the most essential information.

Tech-enabled inquiry

Scaffolded video support

EDpuzzle (https://edpuzzle.com) is a free online service that allows you to customize videos for your students to watch. With EDpuzzle, you can choose existing videos or create your own. Enhance the videos by recording your voice to ask questions or insert written questions and comments at specific points. This scaffolded support can provide a customized learning experience for students of varying skills and abilities. If more repetition is needed, the video can be viewed again, putting the learning within the students' control. This tool is a game changer for grades 1–3 students. EDpuzzle also offers pro accounts to schools and districts needing more storage space and resources.

Picture book sources

Students of any age can benefit from having a picture book read to them or by exploring it on their own. The "kid friendly" language will sound familiar and in most cases will be easily understood. The pictures and photos in both fiction and nonfiction texts are essential for supporting pre-literate students. In this case, a picture really is worth a thousand words. The visuals in picture books can help to build background knowledge and inspire more questions. A picture book is great for the purpose of communicating a challenging or abstract idea in context. You can take the opportunity to review reading comprehension strategies during the read aloud of a picture book to meet your literacy requirements. And students can practice activating prior knowledge, questioning, visualizing, making connections, inferring and synthesizing. Sometimes a picture book can be more effective than a textbook or encyclopedia entry for illustrating key elements of a topic.

CONTEXT

How do you currently balance audio, visual and textual information in your classroom to support student learning? What else could you do?

Primary sources

An often overlooked type of information for grades 1–3 are primary sources. Primary sources include things like photographs, artwork and objects. These can easily be brought into class and are usually very engaging for students (see figure 4.11). Historical artifacts, for example, act like clues to the past.

Another type of primary source is guest speakers. Making a request to families or the community can often result in finding someone with first-hand knowledge on a particular topic. A relative of a student in the class could come in and talk about prior work experience that connects to an inquiry students are in the midst of researching. Reaching out on social media or other online communities can also prove to be fruitful. Many experts are more than happy to share their expertise with a group of eager students, either in person or during a virtual meeting online.

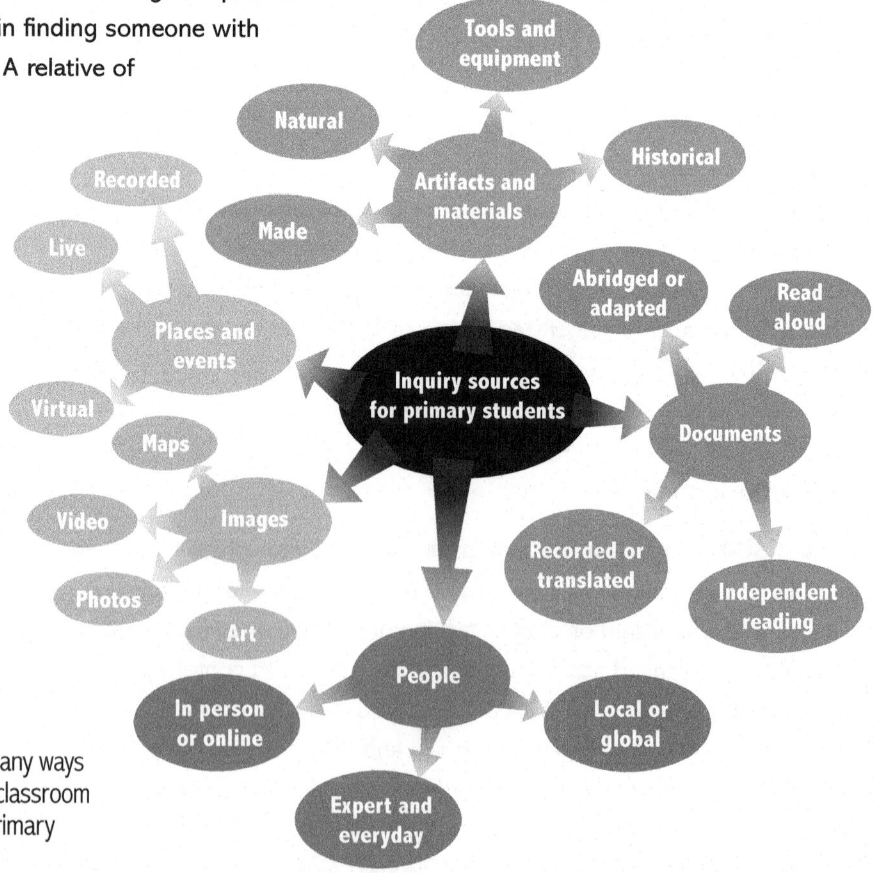

FIGURE 4.11 There are many ways to bring the world into your classroom to enliven and enrich your primary students' inquiries.

Digital Human Library (dHL; www.digitalhumanlibrary.com) is a website that connects experts with classes. The dHL is a nonprofit organization that connects North American teachers and students with hundreds of industry experts around the world for free. Field trips can also enhance the knowledge of students. Many venues provide age-appropriate information and interactive features to support student learning.

Other primary sources of information are *Google Maps* and *Google Earth*. Students can zoom in and explore an aerial view of their surroundings. In some municipalities, organizations have made interactive Geographical Information Systems tools available that show different "layers" of maps of a particular region such as topography, imagery and streets. Historical maps from different eras are also available to online visitors.

Ensuring success for primary learners

Having content readily available for primary students is essential. However, in many situations this alone may not be enough for students to succeed. Our youngest students will need to have text read to them. Often you will be the one to read and explain the material that students need to explore. But if you have reading buddies that support your students in the classroom, these older students can serve this purpose. Technology can be a solution as well. Every handheld device such as a tablet or smartphone has the ability to "read aloud" content using a text-to-speech tool that is integrated into the tool itself or can be added through an app. There are also text-to-speech tools on various internet browsers. Some search tools online have a microphone icon to demonstrate their voice search functionality.

THINQ

- What sources have you used successfully with primary students in the past?
- What is one new primary source idea that you will take from this chapter to use with your students?
- How might you use picture books both within an inquiry and to meet your literacy protocols?
- Consider challenging yourself to integrate one new technology idea per term to focus on with students. Which of the tech ideas presented in this chapter would you like to integrate in your classroom first?

Inquiry for ALL

Variety and choice matter

It's important to provide students with resources in a variety of different formats. Audio recordings in the form of podcasts or audiobooks may be a new source of information for students and teachers. These types of audio resources provide important opportunities to practice oral language skills and are particularly effective for students with emergent literacy skills or multilingual learners. Consider, too, the balance between text and visual sources. The greater variety of sources and formats, the more likely we will be to support a broad range of students' interests and capacities.

4.4 How can I ensure my students use information that is reliable and credible?

Big Idea
Young students have the capacity to learn how to think deeply and critically.

If your primary students are emergent readers, you will provide information to them in a source bundle. If your primary students are confident and capable readers, with guidance, they will be able to locate some information themselves. In either case, there are a number of skills you can help them develop to organize, evaluate and make sense of information. Gradually, they will begin to sift through information and vet sources before taking notes (text, audio or visual). With consistent modeling, guidance, support and strategies, young learners will have a much greater chance of understanding and applying the material (see figure 4.12). In this section, we consider how to help students record and understand information, consider multiple perspectives and determine the quality of sources.

Recording and understanding information

Students can collect and track their learning in a variety of ways. Our youngest learners could be invited to draw sketches either on paper or digitally while listening to the teacher read and discuss fiction or nonfiction text. There are many apps and digital tools that are designed to make students' thinking visible. Some examples are the apps *Book Creator* (https://bookcreator.com) and *Draw and Tell* (https://bit.ly/3ScBlUW).

In order to avoid the common pitfall of students copying information verbatim or merely changing a word or two, they must learn how to process the knowledge first and then restate it in their own words. It helps to encourage students to do so without looking at the text. Then they can check back to verify their work and include any important vocabulary. By carefully going through the steps of read, stop, summarize and review, students will be on their way to learning how to do research effectively (Lehman, 2012).

Note-taking can be done with paper and pencil, through sketching or by using digital tools to create an audio recording of summarized information. Speech-to-text tools enable students to create notes or complete a mind map type of graphic organizer. Every handheld device and most computer operating systems have the means to

Helping students locate appropriate sources

1. Provide students with evidence bundles.
2. Direct learners to three to five sources (e.g., books or websites) that have been previewed and determined useful and credible.
3. Use a virtual bulletin board (e.g., Padlet) or online document to collect and share appropriate bookmarks.
4. Have learners work within walled garden websites (a browsing environment with restricted access to materials).
5. Include the use of at least one human resource (e.g., librarian, museum curator, community member, parent) in your list of search criteria.

FIGURE 4.12 There are many ways to help students gather appropriate sources.

translate clearly articulated spoken words into text. Some apps or extensions are available to be installed on web browsers in order to accomplish this task. Once again, it is essential that teachers model this process for their young charges. Some students will need an extended period of time in the "modeled" phase, or in the "shared" stage of the gradual release model, before they are able to document their thoughts with a partner or on their own.

CONTEXT

How do you ensure classroom instruction encourages multiple perspectives?

Considering multiple perspectives

When any student searches for an answer to an inquiry question, we always want them to look for and consider multiple points of view. We want our students to learn not to rush to judgment. In a world where we have unlimited access to information, this is one of *the* most important critical thinking skills this generation of students needs.

Once again, at the primary level, you will most likely need to take the lead on this aspect of the inquiry and rely on extensive modeling and scaffolding. At its most basic level, the information students consider, whether located by themselves or provided by you, will ideally meet the following criteria (see figure 4.13):

- Resources include at least two different points of view or perspectives (e.g., an adult's perspective, a student's perspective, an Indigenous perspective, an economic perspective, an environmental perspective).
- Information includes samples from a variety of sources.
- If applicable, information includes at least one position in support of, one position against, and one undecided (or neutral).

We realize that gathering resource material for your students takes time. However, it is critical that we promote the idea that issues are not black and white. If time is an issue, we recommend doing a smaller number of rich inquiries that explore an issue in depth and reflect multiple perspectives, rather than numerous inquiries that do not dig as deeply.

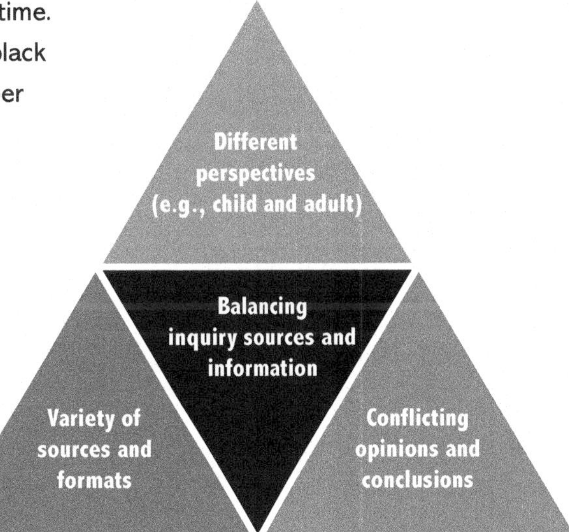

FIGURE 4.13 Sources should be chosen to promote insight, thinking and discussion.

Determining the quality of sources

As with any of the prerequisite skills involved in student inquiry, teachers will have to be very intentional and use a high level of support when it comes to helping students determine whether or not information is reliable and credible. In the early primary grades, teachers can use a "think aloud" approach while modeling the use of one of the tools for evaluating sources and evidence (see Reproducible 4A, *Evaluating sources and evidence: P.A.S.S.*, page 105, or Reproducible 4B, *Evaluating sources and evidence: R.A.D.A.R.*, page 106; see figure 4.14). While projecting one of these reproducibles on a whiteboard, or enlarging it on chart paper, you can talk students through the process of checking to see that a source is reliable and credible. Some students may be ready to accomplish this task on their own by the time they enter the upper elementary grades.

A transitional phase, as students gain independence, could involve the teacher providing sources of information of varying degrees of credibility. Students would be challenged to begin to think critically about which ones to use.

> **CONVICTION**
>
> Does using strategies you're accustomed to, such as "think aloud," to model for students how you would determine the quality of a source of information, make this seem more doable with primary learners?

Tools for evaluating sources and evidence

There are many tools you can use to help your students think about the quality and usefulness of the information they find. Here are two examples.

P.A.S.S. (See Reproducible 4A, *Evaluating sources and evidence: P.A.S.S.*)

- **Purpose:** Why and when was it created?
- **Accuracy:** Is the information current, truthful and unbiased?
- **Source:** Who created it? Are they an expert?
- **Support:** Is it supported by other information and sources?

R.A.D.A.R. (See Reproducible 4B, *Evaluating sources and evidence: R.A.D.A.R.*; Mandalios, 2013; Tanner & McPhee, 2015)

- **Relevance:** Is this information related to my inquiry topic?
- **Authority:** Is the author an expert on this topic?
- **Date:** Was the information created recently? Is it the most current information?
- **Appearance:** Is the information presented in a way that looks professional?
- **Reason:** Why was this information created?

FIGURE 4.14 You can introduce primary students to frameworks for evaluating sources and information and model their use.

A curated list of resources can be made available to students in a variety of ways. One method that can be implemented even with non-readers is QR codes. These black and white images, similar to barcodes, can be placed around the room. The method for creating QR codes directly from a web browser changes with version updates. Among the options often provided for sharing a particular website will be to "Create a QR code." Do an internet search to determine the procedure for the current version of your web browser. Using a tablet, students can scan the code, which will take them to a specific website, video or interactive online tool. Class blogs or learning management systems such as *Seesaw* (https://seesaw.com), *Google Classroom* or *D2L's Brightspace* (www.d2l.com/brightspace) provide great places where teachers can collect hyperlinks to resources students can access easily from school or home, in the classroom, or outdoors. Alternatively, a teacher can create a custom Google search, meaning that certain websites are chosen and the specialized search box will only send visitors to those sites for accessing information matching their search terms.

Students who are ready for greater autonomy in the inquiry process can be given more independence over their research (see figure 4.15). Some may be ready to vet sources with minimal support before taking notes. Two handy tools that are available in most school districts for collecting notes and gathering sources are *Google Keep* and *Microsoft OneNote*. They integrate well with their respective online word processing companion tools and act as virtual sticky notes for collecting comments, questions, website links, lists, photos, audio, videos and even sketches either on a laptop or a handheld device. This task of curating will advance students' understanding of their inquiry topic.

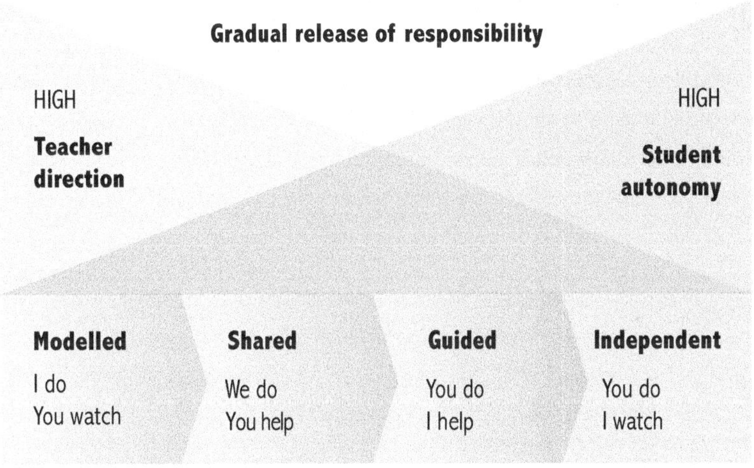

Source: Pearson & Gallagher, 1983.

FIGURE 4.15 The gradual release model is useful for primary teachers as they consider the level of support to offer students in an inquiry. This will be especially true in helping your students investigate and explore.

THINQ

- What "networking" do you already have in place (e.g., parent volunteers, teacher-librarian support, special education support, learning buddies) that might provide support to your students while investigating and exploring?
- How would you convince a colleague to form a new collaboration with you and your students to advance their comfort with inquiry?
- In what ways would you need to prepare mentors so their support would be the most beneficial to your students?

Inquiry in Action

Learning Buddies to the rescue!

Earth Day inquiry

Often, primary classes are paired with older students for support with reading skills. Some teachers have gone beyond this traditional relationship and renamed the partnership "learning buddies." Such was the situation with Mel's grade 8 students and Lyne's grades 1 and 2 students. The younger students were embarking on an inquiry to explore questions around Earth Day and planned to use an iPad app called *Adobe Spark Video* to share their learning. Lyne approached Mel to ask if the learning buddies could assist.

On several occasions, students paired up to work on this inquiry (see figure 4.16). They started by generating a list of what the younger students thought they knew about environmental topics. Next they selected ideas upon which to build, leading them to do research. The older buddies performed *Google* searches and then read information to their young partners to help answer any inquiry questions they had generated. The grade 8s were able to develop their own research skills, in this case, by brushing up on *Adobe Spark Video* and sharing it with their own teacher. The final product, created in learning buddy pairs, was a slideshow highlighting the supported new learning.

Environmental science inquiry

Another powerful collaboration developed between Kerri-Ann's grade 5 students and Sarah's grade 1 class. The younger learners were concerned about a bad smell coming up from the driveway at the front of the school into their second floor classroom. The class began an inquiry to find out more about what they later learned were emissions from the vehicles waiting to pick up students.

It was a challenge to find resources at a suitable level for the primary students, so a partnership was formed to facilitate the learning. The older students joined the inquiry and did some investigating online. Using the research they gathered, they created instructional videos explaining the impact of this particular form of air pollution on people. Inspired by their new learning, the primary students hung a huge banner in the window to persuade the drivers below to "Turn off your car!"

FIGURE 4.16 Older students can model and facilitate the inquiry process for younger students.

4.5 How do I assess the investigation and exploration stages of the inquiry process?

Big Idea

Assessment for learning during the investigation and exploration phases is important to student success.

In this chapter, we have recommended that primary teachers gather and organize rich, age-appropriate resources for, or with, their students using the appropriate level of scaffolding. It's important to understand what your students can and can't do in this regard and provide ongoing feedback and support.

This is a stage when observation and conversation are essential to understanding how primary learners are doing as they investigate and explore. If they can't express it orally, they probably don't understand it. So you will need to base your assessment on triangulated evidence: reflections on **conversations** with students; **observations** of students at work; the evaluation of student-created **products**; and a system for tracking information (either digitally or using a hard copy). Part of the process of gathering evidence to strengthen new learning involves designating time for sharing the acquired understandings. Giving students time to exchange new ideas strengthens the learned information, gives opportunity to clarify any confusion about new concepts, and helps students of varying abilities learn from each other. Educators can assess oral language as well as the skills that students demonstrated in the investigation phase of the inquiry process.

Reproducible 4C, *Assessment planning template: Understands what is currently known* (page 107) can be used to plan your triangulated assessment evidence collection. Reproducible 4D, *Inquiry rubric and self-check: Understands what is currently known* (page 108) can be used as a guide by you and your students to assess and evaluate the skills of investigation as found in each of the six essential abilities of inquiry learners.

THINQ

- Where might you be able to inject more assessment for learning into class time devoted to the investigation phase of the inquiry process?
- What would be the benefits of doing so?
- What else would you like to know about assessing learning at this stage?

Revisit and reflect

In this chapter, we argued that teachers can foster and support an investigative mindset that sees problems and questions as challenges and views the search for answers as interesting and exciting. We also stressed that primary students can begin to learn the important skills and abilities required to investigate and explore information to find answers to questions.

We explored how teachers can assist students with the investigative process, including:

- the need to foster an investigative mindset
- how to create classroom conditions that encourage an investigative mindset
- scaffolding the process of gathering information while investigating and exploring
- introducing the importance of using information that is reliable and credible
- how to use technology effectively during this phase

We examined how source evidence can be prepared and shared with students in a variety of ways and concluded by reviewing a number of assessment tools designed to measure students' abilities to begin to navigate the investigative phase of the inquiry process.

To conclude your exploration of this chapter, take some time to complete Reproducible 4E, *Teacher checklist: Investigative mindset in my classroom* (page 109).

Big Ideas

4.1 Students are naturally curious, and their interests will drive them to want answers to questions.

4.2 Literacy protocols fit naturally into inquiry-based learning.

4.3 Teachers need to model how to find answers to ensure student success.

4.4 Young students have the capacity to learn how to think deeply and critically.

4.5 Assessment for learning during the investigation and exploration phases is important to student success.

THINQ

- What are one or two specific strategies you could implement in your classroom to signal to your students that your classroom is a place for investigation?
- How might you encourage your students to gradually acquire greater independence while investigating and exploring their inquiry questions?
- How might you improve how you integrate multiple points of view in response to the questions, issues or problems explored in your classroom?
- How will you ensure that you are accurately assessing students' skills demonstrated in the investigation phase of the inquiry?

Reproducible 4A

Evaluating sources and evidence: P.A.S.S.

Name: ______________________________ Date: ______________

Inquiry focus: ______________________________

Evidence being evaluated: ______________________________

Key questions		My evaluation of the evidence
P	**PURPOSE** Why and when was it created? Is it important to my inquiry?	
A	**ACCURACY** Is the information correct, truthful and unbiased? Should I use it?	
S	**SOURCE** Who created it? Are they an expert? Are they believable?	
S	**SUPPORT** Is it supported by other information and sources? What does this tell me?	

Reproducible 4B

Evaluating sources and evidence: R.A.D.A.R.

Name: ______________________ Date: ______________

Inquiry focus: ______________________

Evidence being evaluated: ______________________

Key questions		My evaluation of the evidence
R	**RELEVANCE** Is this information related to my inquiry topic?	
A	**AUTHORITY** Is the author an expert on the topic?	
D	**DATE** Was the information created recently? Is it the most current information?	
A	**APPEARANCE** Is the information presented in a way that looks professional?	
R	**REASON** Why was this information created?	

Source: Mandalios, J. (2013). RADAR: An approach for helping students evaluate Internet sources. Journal of Information Science, 39*(4), 470–478; Tanner, K., & McPhee, K. (2015).* A new approach to evaluating information: A reflection on RADAR *[Conference presentation]. 2015 Research on Teaching and Learning Conference, Hamilton, Ontario, Canada. Accessed at https://ir.lib.uwo.ca/wlpres/50 on February 29, 2024.*

Reproducible 4C

Assessment planning template: Understands what is currently known

Name: ______________________________ Date: ________________

Essential inquiry ability — Understands what is currently known	Evidence gathered		
	Conversations	Observations	Products
Demonstrates curiosity • Actively asks many questions during the investigative stage. • Demonstrate an eagerness to explore, find things and learn.			
Understands what is currently known • Has the necessary facts and information. • Is able to understand different points of view in the research.			
Puts it all together • Understands when "enough" evidence has been collected and/or considered.			
Thinks together • Listens to, builds on, considers and assists others during the investigative process. • Asks relevant questions of other people to further an inquiry (gets an opinion or some advice, disagrees, inquires, brainstorms).			

Reproducible 4D

Inquiry rubric and self-check: Understands what is currently known

Name: ______________________________ Date: ______________

Areas that need work	Standard for this criterion	How work exceeds expectations
	Demonstrates curiosity • Actively asks many questions during the investigative stage. • Demonstrate an eagerness to explore, find things and learn.	
	Understands what is currently known • Has the necessary facts and information. • Is able to understand different points of view in the research.	
	Puts it all together • Understands when "enough" evidence has been collected and/or considered.	
	Thinks together • Listens to, builds on, considers and assists others during the investigative process. • Asks relevant questions of other people to further an inquiry (gets an opinion or some advice, disagrees, inquires, brainstorms).	

Source: Rubric based on ideas from Dietz, M. (2000). Single point rubric idea. *INTASC Academy, Milwaukee, WI, as cited by Gonzalez, J. (2015, February 4).* Meet the single point rubric. *Accessed at www.cultofpedagogy.com/single-point-rubric/ on February 29, 2024.*

Reproducible 4E

Teacher checklist: Investigative mindset in my classroom

Check which of the following statements represent your current teaching practice. The focus of this checklist is on the investigative step of the inquiry process. You may want to use this checklist for self-reflection, for planning and sharing with colleagues, and to determine next steps in deepening inquiry practice.

- An investigative mindset is fostered in meaningful ways in my classroom.
- Conditions in my classroom encourage an investigative mindset.
- I give my students the opportunity to activate and demonstrate their background knowledge on a topic of inquiry.
- I locate age- and grade-appropriate resources for my students to drive their inquiry learning.
- I provide just the right amount of scaffolding for my students to assist them while seeking information.
- I make sure that students are exposed to multiple perspectives during their inquiries.
- Students know that they cannot draw a conclusion before they have considered multiple perspectives.
- I am starting to demonstrate to my students how to determine the quality of sources.
- I know how to facilitate the investigative portion of an inquiry.
- I use a variety of provocations to pique and sustain student curiosity, wonder and questioning during the inquiry.
- I build in collaboration opportunities during the investigative phase of inquiry.

Chapter 5
MAKING SENSE:
Helping primary students synthesize, consolidate and reflect

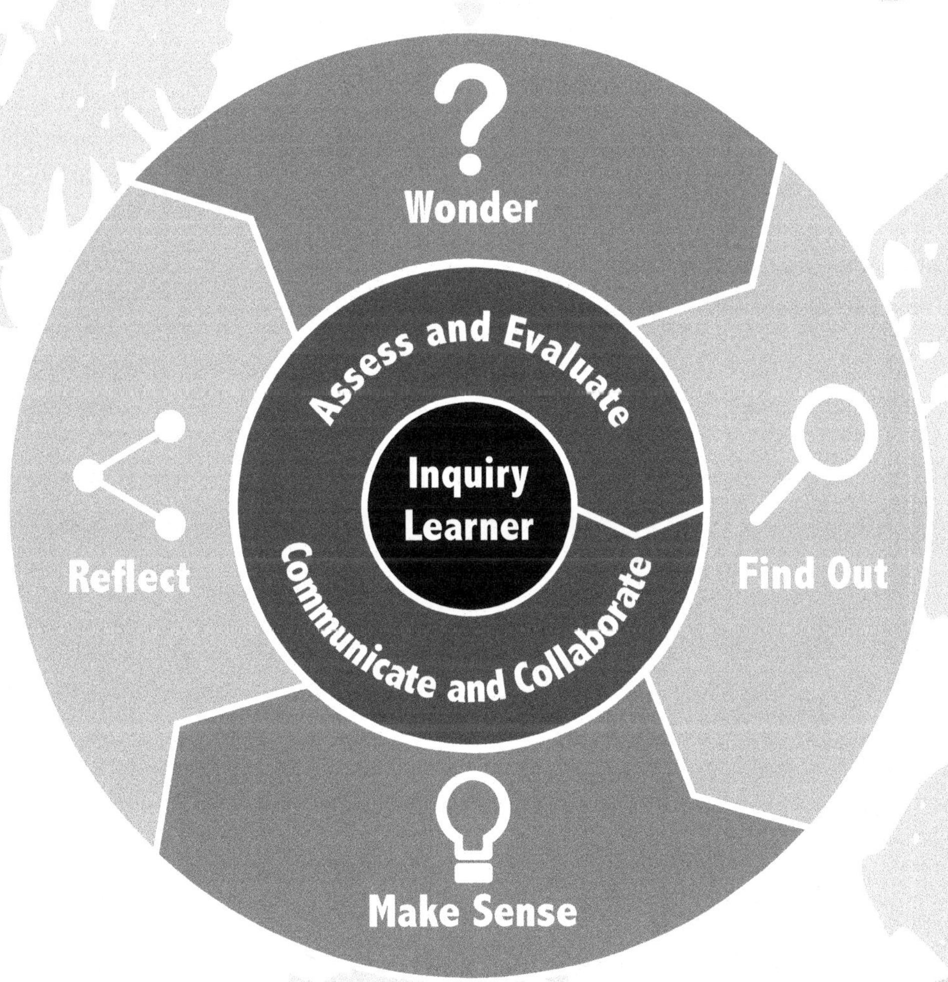

People do not like to think. If one thinks, one must reach a conclusion. Conclusions are not always pleasant.

—Helen Keller

In this chapter, we look at several ways to help primary students move from simply knowing facts to synthesizing ideas to create a new understanding and to consolidate and reflect on their knowledge. Understanding that our thinking changes with new information is the key to supporting students in making sense out of seemingly disconnected pieces of data.

5.1 What does the "making sense" part of inquiry involve?

One of the most exciting parts of inquiry learning for primary students is when they arrive at the place where they can create new knowledge and innovative solutions. This is a generative stage of inquiry. Students have examined and explored what is already known; now they engage with this knowledge again in a new, creative and highly personalized way (see figure 5.1).

You may recall that hopefulness is one of the five inquiry dispositions that we believe is essential to inquiry learning. Hopefulness is put into action when students can consider what is known and how things are in the world and suggest innovations and alternative ways of thinking and being. In other words, when they create new knowledge. This is the empowering stage of learning, where we consolidate, synthesize and take action.

FIGURE 5.1 The synthesis process allows us to make meaning out of seemingly disconnected pieces of information and data.

Big Idea

New knowledge and understandings emerge after we "make sense" of information.

Educators Ask

Shouldn't we hold off trying to develop synthesis skills until upper elementary?

Some teachers we have talked to feel that since synthesis is at the top of Bloom's (1969) taxonomy, other "lower order" skills have to be in place before they can address this important "higher order" skill. When educators view learning in this way they rarely "make it" to synthesis. This is detrimental to our ultimate goal of fostering critical thinking in our students. Analyzing, evaluating and synthesizing are important critical thinking skills required to push learning deeper for our students.

Inquiry in Action

Using question prompts during a patterning activity for grades 1–2

Allison wanted to see if she could help her students in her grades 1–2 class develop their critical thinking skills through a patterning exercise (see figure 5.2). She asked her students, "How many different patterns can you make with two colors?"

The students worked with a strategically chosen partner (students similar in their current level of understanding), and the task was differentiated through the materials (some pairs received bins with only two colors of cubes) as well as recording sheets.

When asked to describe the patterns, the pair replied by naming the colors. When asked to describe the core, the students did not know. Allison explained that the core is the part that repeats, and the students were able to isolate the pattern, naming the colors involved.

The top pattern, which was the last pattern built, resulted from a challenge she gave the pair to build a pattern where one of the terms included more than one block.

FIGURE 5.2 Allowing students to experiment with block patterns is a great way to invite inquiry.

Teacher: "What is the same about the top pattern and the second pattern?"

Student 1: "They both use two colors."

Teacher: "Tell me in a different way."

Student 2: "They're both pink green patterns."

Teacher: "What if you are using letters to describe the pattern? What would this one be?" (pointing to the second pattern). The girls were silent for a moment, looking at the pattern.

Student 2: "It's an AB pattern."

Teacher: "Tell me more about that."

Student 2: "This one is A and this one is B because it is a different color."

Teacher: "Okay, so now look at the top pattern." (silence)

Student 1: (very excited) "They are both AB patterns! See! This one is A and this one is B!"

THINQ

- How did this teacher use question prompts to assist her students' thinking?
- In this example, the teacher chose to pair students with another of similar abilities. Why do you think she did this rather than pairing students of differing abilities?

It doesn't matter whether we are working with primary learners, preschool learners or adult learners: learning something new is really hard. In their book *Intentional Interruption: Breaking Down Learning Barriers to Transform Professional Practice*, Stephen Katz and Lisa Ain Dack (2013) remind us that there are a number of psychological barriers that hinder new learning for most individuals, as presented in figure 5.3.

Young people can be susceptible to the same cognitive biases as adults (Dibbets, Fliek, & Meesters, 2015). It's important for us, as teachers, to be aware of these psychological barriers to learning so we can help our students avoid them.

Words Matter

You may want to post these words in your room under the heading "Making Sense."

Arrange
Organize in a particular order

Assemble
Put or fit together

Combine
Bring or join together

Construct
Build by putting parts together

Make sense
Explain or understand something

Synthesize
Make something new by combining different things

Brain barriers to learning	
We find thinking hard. People really dislike hard thinking and therefore avoid it.	**We can't see all options.** People aren't very good at thinking through all possible options when making decisions.
Our thinking is biased. People tend to accept information and ideas that confirm what they already think, believe, know and do, and dismiss evidence to the contrary.	**We believe being wrong is weak.** People keep their questions to themselves because they believe not knowing or being wrong is seen as a weakness.

Source: Katz & Dack, 2013.

FIGURE 5.3 Human beings are flawed thinkers, and that can create barriers to learning.

THINQ

- In your experience, do primary learners find it difficult to synthesize or consolidate a body of evidence?
- Do you have strategies to assist your students with the synthesis process, or is this an area you would like to improve in your practice?
- Are there opportunities within your school for teachers to share effective strategies with one another? If not, could this be a useful target for a future staff meeting?

5.2 What are some obstacles to the synthesis process?

Big Idea
The human brain often makes errors when processing information.

As teachers, we often caution our students about the synthesis process. We tell students to make sure they consider all their evidence carefully, we tell them not to jump to conclusions and we tell them to consider bias in the information they have collected. We certainly give the impression that "making sense" is a minefield of trouble!

We feel that it is worthwhile exploring this phenomenon with primary learners so that they begin to have a better understanding of how their brains work. If students understand that the human brain makes errors when processing information, they may proceed more carefully when synthesizing and drawing conclusions.

One way that the human brain makes "errors" is by making inferences and then treating those inferences as facts. You can explore this phenomenon with your students by doing a few simple optical illusion experiments in class. We have provided two images here to get you started (see figures 5.4 and 5.5), but you can use Google Images in your classroom for the same result. When we stare at each of the images, our brains play tricks on us. Students will want to know how this happens!

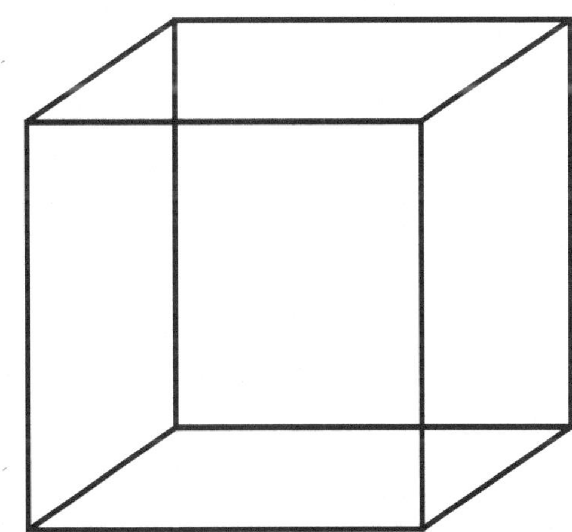

FIGURE 5.4 When you stare at this Necker cube, the faces of the cube move forward and backward. This "brain error" occurs as a result of the fact that this is an ambiguous line drawing that does not include any depth cues.

Students know that these optical illusions don't make sense, but they also know that they see them! There is a scientific explanation for both of these illusions, which you can discuss with your students if you choose, but the big idea we want to emphasize is that our brains are constantly making inferences and drawing conclusions when processing information. Often the inference is correct, but sometimes it isn't. When our brains make an incorrect inference based on *visual* information, then an optical illusion is the result.

After doing a few optical illusions with your students, you may choose to broaden the discussion by exploring other phenomena that result in brain errors: lack of sleep, hunger, poor nutrition and extremes of temperature, to name a few.

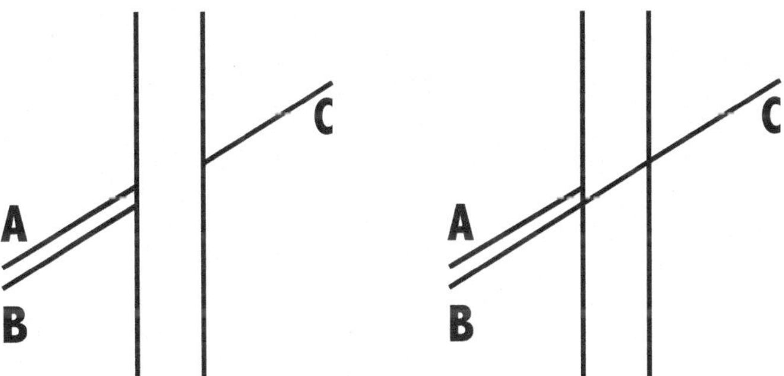

FIGURE 5.5 Look at this Poggendorff illusion. In the diagram on the left, can you tell which diagonal line connects: line A-C or line B-C? If you look at the diagram on the right, you can see that it's line B-C. This optical illusion is the result of the brain's misperception of the interaction between diagonal lines and horizontal and vertical edges.

At the conclusion of this exploration you'll want to make an explicit connection back to the issue at hand: the synthesis of new information (see figure 5.6). In particular, if the human brain can make errors processing "factual" visual information, then of course the brain can make errors while trying to make sense of new information.

THINQ

- How might this information about brain errors be helpful to primary students in their learning journey?
- How might knowledge about brain errors be useful to you when you are leading students through the synthesis process of an inquiry?

FIGURE 5.6 Students can work together with teacher guidance to synthesize pieces of new information.

5.3 How can I help students consolidate their information?

Big Idea
The development of synthesis skills requires teacher modeling and support.

CONVICTION
Are you convinced that, with support, primary students are capable of synthesizing and consolidating?

Once students have finished the investigation phase of an inquiry and have gathered a variety of information, data or materials, they must make sense of it through consolidation. *Consolidation* means to bring together different ideas into a coherent whole.

Many primary learners are still emergent readers, so they will need support from you, another student or a learning buddy in this process. Even if our primary students struggle with this task, it is still important that we ask them to consolidate and draw conclusions as these are key elements of critical thinking. They will get better at this over time and with practice. To help students get started with consolidation, we recommend revisiting the inquiry question and identifying trends, patterns, and ideas.

Revisiting the inquiry question

There are a number of ways teachers can help with the consolidation phase of the inquiry process. The first is to have students return to their inquiry question. Students need to determine what the evidence they have collected tells them about their inquiry question. We have created a number of templates to help your primary learners with this process (see Reproducibles 5A, 5B and 5C on pages 129–131).

Identifying trends, patterns and ideas

One way for students to consolidate or make sense of their evidence is to identify patterns or trends in the information they have collected. Patterns or trends are ideas, themes or arguments that repeat throughout the evidence. Students can be prompted to identify patterns and trends by considering questions such as the ones in figures 5.6 and 5.7.

When making sense of evidence, students can also look for connections between ideas. These connections can be between their own ideas and the evidence or connections between the ideas expressed in the evidence they have collected. For example, students make connections between their own ideas and the evidence when they respond to the questions: "What did I wonder?" and "What did I find?" Students will also make connections when they find similar ideas expressed in the evidence they have collected.

> **CONTEXT**
> As a co-learner, how are you modeling synthesis and consolidation for your students? How could you be more effective?

Questions to develop consolidation skills

- What was our question or problem?
- What did we think we might find?
- What did we find?
- What patterns or trends did we see?
- Did we find anything surprising?
- Did we miss anything?
- What might we conclude?
- What other questions do we have?
- How could we explore this further?

FIGURE 5.7 Careful consolidation of information helps students to draw stronger conclusions.

What is **similar** about the information we gathered?

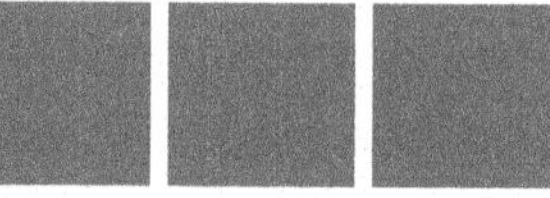

What is **consistent** about the information we gathered?

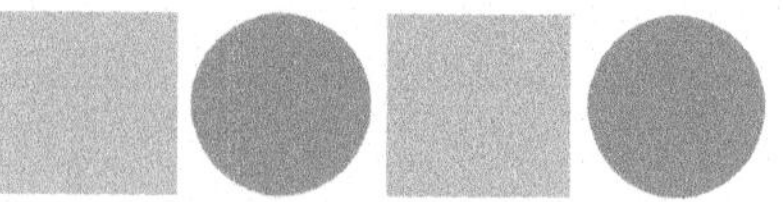

Can we see any **patterns**? What do they tell us?

Can we see any **trends**? What do they tell us?

FIGURE 5.8 Pausing and asking a few key questions can help your primary students make sense of a body of information. You could use colored shapes like these to illustrate for students the concepts of similarity, consistency, patterns and trends.

Inquiry in Action

Consolidating during a primary math inquiry — How big is a foot?

A grades 2–3 class had been exploring proportional reasoning in mathematics. The teacher, Elinor, decided to capitalize on her students' interest in literature and fairy tales to build their understanding of units of measurement. Using the student wonderings and the picture book *How Big Is A Foot?* by Rolf Mylier (1990) as a provocation, Elinor designed a mini-math inquiry to build her students' understanding of proportional reasoning.

In the story, the King decides to create a bed for the Queen as a birthday present. But, no one knew how big the bed should be because beds hadn't been invented yet. The King insisted that the builder should use the measure of his own foot in creating the bed. But the bed did not fit the Queen properly and the students were invited to figure out why.

The inquiry question became: "Why doesn't the bed fit the Queen?"

Students hypothesized:

- The Queen had not hired a good builder
- The Queen had grown while the bed was being built
- Maybe the builder didn't use the King's foot as a measure

In trying to solve the problem, students suggested they needed to make pictures and talked about how helpful it would be to have actual feet to help them figure it out (see figure 5.9).

FIGURE 5.9 While the teacher read and invited inquiry, students hypothesized about the story and talked about possible visuals.

Elinor drew an outline of the Queen and then made feet in two different sizes based on student observations and predictions. Once students saw the bed size outlined on the floor with two different feet sizes, they began to think about the relationship between the length of the bed and the size of the feet used to measure it.

Elinor heard thinking like:

- The bed doesn't fit the Queen because the apprentice's feet were smaller
- He did exactly what he was told to do but the Queen was bigger
- The King's feet were bigger than the apprentice so the bed was too small
- The King didn't think about the sizes of everyone's feet

Capturing and consolidating the students' thinking was a key focus in this learning. The teacher had students record their thinking on paper while revisiting the inquiry question (see figure 5.10). Some students needed scribing in order to capture their questions and thinking.

After the prediction and measurement activity, Elinor returned to the math concept of proportional reasoning and the students were able to apply what they learned from the fairy tale mini-inquiry.

THINQ

- Where might literature activities support your mathematics programming?
- What do you feel are the benefits of an inquiry that is cross-disciplinary?
- How might you be able to use, or modify, this example for your own students?

FIGURE 5.10 Students worked individually to come up with possible solutions.

THINQ

- Two effective consolidation strategies for primary students are revisiting the inquiry question and identifying trends and patterns in data. What other consolidation strategies have you used effectively?
- How much time do you think you would need to devote to consolidation during an inquiry? What might you say to a colleague to convince them that this is time well spent?

5.4 What are some simple tools to help students draw conclusions?

Big Idea
Sound conclusions can be drawn after evidence is carefully considered.

At the most basic level, drawing a conclusion is really about weighing the evidence related to a question under investigation. Most inquiries will have a number of branches of exploration and associated evidence. After students have consolidated their information they will have to make a decision about the inquiry question being explored. Keeping in mind that our primary students are young and just beginning to learn how to draw conclusions, so any tools we use in our classrooms should be clear and uncomplicated. In this section, we discuss applying self-reflection tools, using question prompts, choosing other tools to help students synthesize and conclude, and weighing the evidence and concluding.

Self-reflection tools

One way to help students draw conclusions is to involve them in self-reflection. Self-reflection is an important critical thinking skill and assessment protocol, and it also teaches students how to learn. In light of this, it is important to make time to allow our primary learners to work through the self-reflection and/or self-assessment process. We have found it helpful to project a "slice" of a checklist like the one in figure 5.11 to help students reflect on their own progress during the synthesis and conclusion process (see Reproducible 5D, *Student self-check: Making sense,* page 132).

Using question prompts

Another way we can help students draw conclusions is to provide question prompts along with success criteria to push understanding to a new level. For example, asking students, "Did this new information change your thinking?" or "What are you thinking now?" encourages a growth mindset among students by demonstrating that our thinking evolves as we learn.

Consolidation self-check	Yes	Mostly	A little	Not yet
I made a thoughtful conclusion from the information I gathered.				
I shared and discussed my conclusion with my peers.				
I used feedback from my peers to improve my conclusion.				

FIGURE 5.11 Making sense of things is a process that benefits from reflection, sharing and feedback.

Inquiry in Action

Consolidation tools for primary classrooms

Grade 3 mathematics

In her mathematics classroom, Stacia worked to develop problem solving success criteria to support her students in both consolidating their mathematical learning and making judgments about what they know and how they are doing. When students have to think about and reflect on the strategies and tools they are using to solve problems, they build understanding and consolidate thinking (Dean, Hubbell, Pitler, & Stone, 2012). Developing effective success criteria supports the goal of pushing the learning deeper (see figure 5.12). This also gives educators opportunities to gather current thinking and give timely, descriptive feedback to support them in the development of more sophisticated tools, models and strategies.

Problem Solving Success

- ☐ 1. We read over the problem a few times so we knew what we were being asked to do.
- ☐ 2. We made a plan and chose this strategy and this tool: ____________________
- ☐ 3. We recorded all of our math thinking in number sentences and diagrams (if needed).
- ☐ 4. When we got stuck we____________________
- ☐ 5. We wrote clear sentences that answered all of the questions in the problem.
- ☐ 6. We used estimation to be sure our answers were reasonable.
- ☐ 7. We decided that if we did a similar problem like this, we would ______ ____________________

FIGURE 5.12 Problem-solving success criteria.

Grade 1 language arts

In Terry's grade 1 class, she uses RAN charts to help her young primary students draw conclusions. RAN charts (short for Reading and Analyzing Nonfiction) are designed to track changes in student thinking over time as they are introduced to new information (see also page 71).

You can see in figure 5.13 a RAN chart in its beginning stages. As her grade 1 students wondered about clouds on an overcast day, Terry recorded the students' understandings and then chose a nonfiction book to find out more and to confirm what they thought they knew. The students decided if information from the text was new learning, confirmed prior knowledge or uncovered a misconception. In the confirmed column, the page number and title of the resource can be recorded, along with a rephrasing of relevant information. Wonderings are recorded to spark further learning using a variety of sources.

The RAN chart can be used as a launch into a larger inquiry, or as a way to help young students consolidate their thinking and draw conclusions.

Reading and Analyzing Nonfiction
RAN Strategy

Prior Knowledge	*Confirmed*	*New Learning*	*Misconceptions*	*Wonderings*
What I think I knew	Yes, I was right!	What I learned	What I couldn't prove	Questions I still have
1.				
2.				
3.				

FIGURE 5.13 Tracking changes in students' thinking.

Educators Ask

How can I help my primary students draw conclusions when many of them are still struggling readers?

It is good practice to model a task or tool with your entire class through a think aloud protocol before asking students to attempt the task or use the tool on their own. If you are going to ask pairs of students to complete a worksheet to self-reflect, then you can project the worksheet onto the white board and share your own thinking and answers out loud while you complete it in front of the students. Alternatively, you can prompt a pair of students to talk through their thinking and complete the sheet based on their answers in front of the class.

And remember, at the primary level we are building the foundations for critical thinking. It is fine if your students are not able to "perfectly" draw a sound conclusion. It is a significant achievement if they learn that pausing and drawing a conclusion is an important part of inquiry learning.

Other tools to help students synthesize and conclude

Graphic organizers are very helpful to the inquiry process. Venn diagrams are useful to compare and contrast and to consolidate evidence. Many teachers use a fishbone graphic organizer to help students draw conclusions (see figure 5.14). The lines or bones at the top of the fish are where students record "what I know" in alignment with the bones at the bottom of the fish, where students record "what the evidence is telling me." The head of the fish is the conclusion that arises after consideration of the all the fishbones.

The ladder of inference (see figure 5.15) is another organizer that uses a thinking process to move from acquiring simple facts to inferring meaning and from there to making conclusions. Each thinking stage can be seen as a rung on the ladder.

CONFIRMATION
What are your favorite tools to help students organize their thinking?

Fishbone diagram

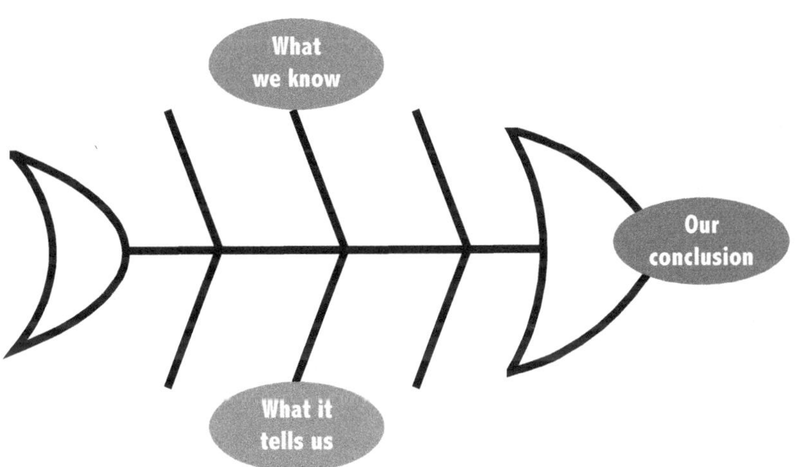

Source: Adapted from Ishikawa, 1968.

FIGURE 5.14 You can use a fishbone graphic organizer to help students summarize findings, determine significance and draw conclusions.

Ladder of inference

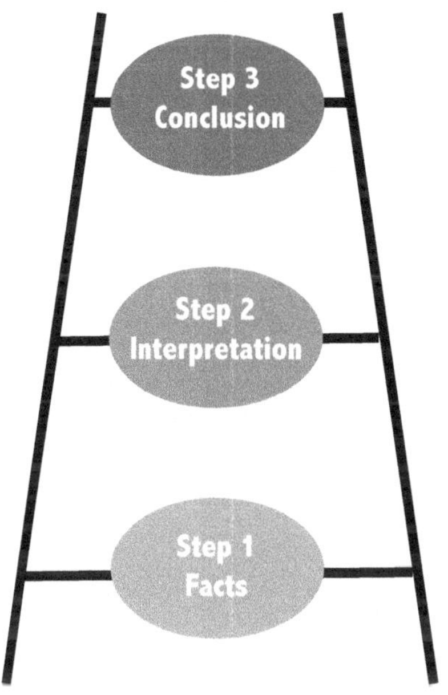

Source: Adapted from Argyris, 1986; Senge, Kleiner, Roberts, Ross, & Smith, 1994.

FIGURE 5.15 The ladder of inference describes a thinking process from acquiring simple facts, through inferring meaning, to making conclusions. Each thinking stage can be seen as a rung on the ladder.

Many teachers also use PMI charts help them with the inquiry process (see figure 5.16). The PMI (Plus, Minus, Interesting) chart was developed by Edward de Bono (2007) in 1982. De Bono was an early proponent of the deliberate teaching of thinking in schools. The PMI chart has many applications, but it was designed to be a quick tool (three to five minutes in length) to weigh the pros and cons of an issue, widen the perception of a problem or decision, or uncover issues that might have been overlooked.

In the context of inquiry, we have found that many teachers use PMI charts (without a five-minute length limit) to help students draw conclusions. A blank template is provided as Reproducible 5E (page 133), but a simple web search will provide you with a number of other formats to choose from.

Another organizer to help students draw conclusions is the "What? So What? Now What?" chart (see figure 5.17). In the "What?" category, students summarize their evidence. In the "So What?" category, they identify the relevance of the evidence and draw conclusions. In the "Now What?" category, students consider possible actions and innovations.

PMI chart

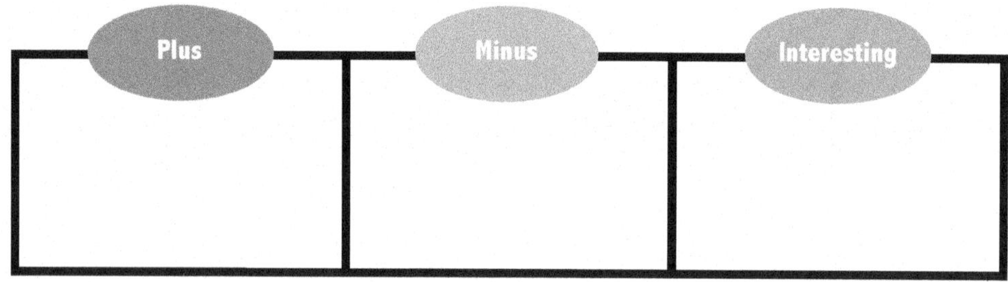

Source: de Bono, 2007.

FIGURE 5.16 A PMI chart can help students see the pros and cons of an issue and identify what may have been overlooked.

What?	So what?	Now what?
Summarize the evidence: • What happened? • What is known and not known? • What is agreed or not agreed on? • What did you expect and what was different?	Assess why the evidence is relevant: • What can be learned? • What was the impact on people and events? • Why does it matter? • What are the consequences and outcomes? • Who cares and why?	Consider possible actions and innovations: • What else do you need to find out? • What can you do with what you have learned? • What are the possibilities and opportunities? • What conclusions can you make, if any? • What can you do now that you couldn't before?

FIGURE 5.17 How and when might you use this organizer to help your students evaluate evidence and draw conclusions?

Weighing the evidence and concluding

Not all of the information students consider will be equally important or useful. Students need to make sense of information if they are to sort and filter their data. Figure 5.18 offers some criteria to consider. Reproducible 5F, *Balance of evidence* (page 134) asks students to "pile up" the evidence they have in support of the inquiry question under investigation. The side with more evidence is the side they would argue answers the inquiry question. Although we do not want students to see inquiry questions as either "right" or "wrong," for the primary learner it is likely best not to complicate the process of drawing a conclusion with too many layers, at least in the beginning. Our hope is that as primary learners gain sophistication with the consolidation process, they will start to consider evidence that is ambiguous and illustrates the gray areas of their inquiry question.

Is some information **more important** or useful in answering the inquiry question than others?

Is there **more information** supporting one conclusion over others?

Does any of the information **conflict** or support totally different conclusions?

FIGURE 5.18 You can help your primary students begin to appreciate that all information may not be be equally important or useful.

THINQ

- Do you find your primary students are able to stop and pause before drawing a conclusion? Or do they instinctively seem to know they should wait to learn more?
- What are two strategies you already use to help students weigh evidence and draw conclusions? Which of the strategies and tools suggested here would you like to add to your current practice?

Inquiry in Action

A tool to help with drawing conclusions: Ladder of inference activity

In her grades 2–3 class, Hind found success using the ladder of inference as a teaching tool to support deeper thinking about characters in a story. Using the book *Chrysanthemum* by Kevin Henkes (1991), she explored conclusions that students could make about the character Victoria.

Step 1: Reality and facts

How did Victoria treat Chrysanthemum because of her name? What did she say? What did she do? What specific actions did she take?

Step 2: Interpretation

What do you know about the way Victoria was behaving? (Students shared that they thought Victoria was being unkind, bullying, and making fun of Chrysanthemum).

Step 3: Conclusions

What should the following people do about a situation like this?

- Teacher?
- Chrysanthemum?
- Victoria?
- Other students?

Hind co-created the following success criteria with her students to consolidate the learning and draw strong conclusions.

Success criteria

1. My observations are based on fact and not opinion.
2. My facts are solid pieces of evidence.
3. My interpretation matches my facts and is based on my own experiences and information from the story.
4. My conclusion is solid. I did not go up the ladder too quickly.

Hind used a very simple worksheet to assist students with this activity (see figure 5.15, page 123, and page 135 for the reproducible).

5.5 How do I assess the "making sense" phase of the inquiry process?

In chapter 2, *Assessing and evaluating*, we suggested that the six essential abilities of inquiry learners are at the core of inquiry activities and inquiry assessment. The abilities to make sense, synthesize and consolidate are crucial at every stage of an inquiry. For example, a student cannot formulate a response to an inquiry question without "asking questions" about the evidence they have collected, and they cannot conclude an inquiry without consolidating or "putting it all together." Reproducible 5E, *Assessment planning template: Puts it all together* (page 133) can be used to plan your triangulated assessment evidence collection. Reproducible 5F, *Inquiry rubric and self-check: Puts it all together* (page 134) can be used as an assessment for and as learning tool.

Further useful tools are available in Reproducible 5G, *Drawing a conclusion: The ladder of inference* (page 135), Reproducible 5H, *Assessent planning template: Puts it all together* (page 136), and Reproducible 5I, *Inquiry rubric and self-check: Puts it all together* (page 137).

THINQ

- How do you encourage student ideas and experiences as a part of the synthesis and consolidation process?
- How would being able to develop and appreciate multiple perspectives support deep thinking?
- What do you need to consider in order to further develop your own instructional and assessment toolkit to support deep thinking for your students?

Big Idea

Assessment for learning during the making sense phase is important to student success.

Inquiry for ALL

Proficiency takes time and practice

It is worth remembering that like all important skills, consolidation and synthesis skills take time to develop. Providing plenty of class time to complete tasks can increase success. Thinking takes time, and we need to provide it. For many of us, this will require pushing back against overly packed classroom schedules that demand a certain number of minutes for each subject in a cycle.

You can also model these skills for students before asking them to try it. This doesn't have to take a huge amount of preparation. A simple think aloud where you try to solve a riddle or put the pieces of a puzzle together to reveal the "whole" can be enough to illustrate what consolidation looks and sounds like. After that, walking students through whatever consolidation tool you are asking them to use (such as a PMI chart or Balance of Evidence graphic [see pages 133 and 134]) will be a big help.

Revisit and reflect

This chapter looked closely at synthesis, consolidation and drawing conclusions and ways that educators can push the learning deeper for their students. We shared our belief that synthesizing is a process of first analyzing and then consolidating learning and creating new understandings based on information. Working with an inquiry framework enables students to make sound conclusions, and these processes must be intentionally taught, modeled and practiced. We explored the idea that our students think critically when we present opportunities for them to make decisions and judgments. We explored a number of ways that teachers can assist students with the synthesis process, including:

- having students explicitly revisit the inquiry question under investigation
- identifying patterns and trends in evidence and making connections between ideas
- using success criteria to support self-reflection and synthesis in language and in math
- using prompting questions to push the learning deeper
- using a variety of tools such as RAN charts to support student consolidation and synthesis

To conclude your exploration of this chapter, take some time to consider Reproducible 5J, *Teacher checklist: Synthesis and consolidation in my classroom* (page 138).

THINQ

- How can you collaborate with other educators to increase your confidence and expertise at pushing the learning deeper for your students?
- What are you thinking now about supporting student thinking? What has been confirmed? What is new learning?
- Which of the big ideas from this chapter do you feel are the most important enduring understandings for you? What about for your students?

Big Ideas

5.1 New knowledge and understandings emerge after we "make sense."

5.2 The human brain often makes errors when processing information.

5.3 The development of synthesis skills requires teacher modeling and support.

5.4 Sound conclusions can be drawn after evidence has been carefully considered.

5.5 Assessment for learning during the "making sense" phase is important to student success.

Reproducible 5A

Putting it all together

Name: ______________________________ Date: ______________

My inquiry question: ______________________________

At first I thought: ______________________________

____

____

Then I read, listened to, or watched: ______________________________

I learned: ______________________________

____

Now I am thinking: ______________________________

____

____

Then I read, listened to, or watched: ______________________________

I learned: ______________________________

____

Now I am thinking: ______________________________

____

____

Reproducible 5B

Support for my inquiry question/big Idea

Name: ______________________________ Date: ______________

Synthesis means using **important ideas** to support an **inquiry question** and **big idea**.

My inquiry question:

____

This is my big idea:

____

First source: ____

Important ideas from the source to support my thinking: ______________________

____

____

Second source: ____

Important ideas from the source to support my thinking: ______________________

____

____

Third source: ____

Important ideas from the source to support my thinking: ______________________

____

____

Reproducible 5C

Making sense of my inquiry question

Name: ______________________________ Date: ______________

My inquiry question: ____

1. What do you know about this topic?	2. Watch/read/listen to your first source. What did you learn? Write down one or two thoughts.
3. Watch/read/listen to your other source(s). What new ideas do you have? What has changed in your thinking?	4. What questions do you still have about this topic? How has your thinking changed?

Reproducible 5D

Student self-check: Making sense

Name: ______________________________ Date: ______________

My inquiry question: ____

Synthesis self-check	Yes	Mostly	A little	Not yet
We made a thoughtful conclusion from the information we gathered.				
We shared and discussed our conclusions with our peers.				
We used the feedback from our peers to improve our conclusion.				

Reproducible 5E

PMI Chart

Name: ______________________ Date: ______________

Inquiry focus: ______________________________

Use this template to help you draw a conclusion about the question you are investigating.

+

Evidence that SUPPORTS my conclusion

Evidence that DOES NOT support my conclusion

–

Other interesting evidence I uncovered

Source: Adapted from idea by de Bono, E. (2007). Tactics: The art and science of success. *New York: HarperCollins.*

Reproducible 5F

Balance of evidence

Name: ______________________________ Date: ______________

My inquiry question: ______________________________________

Possible conclusion A:	Possible conclusion B:

Evidence for conclusion A:	Evidence for conclusion B:

Key questions

- Is some information of better quality than others?
- How much weight do you give to those pieces of information?
- What did you do with information that doesn't support either of your predicted conclusions?

Reproducible 5G

Drawing a conclusion: The ladder of inference

Name: ______________________________ Date: ______________________

Step 3 So my conclusion is: ______________________________

____

____

____

____

Step 2 So this tells me: ______________________________

____

____

____

____

Step 1 I saw/heard/read: ______________________________

____

____

____

____

Step 3
Conclusion

Step 2
Interpretation

Step 1
Facts

Source: Adapted from idea by Argyris, C. (1986). Skilled incompetence. *Accessed at https://hbr.org/1986/09/skilled-incompetence on February 29, 2024; Senge, P. M., Kleiner, A., Roberts, C., Ross, R. B., & Smith, B. J. (1994).* The fifth discipline fieldbook. *New York: Currency.*

Reproducible 5H

Assessment planning template: Puts it all together

Name: ______________________________ Date: ________________

Essential inquiry ability — Puts it all together	Evidence gathered		
	Conversations	Observations	Products
Asks questions • Asks and refines relevant questions about a body of evidence, inconsistencies in the evidence, and the weight of different pieces of evidence.			
Demonstrates curiosity • Actively asks many questions during synthesis and consolidation that demonstrate eagerness to learn.			
(Gives and) asks for reasons • Asks for justification of evidence and gives reasons for a conclusion.			
Understands what is currently known • Is able to synthesize/consolidate "what is already known" (i.e., facts, data, theories).			
Puts it all together • Can synthesize a body of evidence into a coherent "whole." • Looks for patterns and trends in evidence. • Makes connections between ideas.			
Thinks together • Listens to, builds on, considers and assists others during the synthesis process. • Asks relevant questions of other people to further an inquiry (gets an opinion or some advice, debates, disputes, inquires, brainstorms).			

Reproducible 5I

Inquiry rubric and self-check: Puts it all together

Name: ______________________________ Date: ____________________

Areas that need work	Standard for this criterion	How work exceeds expectations
	Asks questions • Asks and refines relevant questions for different purposes (about a body of evidence, about inconsistencies in evidence, about the weight of different pieces of evidence) and from different perspectives.	
	Demonstrates curiosity • Actively asks many questions during synthesis and consolidation that demonstrate eagerness to learn.	
	(Gives and) asks for reasons • Asks for justification of evidence and gives reasons for a conclusion.	
	Understands what is currently known • Is able to synthesize/consolidate "what is already known" (i.e., sources, data, strategies, theories).	
	Puts it all together • Can synthesize a body of evidence into a coherent "whole." • Looks for patterns and trends in evidence. • Makes connections between ideas.	
	Thinks together • Listens to, builds on, considers and assists others during the synthesis process. • Asks relevant questions of other people during the synthesis process (gets an opinion or some advice, debates, disputes, inquires, brainstorms).	

Source: Rubric based on ideas from Dietz, M. (2000). Single point rubric idea. *INTASC Academy, Milwaukee, WI, as cited by Gonzalez, J. (2015, February 4).* Meet the single point rubric. *Accessed at www.cultofpedagogy.com/single-point-rubric/ on February 29, 2024.*

Reproducible 5J

Teacher checklist: Synthesis and consolidation in my classroom

Check which of the following statements represent your current teaching practice. The focus of this checklist is on the consolidation step of the inquiry process. You may want to use this checklist for self-reflection, for planning and sharing with colleagues, and to determine next steps in deepening inquiry practice.

- Synthesis and consolidation skills are fostered in meaningful ways in my classroom.
- Conditions in my classroom encourage the development of synthesis and consolidation skills.
- I purposefully plan our classroom experiences to minimize the impact of brain errors on the synthesis and consolidation phase of inquiry.
- I use age- and grade-appropriate templates to drive the inquiry learning of my students.
- I make sure that students have considered multiple perspectives while consolidating their evidence.
- Students know that not all evidence is of equal weight.
- Students are learning how to weigh both the amount and quality of evidence while drawing a conclusion.
- I know how to facilitate the synthesis portion of an inquiry.
- I use a variety of provocations to pique and sustain student curiosity, wonder and questioning during the synthesis phase of inquiry.
- I build in collaboration opportunities during the synthesis phase of inquiry.

Chapter 6
REFLECTING AND SHARING:
Pushing learning to a deeper level

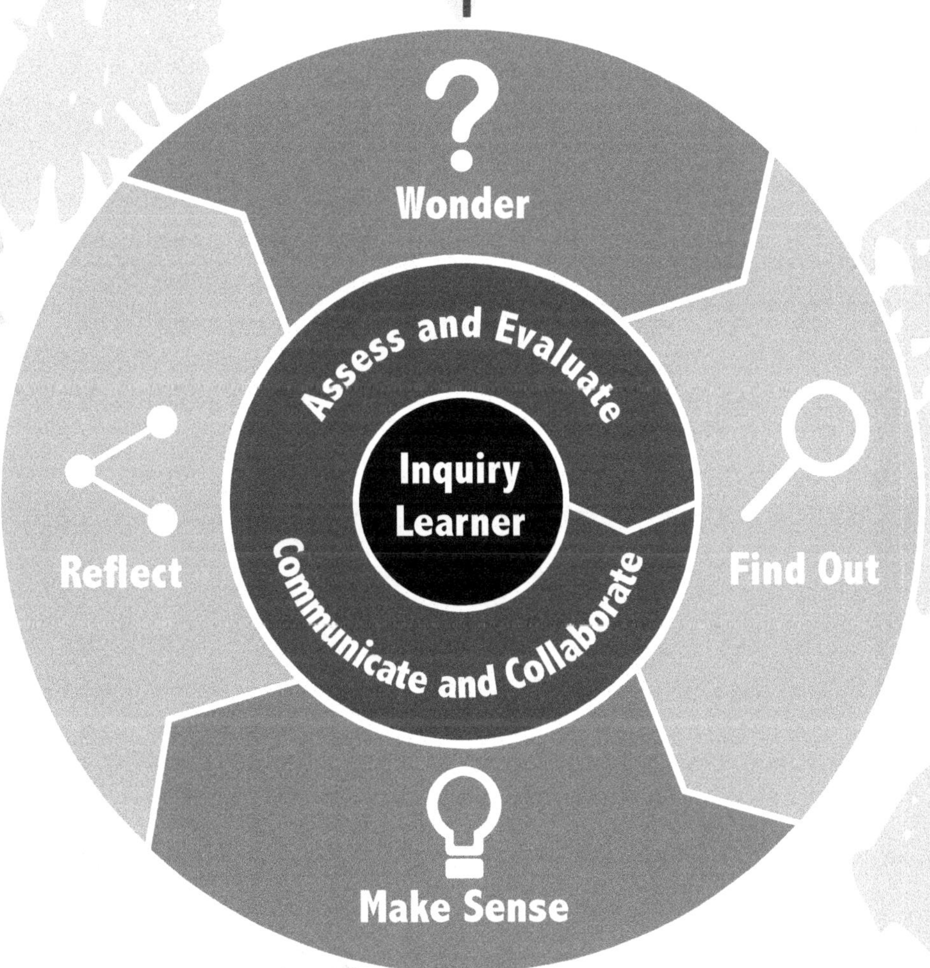

We don't learn from experience; we learn by reflecting on experience.

—John Dewey

Big Idea
Inquiry learning becomes deep learning through reflection and sharing.

In this chapter, we explore an important but often overlooked element of the inquiry process: reflection and sharing. When students explicitly reflect on and share their thinking, it is not only a celebration of their learning but also an invitation for others to participate and engage in the same question or problem.

CONVICTION
How convinced are you that reflection and sharing can deepen learning?

6.1 Why do reflection and sharing matter?

You'll notice that in our inquiry process cycle (figure 6.1), we have reflection and sharing as a final, explicit component. The goal of this endpoint reflection and sharing is to push student thinking to a deeper level. Sharing and reflection activities are an essential element of *all stages* of an inquiry, for example, during the questioning, investigating or making sense "stages" of the inquiry process. However, at an endpoint of an inquiry it is particularly important that students are given time to consolidate and articulate key lessons learned.

Without this opportunity to synthesize and consolidate through reflection and sharing, students may be left with the impression that inquiry is a series of isolated steps or disconnected activities that end in the creation of some kind of product. Primary students, in particular, benefit from ongoing reflection and sharing because their verbal skills are often stronger than their written skills.

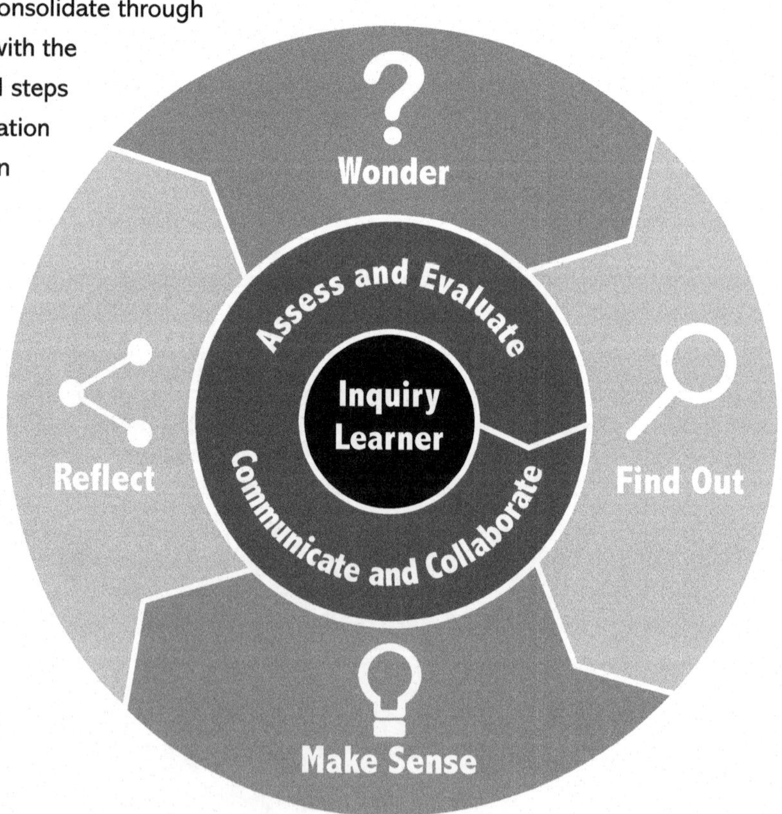

FIGURE 6.1 Even though reflection and sharing occur throughout an inquiry, setting it out as a final step is intended to emphasize the need for, and critical importance of, helping students consolidate what they have learned.

6.2 What do effective refection and sharing look and sound like?

Big Idea
Both students and teachers need concrete examples of what good reflection and sharing look and sound like.

To paraphrase John Dewey (1933), we do not learn from inquiry experiences — we learn from reflecting on inquiry experiences. Reflection asks us to pause and attend deliberately to our thinking processes and our lived experiences. It is at these crucial mental "check-in" points that we "go over" and "re-live" our experience. During reflection we may contemplate other possible choices, ask further questions and consider future courses of action based on the conclusions of our reflective process. When supporting student reflection and sharing, teachers should consider what engaging in effective reflection looks like as well as sharing at the end of an inquiry.

CONFIRMATION
How have sharing and reflection with colleagues helped clarify your thinking and improve your professional practice?

Effective reflection

Reflection can take many forms. Reflection can happen during an action ("Let's pause and think.") or after an action ("Let's think about what I did and why."). Reflection occurs throughout all stages of an inquiry process and again at the end of the process.

Reflection works well when teachers model it and students practice it on a regular basis (see figures 6.2–6.4). Reflections can be written on an exit card, in a journal or on a simple graphic organizer. Oral reflections can be shared with a teacher, students or family members. Reflections are most effective when students can see the impact of the reflection in helping them to improve their skills and deepen their learning. Reflections should be motivating and build confidence in primary learners.

Check in with your learners and ask them what type of reflection they like the best and the reasons for their preferences. Sometimes, reflection is considered by primary learners as the throwaway part of an activity, an unpleasant necessity that seems to interrupt their learning.

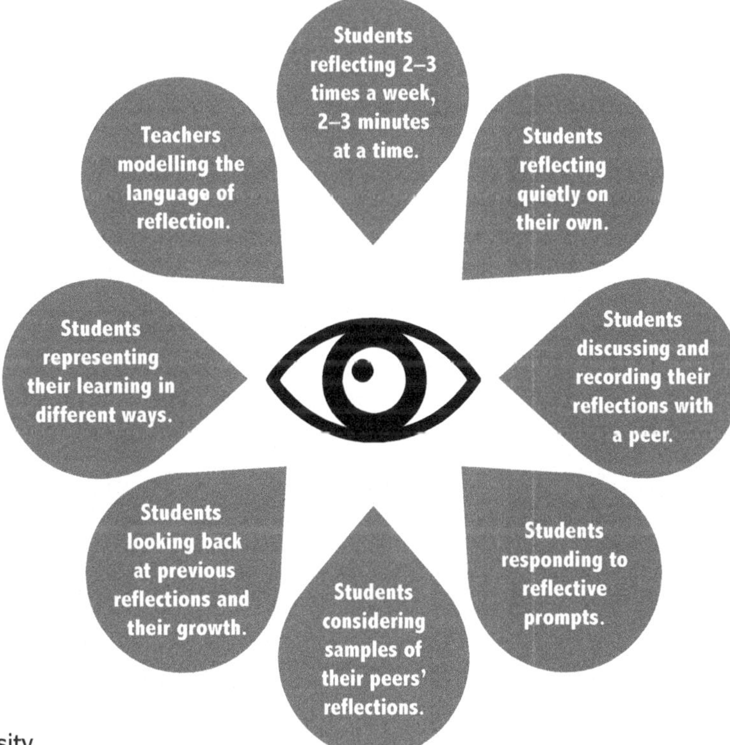

FIGURE 6.2 Reflection doesn't just happen. Teachers need to carve out time and space if it is to become a regular part of their inquiry classroom.

Your goal should be to make reflection as seamless as possible in your inquiry activities, and, especially at primary, to use oral formats to increase student interest in, and engagement with, what is being learned. Some teachers we have met use motivational and/or mindfulness techniques such as reflection music and/or reflection images (e.g., of nature, abstract art, people thinking) in addition to reflection prompts to cue students to the fact that it is time for quiet, individual, serious thought. Once students have had time for individual reflection (which may or may not include writing), there should be time for students to share one aspect or part of their reflection with a peer or the teacher.

Reflecting during inquiry sounds like …

This doesn't make sense so I should think this through again.

I am still confused by …

Can you help me think this through? What about this?

I am not sure this is the best conclusion.

I wonder if there is a better way to do this?

Why is this so hard? We must be doing something wrong.

But that information is different from the other ones.

I am changing what I think about this topic.

FIGURE 6.3 As students reflect during their inquiry, you should hear expressions of confusion, rethinking, wondering, questioning and analysis.

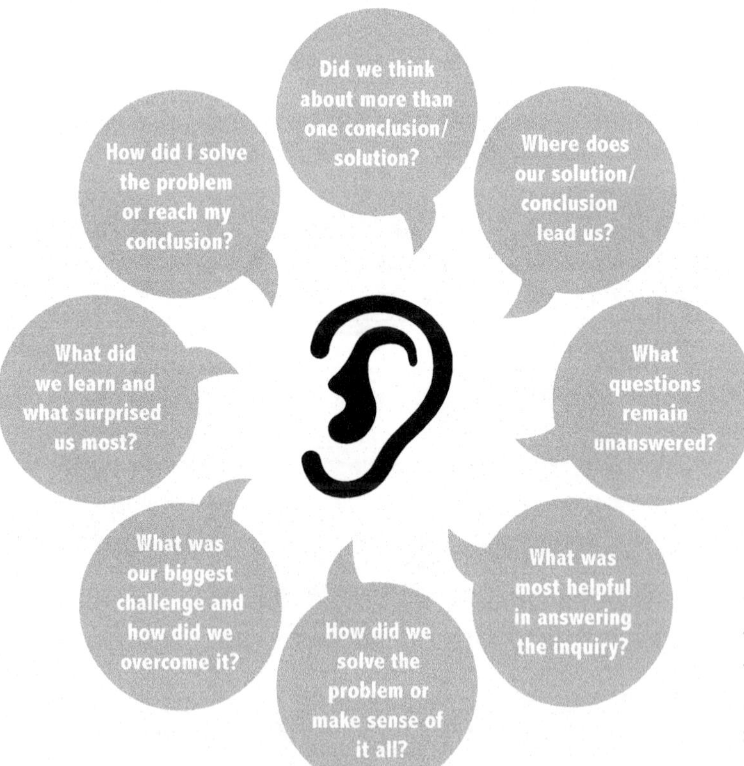

FIGURE 6.4 For the primary learner, reflection at the end of the inquiry may be as simple as sharing the answers to these questions, being open to suggestions from others and acting on those suggestions.

Sharing at the end of an inquiry

Sharing the outcomes of an inquiry should be an exciting and celebratory time for primary learners. This is the time to highlight their unique thinking, solutions and creations. It should also be a time of support because inquiry demands a double check of thinking, solutions and creations by peers. Student work is not just presented as a static finished work; it becomes an invitation for others to participate and engage in the same question or problem (see figures 6.5–6.7).

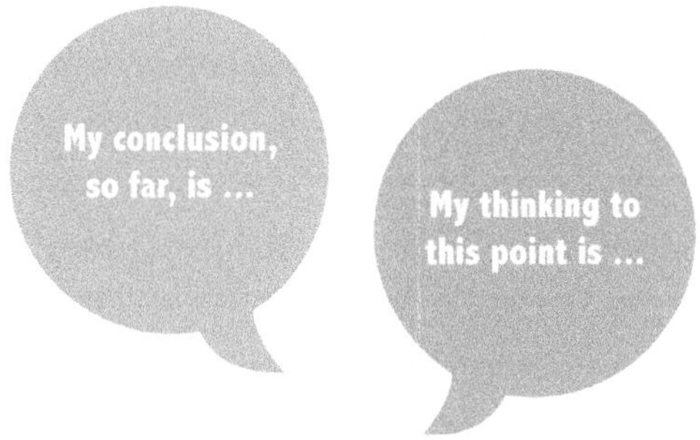

My conclusion, so far, is ...

My thinking to this point is ...

FIGURE 6.5 When conclusions are shared, they should be presented as a learner's thinking "up to this point" and as an invitation for others to engage. This highlights the fact that learning is an ongoing process and that conclusions change and evolve as we learn more.

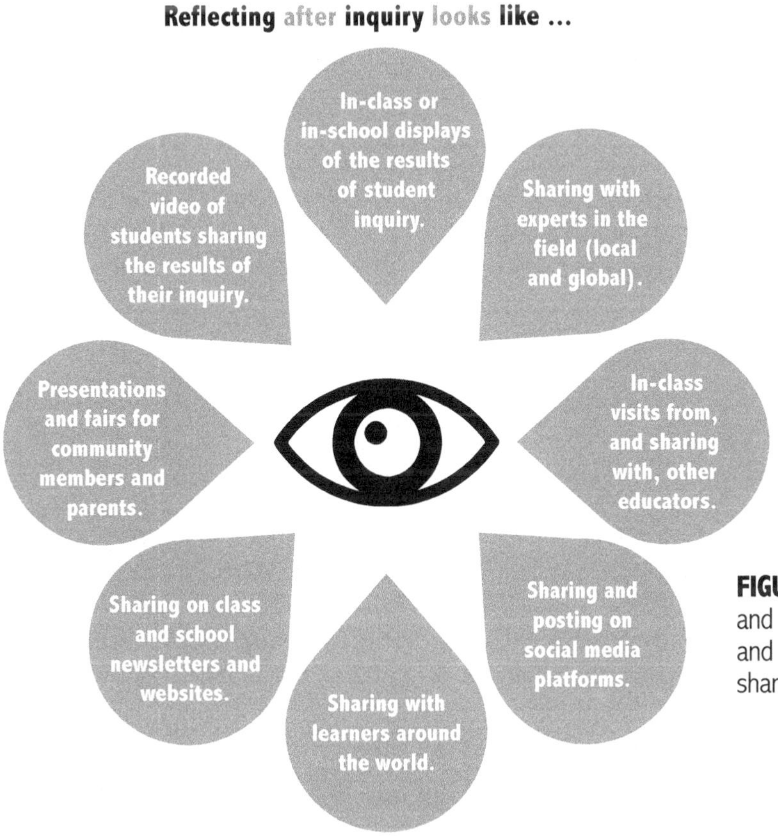

Reflecting after inquiry looks like ...

In-class or in-school displays of the results of student inquiry.

Sharing with experts in the field (local and global).

In-class visits from, and sharing with, other educators.

Sharing and posting on social media platforms.

Sharing with learners around the world.

Sharing on class and school newsletters and websites.

Presentations and fairs for community members and parents.

Recorded video of students sharing the results of their inquiry.

FIGURE 6.6 Sharing works best when teachers and schools create places, venues, connections and events specifically designed to help students share their inquiry work.

FIGURE 6.7 Public presentations and discussions of the results of an inquiry offer many opportunities to reflect and share.

Some of the common terminology used for this endpoint of an inquiry method is "sharing findings," "taking action," "improving" and "checking and extending." What each of these terms share is the idea that the conclusions of the inquiry are open for consideration and can be further deepened through collaboration with other students as learner-experts (see figure 6.8). These learner-experts help to ensure the quality of the product. Students are learner-experts when they understand and can apply the criteria of an effective inquiry. Students who have participated in the co-creation of criteria for an effective inquiry and have had multiple opportunities to self-assess and peer-assess are skilled learner-experts.

CONTEXT

Can you imagine your inquiry classroom full of the sights and sounds of reflection and sharing?

The sharing stage of an inquiry is an opportunity to highlight inquiry dispositions for your students. Students should be encouraged to demonstrate curiosity, wonder and open-mindedness toward the learning of their peers. They can once again question, critique and provide new perspectives. An important aim in the sharing stage is for students to be amazed at the new learning discovered by their peers and to learn more about themselves as learners while witnessing the learning of others.

THINQ

- How might your students benefit from more frequent opportunities for sharing and reflection in your classroom?
- Do you anticipate obstacles or barriers to building reflection and sharing into your classroom routines?
- Which of the strategies listed in this section might prove to be the most successful for your students?

FIGURE 6.8 At the end of an inquiry you can use these questions and comments to model, facilitate and gauge the nature of student sharing.

6.3 How can I help primary students to listen and respond appropriately during sharing?

Big Idea
Reflecting and sharing should be regular occurrences in any inquiry classroom.

COMMITMENT
How committed are you to doing more sharing and reflection in your classroom?

It is important to stress that the focus of this section is on helping our primary learners to navigate the sharing process (see figure 6.9). This is a different protocol than peer review or descriptive feedback. We want each primary student to learn from the work of others, and sharing learning is a way to do this. So in this case, we need to work on preparing our students to be good listeners. If you do choose to have the audience respond to, or critique, the student or students who are sharing, then the focus should be on positive reinforcement.

We feel it is important to stress how worthwhile it is to regularly build in reflection and sharing sessions into your classroom routine. Teachers we have worked with tell us they were pleased and surprised by how much their students look forward to these sessions. They appreciate that their students enter the classroom asking, "Are we going to be reflecting and sharing today?" rather than asking, "Are we going to be doing anything interesting today?"

When reflecting and sharing become the norm in your classroom, you'll have created a community of learners. Students will have come to understand that thinking and knowing can be improved by sharing with others and receiving critiques of their work. They will also now appreciate that learning is an ongoing process, which is a very different classroom model than one that is anchored in the presentation of material from the teacher or the textbook followed by the reporting back of the "right" answer by the students.

FIGURE 6.9 Having classmates actually "try out" something that other students have done is a great sharing protocol at the primary level.

If we want sharing and reflecting to feel different than other classroom activities, like presentations for example, then it is important to set different expectations for sharing (see figure 6.10). One way to do this is to have students share, show or demonstrate their learning rather than just tell about it. If possible, having other students actually engage in an activity in some way is the most effective way to share.

While the use of print or digital templates in grades 1 and 2 will not likely be a tool you automatically turn to, by grade 3 students will most likely be able to complete basic templates to assist the reflection and sharing process. These templates can be used to guide reflections or conversations, and they do not necessarily have to be completed with pen or pencil. You may also choose to modify these templates to better meet the needs of your students. See pages 149–151 for Reproducibles 6A, 6B, and 6C.

How to be a good listener during sharing

- Sit still and pay attention.
- Make eye contact with the student(s) who are sharing.
- Nod your head or smile.
- Volunteer if the speaker asks.
- Only put your hand up to ask a question when the speaker asks for questions, or the teacher asks you to do so.

FIGURE 6.10 Simple guidelines for sharing can be posted around your classroom.

FIGURE 6.11 Providing opportunities for students to move, view, and touch during reflection time increases student understanding.

CONFIRMATION

Where might you be able to share the benefits and challenges of helping primary students develop their reflection skills?

Inquiry in Action

Sharing learning after a grade 1 science inquiry

In Jackie's grade 1 class she had her students participate in an "engineering inquiry." Jackie provided a variety of materials as well as photo prompts and challenge cards. Some groups of students needed these visual prompts, but other students designed and create their own custom builds. In many cases, students worked together to build increasingly complex structures, working collaboratively through the many trials and tribulations: redesigning, testing, embracing failures, and celebrating successes (see figure 6.11). This oftentimes translates into greater understanding of numerous science strands.

Jackie wanted students to learn from one another during this inquiry, so she had them regularly share their creations. All student work was left "in place" and students took turns sharing what they had built and how. Having students sit in front of the work being shared proved to be a powerful way to increase learning. In contrast, if Jackie had asked her students to tidy up and put away their work, the sharing experience would have been markedly different.

Revisit and reflect

This chapter made the argument that it is important to build in frequent opportunities for primary learners to reflect and share during the inquiry process. You were asked to consider the benefits of sharing and reflection for student learning.

We explored what sharing and reflection look and sound like in the classroom, and we provided some practical strategies to help students become good listeners during sharing sessions. We also argued that in the primary grades sharing by showing is often the most effective way to keep young students engaged and to extend learning.

In the next chapter, we examine the big ideas of inquiry that underpin a successful inquiry-based learning program in the primary grades. We also provide a planning model that has helped many teachers to integrate more inquiry into their teaching and assessment practice.

Big Ideas

6.1 Inquiry learning becomes deep learning through reflection and sharing.

6.2 Both students and teachers need concrete examples of what good reflection and sharing look like and sound like.

6.3 Reflecting and sharing should be regular occurrences in any inquiry classroom.

THINQ

- How might sharing and reflection push your primary students' learning to a deeper level?
- What is missed if teachers do not find the time to build sharing and reflection opportunities into the inquiry process?

Reproducible 6A

Conclusion of inquiry: Student self-reflection

Name: ______________________ Date: ______________

Self-reflection questions	My response
The inquiry question I explored	
The conclusion I reached	
Reasons for my conclusion (evidence)	
Is there an alternate conclusion I could have reached? If so, what is it? If not, why not?	
What questions remain?	

Reproducible 6B

Pushing thinking deeper: Self-reflection prompts

Name: ________________________________ Date: ________________

Thoughts about my inquiry	
I'm confused by . . .	
I'm imagining that . . .	
I'm "re-thinking" . . .	
I made a good choice because . . .	
I have a valid conclusion because . . .	
The easiest part of my inquiry was . . .	
The hardest part of my inquiry was . . .	
I may have made a mistake when I . . .	
I probably should have done this one thing differently . . .	
I think I am now much better at . . .	
I am left with these questions . . .	
Next time I want to explore . . .	

Reproducible 6C

Critique prompts: Peer feedback

Name: ______________________________ Date: ______________

Student I am critiquing: ______________________________

Important points

- Remember to smile and nod your head while the other student is speaking/presenting.
- Don't give too much feedback during the critique (pick 3 or 4 things from this sheet).
- Only comment on things that will help the student to learn and do better.
- Thank the person for sharing with you!

Things I might say or ask during the critique	My ideas about their inquiry
I learned this from your inquiry . . . presentation/ blog/artwork/invention/solution/etc.	
What if . . . you asked this question/you found more sources/you changed this part?	
I have a similar question/idea/problem! Did you notice that . . . ?	
One thing I wonder is . . . ?	
What do you think should be done about this?	
What questions do you still have?	
What did you learn?	

Chapter 7
WRAPPING IT UP:
What matters most

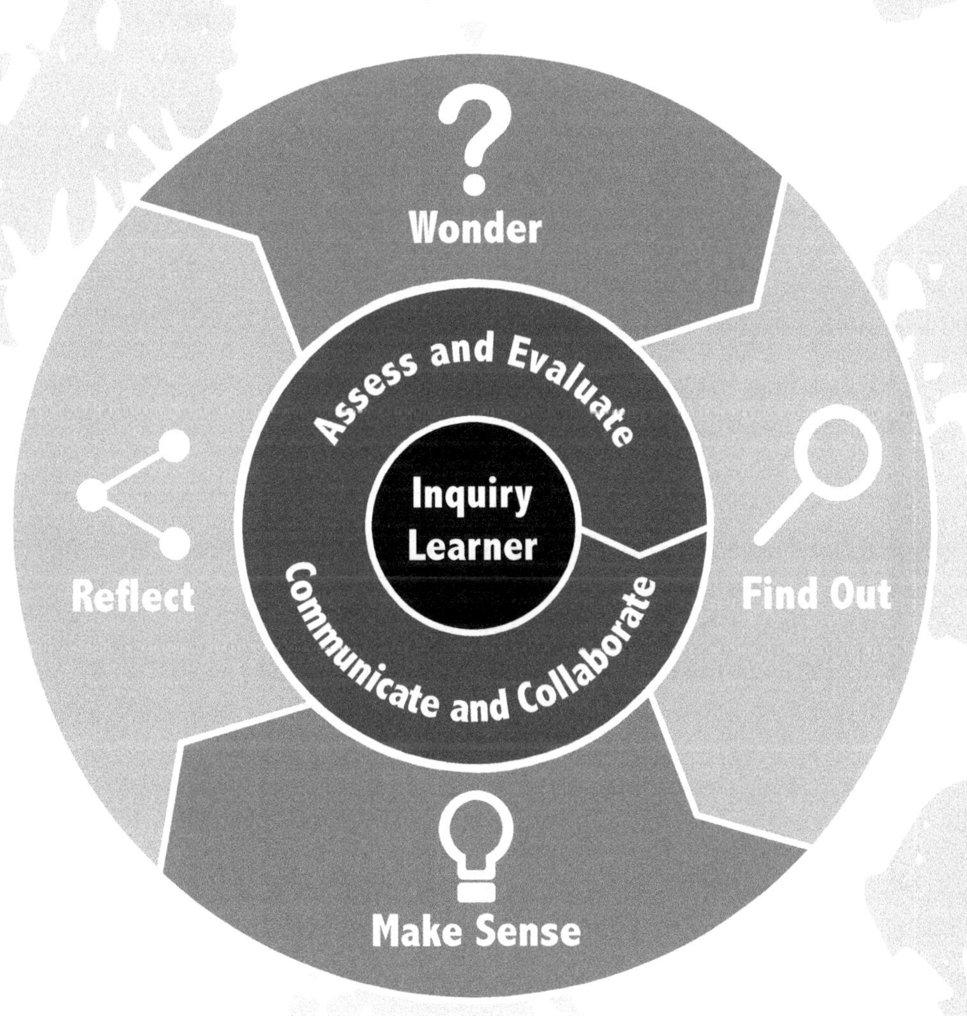

For the things we have to learn before we can do them, we learn by doing them.

—**Aristotle**

In this chapter, we review fundamental principles of inquiry that promote a thriving inquiry-based learning program. We also include a step-by-step planning model to help you seamlessly incorporate more inquiry into your teaching and assessment practices.

Traditional learning	Inquiry learning
Have to learn	**Want to learn**
What to know	**How to know**
Tell and memorize	**Ask and inquire**
Only one right answer	**Many conclusions**
Teacher-directed	**Learner-centered**
One-size-fits-all	**Personalized**
Passive learning	**Active learning**
Assess for marks	**Assess for learning**

FIGURE 7.1 The characteristics of inquiry learning.

7.1 What are the big ideas of inquiry?

THINQ, Grades 1–3: Inquiry-based learning in the classroom has been written specifically for primary teachers and classrooms. Throughout this book, we have argued that inquiry-based learning will capitalize on the curiosity and passion for learning that naturally resides in primary learners.

Inquiry-based learning has a long theoretical history in education but has not been implemented in a consistent, systematic way in most schools and school districts. We believe it is possible to do so. Any new learning is a journey that takes time and effort. Whether you teach in a school or district that hasn't yet encouraged these practices, one that is implementing them but is still finding its way, or one that fully supports inquiry-based learning, our hope is that this book will encourage all educators, regardless of where they are in their journey, to integrate more inquiry into their classroom practice.

THINQ, Grades 1–3 is focused on the big ideas that underpin a successful inquiry learning program in the primary grades and provides practical strategies for planning, instruction and assessment within this context. In this section you will find the twenty big ideas we feel are at the heart of inquiry-based learning. You'll notice that they aren't organized around the stages of the inquiry process. We did this because we believe these big ideas apply regardless of inquiry stage, discipline or educational environment. You can use these big ideas with your teaching partners, staff or senior administrators to implement more inquiry-based learning.

1 We learn by asking questions (inquiring).

Inquiry learning is rooted in our innate desire to make sense of a mysterious world. When we ask questions, determine a problem, and use our heads and hearts to investigate what fascinates us, we are engaged in inquiry (see figure 7.1).

2 Inquiry results in students learning how to learn.

Perhaps the most significant benefit of inquiry-based learning is that the ultimate goal is to create thoughtful, persevering and independent learners. In an inquiry environment, "how to know" counts for far more than "what to know."

3 Inquiry dispositions support risk-taking and a sustainable commitment to inquiry learning.

Curiosity, open-mindedness, hopefulness, reflection and resiliency are inquiry dispositions (see figure 7.2) — or what some call "inquiry habits of mind" (Costa & Kallick, 2008). They are what keep the learner on the journey of inquiry. These dispositions support risk-taking and commitment to inquiry learning.

FIGURE 7.2 Inquiry dispositions.

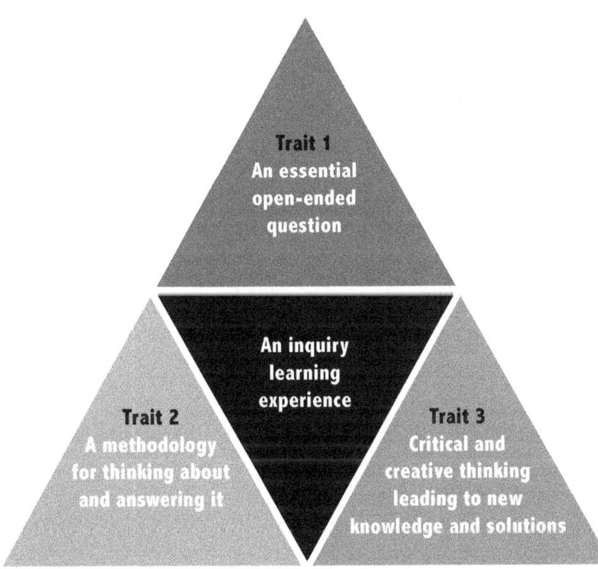

FIGURE 7.3 Essential traits of inquiry learning.

4 Inquiry learning, regardless of grade or subject area, has three common essential traits.

All inquiry learning experience shares three traits (see figure 7.3): an essential question that invites the learner to wonder and think deeply; a methodology to answer the question or solve the problem; and a critical and creative thinking process so that new knowledge is created.

5 Teachers should be co-learners who model their wonder and thinking with students.

In inquiry-based classrooms, teachers take the role of co-learners alongside their students by sharing their own questions and wonderings and admitting that they do not have all the answers (see figure 7.4).

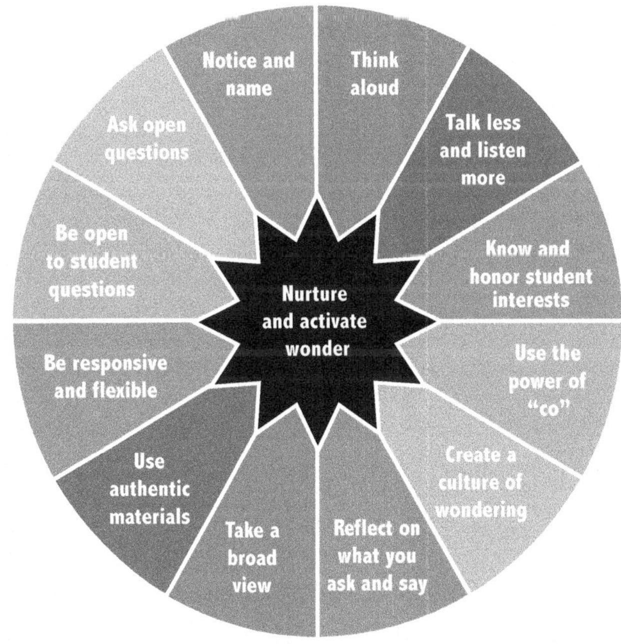

FIGURE 7.4 Strategies for activating learning.

6 Inquiry classrooms focus on big ideas and transferable skills.

Inquiry educators need to be continually asking whether they are: intentionally developing critical and creative thinking; creating learning experiences that are based on student interest; focused on big ideas and essential skills; and knowledge telling or knowledge building (see figure 7.5).

Traditional teaching	Inquiry teaching
Educator is the expert	Educator is a **co-learner**
Educator tells	Educator **models**
Educator controls	Educator **activates**
Educator corrects mistakes	Educator **gives feedback**
Educator gives answers	Educator **asks questions**
Educator is a manager	Educator is a **provocateur**
Educator assesses task completion	Educator **assesses learning**

FIGURE 7.5 The role of an inquiry educator.

7 Inquiry skills and abilities can, and should, be assessed.

The processes and skills of an inquiry are the core of inquiry and assessment. Inquiry should be as varied and unique as each classroom and learner, but the processes and skills should remain constant. We have identified six essential inquiry abilities that capture what inquiry is all about (see figure 7.6).

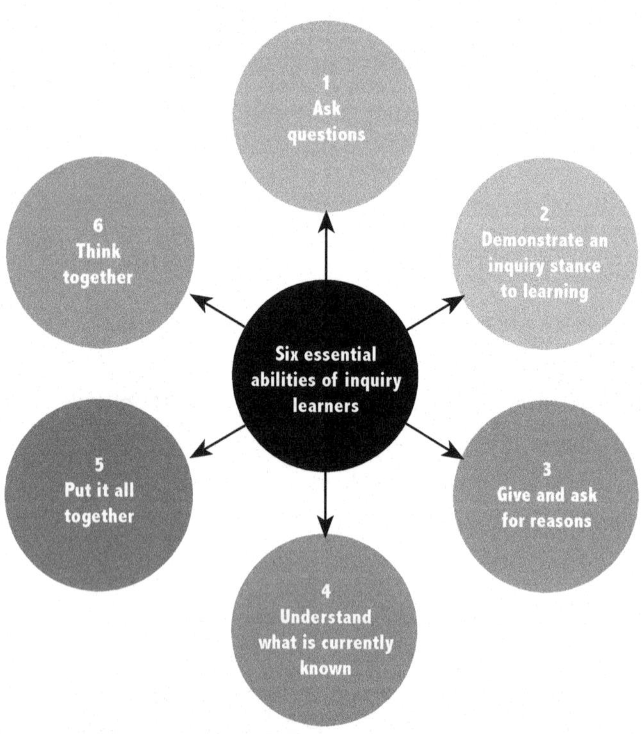

FIGURE 7.6 The essential abilities of inquiry learners.

8 Assessment should be welcomed, not dreaded, by students.

Learning activities and assessment should be as seamless as possible so that students understand that assessment is how teachers determine what students know and can do at a particular point in time. The more we involve students in the assessment process, the more likely they will be to see that assessment is a helpful and natural part of improving as a learner (see figure 7.7).

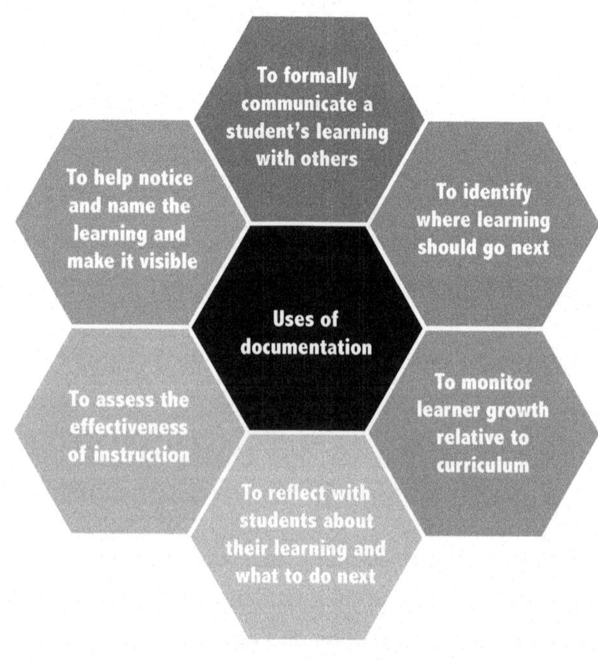

FIGURE 7.7 The uses of documentation.

9 Balanced assessment is essential for equity, reliability and validity.

Given the emergent and diverse nature of literacy development among primary students, it is essential to triangulate assessment data in order to make assessment fair for, and reflective of, all learners. This means collecting evidence through a balance of conversations, observations and products (see figure 7.8).

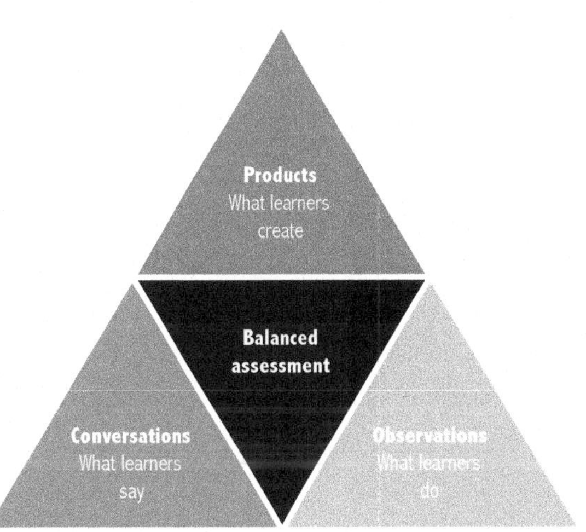

FIGURE 7.8 Balanced assessment.

10 Our curiosity fuels our learning.

Inquiry begins with wondering. Learning begins with questions. We are all curious about the way the world works. Our curiosity fuels our learning. Our curiosity provides purpose to our learning (see figure 7.9).

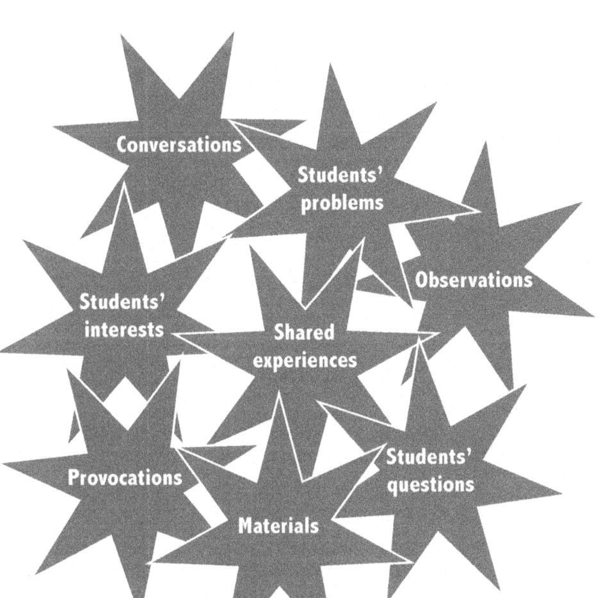

FIGURE 7.9 The spark for inquiry.

11 The purpose of an inquiry question is to get your students to think deeply about a topic being studied.

An inquiry question is a special type of question that helps drive units of learning (see figure 7.10). The purpose of an inquiry question is to entice your students to think deeply about the mysteries of life. These mysteries can be categorized by subject disciplines but are often interdisciplinary in nature.

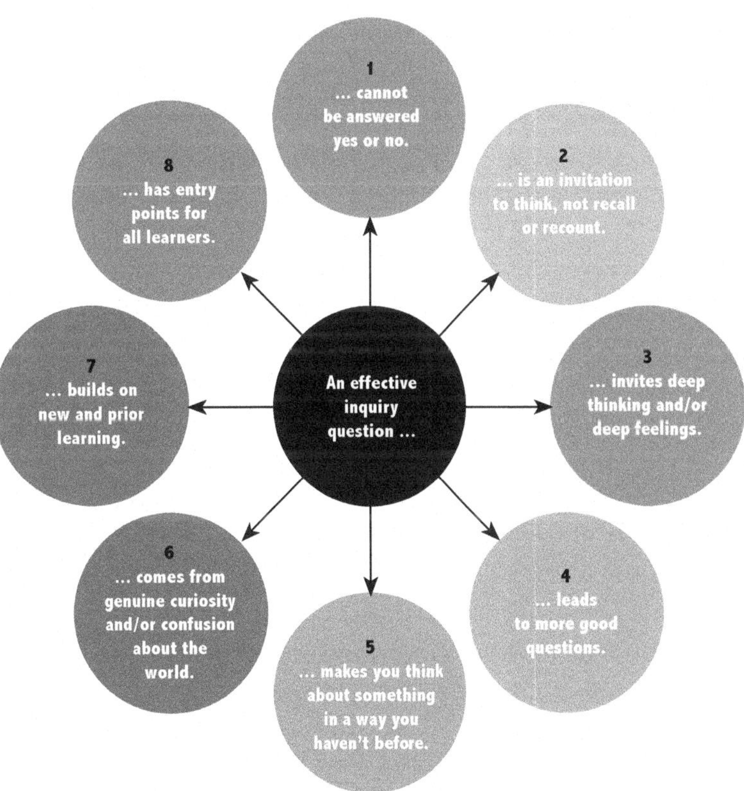

FIGURE 7.10 The characteristics of good inquiry questions.

12 The ability of students to develop strong questions during an inquiry comes with time and practice.

We can't just ask students to "think harder" — we need to describe exactly what good thinking involves and encourage students to be attentive to their own thinking by using guidelines such as the elements of thought. Analytical questions can assist an inquiry learner to "think about and improve their thinking."

Elements of thought (Elder & Paul, 2010):

1. **Purpose:** goals, objectives
2. **Question at issue:** problem, issue
3. **Information:** data, facts, observations, experiences
4. **Interpretation and inference:** conclusions, solutions
5. **Concepts:** theories, definitions, laws, principles, models
6. **Assumptions**: presuppositions, axioms, taking for granted
7. **Implications and consequences**
8. **Point of view**: frames of reference, perspectives, orientations

FIGURE 7.11 The mystery of inquiry.

13 Students are naturally curious, and their interests will drive them to want answers to their questions.

Primary learners love to solve puzzles and mysteries. By putting students in the role of knowledge seekers and problem solvers and giving them some control over their learning, student interest and engagement increase (see figure 7.11).

14 Literacy protocols fit naturally into inquiry-based learning.

Sometimes primary educators view inquiry-based learning as a discrete component of their daily programming, separate from their literacy block. We encourage teachers to incorporate their literacy protocols into the inquiry process itself (see figure 7.12).

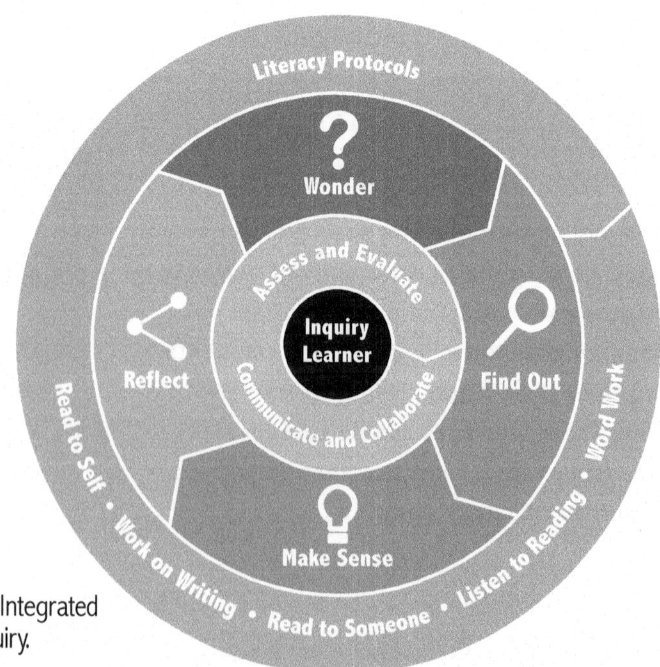

FIGURE 7.12 Integrated literacy and inquiry.

15 Teachers need to model how to find answers to ensure student success.

In a guided inquiry at primary, the responsibility for collecting research and gathering information is focused more on the teacher than the student. Each time the teacher provides more information, students should be invited to revisit their current thinking about their answers to their question (see figure 7.13).

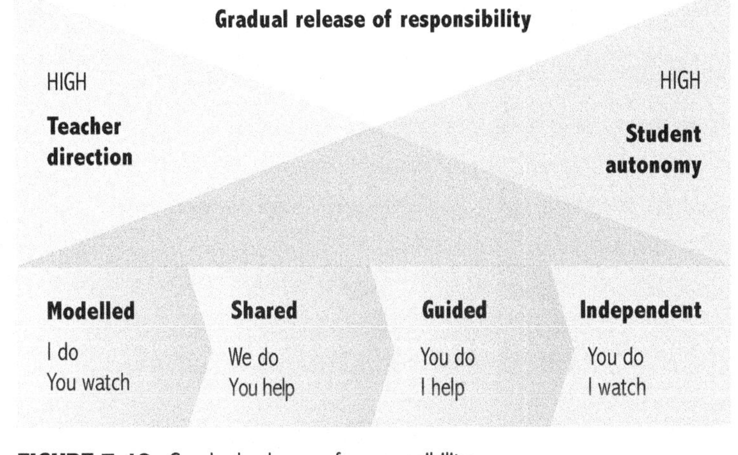

FIGURE 7.13 Gradual release of responsibility.

16 New knowledge and understandings emerge after we "make sense" of information.

One of the goals of inquiry is for students to create new knowledge. The creation of new knowledge comes after a body of information is synthesized and consolidated. This process allows us to make meaning out of seemingly disconnected pieces of evidence (see figure 7.14).

FIGURE 7.14 The synthesis process.

17 The development of synthesis skills requires teacher modelling and support.

Once students have finished the investigation phase of an inquiry, they must make sense of it through consolidation. Consolidation means to bring together different ideas into a coherent whole. Primary learners will need educators to provide consolidation models and tools (see figure 7.15).

Questions to develop consolidation skills

- What was our question or problem?
- What did we think we might find?
- What did we find?
- What patterns or trends did we see?
- Did we find anything surprising?
- Did we miss anything?
- What might we conclude?
- What other questions do we have?
- How could we explore this further?

FIGURE 7.15 Consolidation questions.

18 Sound conclusions can be drawn after evidence has been carefully considered.

At its most basic level, drawing a conclusion is really about weighing evidence. Primary learners will need teachers to model tools and strategies that are clear and uncomplicated (see figure 7.16).

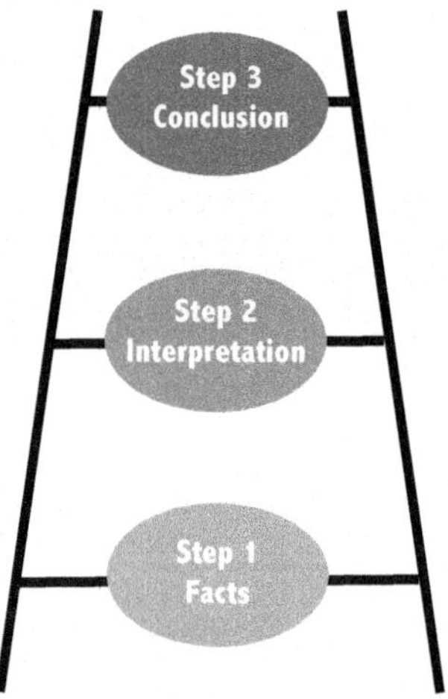

Source: Adapted from Argyris, 1986; Senge, Kleiner, Roberts, Ross, & Smith, 1994.

FIGURE 7.16 The ladder of inference.

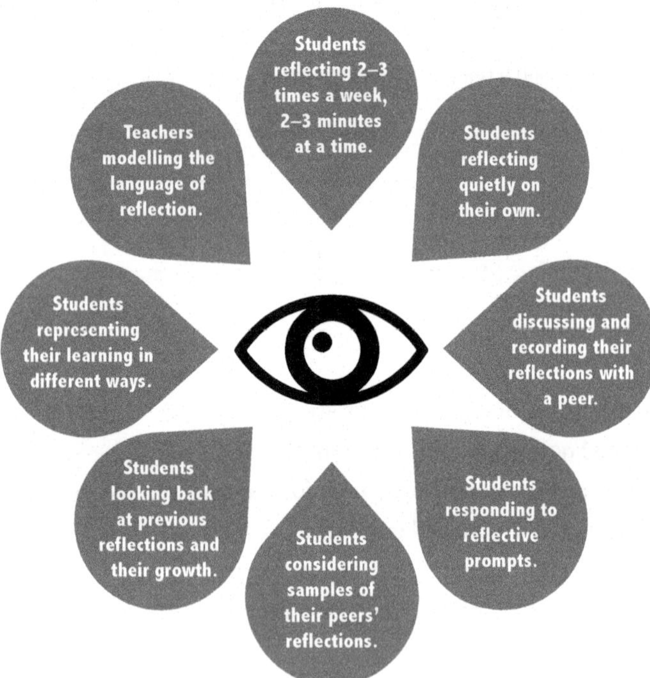

FIGURE 7.17 What reflection looks like.

19 Inquiry learning becomes deep learning through reflection and sharing.

Without the opportunity to reflect and share, students may not move from surface knowledge and skills to the significant changes in cognitive structure that define deep learning (see figure 7.17).

20 Both students and teachers need concrete examples of what good reflection and sharing look like and sound like.

We do not learn from our inquiry experiences. We learn by reflecting on our inquiry experiences (Dewey, 1933). Reflection and sharing work best when they are modeled by teachers and practiced by students on a regular basis (see figure 7.18).

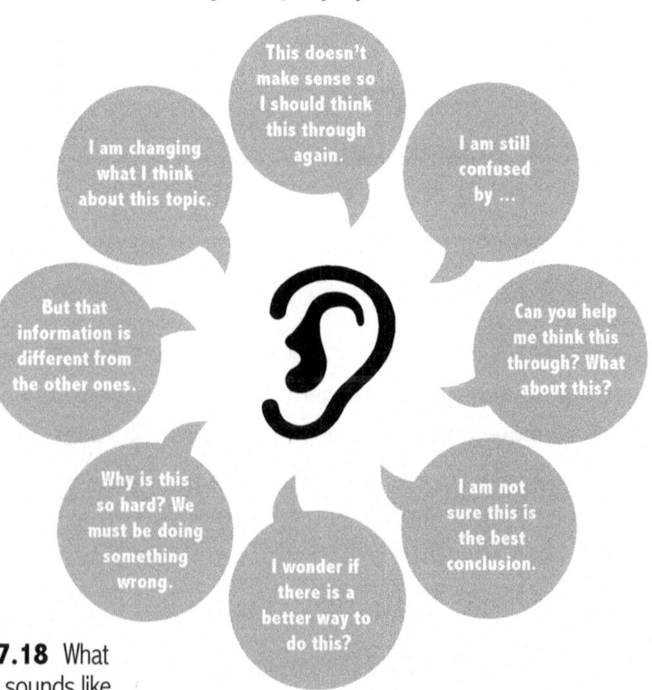

FIGURE 7.18 What reflection sounds like.

7.2 How do I move forward from here?

Many new curriculum guidelines and district directives are embracing inquiry-based learning as a key objective. We believe this is because inquiry-based learning is a bridge to successful teaching and learning in the digital age. It will be well worth the investment to build your capacity to work within an inquiry-based learning framework.

In the end, the only way to learn to do inquiry is to do inquiry. We suggest you plan your early inquiries with the big ideas in mind. If you plan according to the big ideas of inquiry, then rich learning will happen regardless of whether or not the inquiry itself "goes" the way you originally imagined. There are a number of ways to plan an inquiry. We have sketched out one approach that has proven successful for many teachers (see figure 7.19; the following list discusses each step in further detail).

10 steps to doing more inquiry

1. Start with a guided inquiry.
2. Determine your broad curricular targets.
3. Develop rich inquiry questions from your targets.
4. Locate and collect grade- and age-appropriate sources to drive the inquiry.
5. Build in opportunities for ongoing sharing and reflection.
6. Create an assessment and evaluation plan.
7. Create and reinforce vocabulary to communicate inquiry thinking.
8. Help students make sense of the evidence.
9. Assist students in drawing conclusions based on their evidence.
10. Include time to reflect on and share conclusions.

FIGURE 7.19 The goal is to do more inquiry.

1 Start with a guided inquiry.

We suggest you begin with a guided inquiry. There is lots of time for your students to conduct their own student-driven inquiries *after* they have experience and expertise with inquiry-based learning. We believe that starting with guided inquiry is the best way to create the conditions that lead to student success.

2 Determine your broad curricular targets.

All inquiries are about something, and it's up to you to decide which area of the curriculum you want to target. Make sure you are working from broad curricular targets (sometimes called "overall expectations" or "overarching targets" in curricula) rather than the list of small specific expectations that so often fill curriculum guidelines. Working from broad curriculum targets will give students choice within the inquiry experience you design. You can choose from different curriculum areas to build a great inquiry that bridges language arts, social studies and science, for example.

3 Develop rich inquiry questions from your targets.

For inquiry-based learning to work effectively, students must start with an inquiry question that is both exciting and focused on the big ideas of a discipline (see figure 7.20). All effective inquiry questions have certain characteristics. You may choose to have the entire class work together on one inquiry question or have groups of students investigate three or four questions looking at different aspects of the curriculum targets you have selected.

4 Locate and collect grade- and age-appropriate sources to drive the inquiry.

We want to stress that building a "starter" set of inquiry resources is well worth it. It will ensure that students consider resources with a variety of perspectives and increase the chances they will have an enjoyable and successful inquiry experience. Even better, since a rich question can lead to different evidence-based conclusions, you can use a source collection over many years. Sources can be dynamic too, as you add to and update your bundles based on classroom experience.

5 Build in opportunities for ongoing collaboration, sharing and reflection.

One of the fundamental qualities of inquiry is that students work together to make sense of a question or problem. Plan on having students work together at least some of the time. Providing regular opportunities for students to discuss and reflect on their learning, and to loop back to reconsider, revise and/or restructure their thinking, will help them understand more about not only the inquiry but about themselves and their classmates as thinkers and learners.

Questions to drive learning

Social Studies

- Who am I?
- What makes a good friend?
- What is fair?
- What makes a good community?
- Should we have rules?

Language Arts/Literacy

- How can stories change the world?
- How do words help and heal?
- Should there be rules in writing?
- Why does reading give you power?
- Why do people read?

Mathematics

- What kinds of problems can we solve by measuring?
- Where is the math in this room and school?
- How can there be different answers to the same question?
- How do fractions help us in real life?
- How is math just like a puzzle?

Health and Wellness

- How long will I live?
- What are all the ways I can move my body?
- How safe are my food choices?
- How can friends have an impact on my health?
- How are my mind and body connected?

Science

- How are humans the same as and different from other animals?
- What is the impact of machines on the world?
- How can something be both liquid and solid?
- How much have air and water changed?
- Are humans or plants more fragile?

FIGURE 7.20 Possible inquiry questions.

6 Create an assessment and evaluation plan.

Assessment bridges teaching and learning. It identifies where the learner is going (by establishing and sharing big ideas, concepts, fundamental skills, related learning goals and success criteria); where the learner is right now in their learning (by observing students, having conversations and assessing products); and how to get the learner to their goal (through the use of peer, self- and teacher feedback; see figure 7.21). Remember, students need to be partners in the assessment process, providing peer feedback and reflecting and reporting on their own learning. Students should be assessed through observation and conversation, not just an end product.

Three stages of inquiry assessment

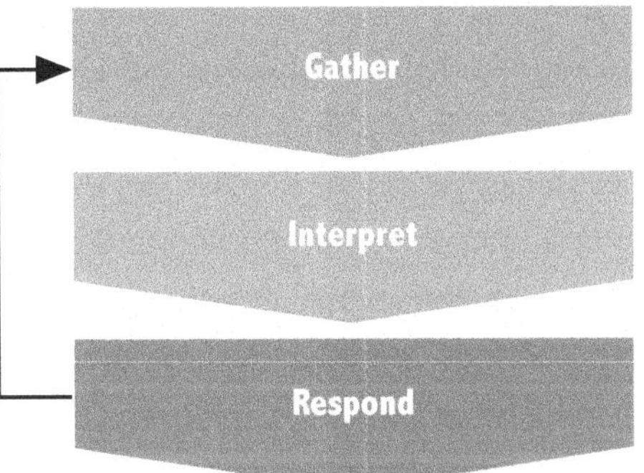

FIGURE 7.21 Three stages of inquiry assessment.

7 Create and reinforce vocabulary to communicate inquiry thinking.

Communication is the way that students make their learning visible. Effective communication requires the integration of inquiry vocabulary into your daily classroom tasks. Over time, you should notice a new and powerful common language being spoken by your students. The strategies in figure 7.22 will help you to develop such a vocabulary among your students.

8 Help students make sense of the evidence.

Whether you provide a full or partial bundle of sources for your students, or have students gather their own evidence, you will need to teach them how to make sense of their data. This includes helping them to consider the quality, reliability, usefulness and perspective of their sources.

Strategies for building inquiry vocabulary

- Create anchor charts or word walls of key inquiry vocabulary.
- Have students complete an inquiry journal where they articulate their understanding of new inquiry vocabulary as it arises.
- When listening to collaborative groups, ask questions that invite students to explain their understanding of key inquiry vocabulary in relation to the work they are completing.
- Students can create T-charts, Venn diagrams or other visuals to define key inquiry vocabulary words or to compare two or more key inquiry vocabulary words.
- Have inquiry vocabulary "check-ins" by asking students comprehension and application questions. You can create the questions, or even better, have students create the questions on specific terms to assess their peers.

FIGURE 7.22 Building inquiry vocabulary.

9 Assist students in drawing conclusions based on their evidence.

Help your students draw conclusions by having them identify patterns and trends, reflect on the quality of evidence, and consider whether the evidence supports one side of the inquiry question or the other (or a bit of both). Remember, a key goal is for students to understand that their conclusions should be based on their analysis of evidence. Others working from the same sources may come up with an entirely different evidence-based conclusion. This is to be encouraged, and it will be a sign that the inquiry question was rich and powerful.

10 Include time to reflect on and share conclusions.

It seems counter-intuitive to us that after a period of rich learning, students would keep their learning to themselves. We advocate that students share and reflect on their learning throughout the inquiry process. Students should also share and critique each other's work at the conclusion of the inquiry. This pushes learning to a deeper level. It promotes the idea that learning is an ongoing process and that new information and discussion could lead to a different conclusion.

THINQ Big

Teamwork, sharing and building networks

There is a saying that "many hands make light work." This is a powerful idea when it comes to doing more inquiry. Designing questions and units, finding and creating inquiry resources, and reflecting on classroom experiences and student learning by yourself is a daunting prospect. Sharing with school colleagues and grade-level teams and creating or joining online networks of like-minded educators is a necessary part of doing more inquiry.

The Internet and social media platforms offer unprecedented opportunities to share the results of your inquiry and to follow other educators. Share, post and blog the results of your efforts and seek out the work of others. Remember that many educators would love to learn about your inquiry experiences.

So whatever else you do, THINQ BIG! Connect yourself to teachers in your school, in your district and around the world. Think of yourself as a member of a team. Join an ever increasing number of educators working to change not only their own instructional practices but the very nature of teaching and learning in a digital age.

References and Resources

Alexander, K., Gonzalez, C. H., Vermette, P. J., & Di Marco, S. (2022). Questions in secondary classrooms: Toward a theory of questioning. *Theory and Research in Education, 20*(1), 5–25. doi.org/10.1177/14778785211043020

Argyris, C. (1986). *Skilled incompetence.* Accessed at https://hbr.org/1986/09/skilled-incompetence on February 29, 2024.

Barell, J. (2003). *Developing more curious minds.* Alexandria, VA: ASCD.

Barron, B., & Darling-Hammond, L. (2008). *Teaching for meaningful learning: A review of research on inquiry-based and cooperative learning.* San Rafael, CA: George Lucas Educational Foundation. Accessed at http://files.eric.ed.gov/fulltext/ED539399.pdf on July 18, 2016.

Barrow, L. H. (2006). A brief history of inquiry: From Dewey to standards. *Journal of Science Teacher Education, 17*(3), 265–278.

Berger, W. (2014). *A more beautiful question: The power of inquiry to spark breakthrough ideas.* New York: Bloomsbury.

Bloom, B. S. (Ed.). (1956). *Taxonomy of educational objectives: The classification of educational goals, Handbook I: Cognitive domain.* New York: McKay.

Boud, D. (2000). Sustainable assessment: Rethinking assessment for the learning society. *Studies in Continuing Education, 22*(2), 151–167.

Brookhart, S. M. (2012). Preventing feedback fizzle. *Educational Leadership, 70*(1), 24–29.

Chappuis. J. (2012, September 1). "How am I doing" feedback for learning. *Educational Leadership, 70*(1), 36–40.

Ciccone, T. (2016, May 29). *So what?* [Blog post]. Accessed at https://reggiokids.blogspot.ca/2016/05/so-what.html on November 29, 2023.

Colyer, J., & Watt, J. (2016). *THINQ 4–6: Inquiry-based learning in the junior classroom.* Toronto, Ontario, Canada: Wave Learning Solutions.

Costa, A. L., & Kallick, B. (2008). *Learning and leading with habits of mind: 16 essential characteristics for success.* Alexandria, VA: ASCD.

Coulombe, H., & Causarano, J. (2018, September 3). *Learning goals: Essential to learning.* Accessed at https://harnessassessment.com/2018/09/03/learning-goals-defined on February 26, 2024.

Couros, G. (2015). The innovator's mindset: Empower learning, unleash talent, and lead a culture of creativity. San Diego, CA: Dave Burgess Consulting.

Dean, C., Hubbell, E., Pitler, H., & Stone, B. (2012). *Classroom instruction that works: Research-based strategies for increasing student achievement* (2nd ed.). Alexandria, VA: ASCD.

de Bono, E. (2007). *Tactics: The art and science of success.* New York: HarperCollins.

Dewey, J. (1933). *How we think: A restatement of the relation of reflective thinking to the education process.* Boston: Heath & Co.

Dewey, J. (1938). *Experience and education.* New York: Macmillan.

Dewey, J. (1944). *Democracy and education.* New York: Free Press.

Dibbets, P., Fliek, L., & Meesters, C. (2015). Fear-related confirmation bias in children: A comparison between neutral- and dangerous-looking animals. *Child Psychiatry and Human Development, 46*(3), 418–425. doi: 10.1007/s10578-014-0481-3

Di Michele Lalor, A. (2012). Keeping the destination in mind. *Educational Leadership, 70*(1), 75–78.

Duck Duck Moose. (n.d.). *Draw and tell.* Accessed at www.duckduckmoose.com/educational-iphone-itouch-apps-for-kids/draw-and-tell/ on November 29, 2023.

Edutopia. (2015, August 24). *Harnessing students' curiosity to drive learning.* Accessed at www.edutopia.org/practice/wildwood-inquiry-based-learning-developing-student-driven-questions on February 23, 2024.

Elder, L., & Paul, R. (2002). *The miniature guide to the art of asking essential questions.* Dillon Beach, CA: Foundation for Critical Thinking.

Elder, L., & Paul, R. (2010). *The thinker's guide to the art of asking essential questions.* Dillon Beach, CA: Foundation for Critical Thinking.

Engel, S. (2013). The case for curiosity. *Educational Leadership, 70*(5), 36–40.

Freire, P. (2017). *Pedagogy of the oppressed.* New York: Penguin Classics.

Frey, N., Hattie, J., & Fisher, D. (2018). *Developing assessment-capable visible learners. grades K–12: Maximizing skill, will, and thrill.* Thousand Oaks, CA: Corwin Press.

Friesen, S., & Lock, J. (2010). *High-performing districts in the application of 21st century learning technologies: Review of the research.* Edmonton, AB, Canada: College of Alberta School Superintendents.

Friesen, S., & Scott, D. (2013). *Inquiry-based learning: A review of the research literature.* Accessed at http://galileo.org/focus-on-inquiry-lit-review.pdf on September 8, 2017.

Fullan, M., & Langworthy, M. (2014). *A rich seam: How new pedagogies find deep learning.* London: Pearson. Accessed at www.pearson.com/content/dam/one-dot-com/one-dot-com/global/Files/about-pearson/innovation/open-ideas/ARichSeamEnglish.pdf on November 29, 2023.

Goodwin, P. (2017). *The articulate classroom: Talking and learning in the primary school.* New York: Routledge.

Greene, P. (2016, October 4). *Should students be able to show what they know?* Accessed at www.huffpost.com/entry/should-students-be-able-t_b_824003 on February 28, 2024.

Handelsman, M. M. (2012, September 20). *Please don't answer your students' questions.* Accessed at www.psychologytoday.com/us/blog/the-ethical-professor/201209/please-dont-answer-your-students-questions on February 28, 2024.

Harlen, W. (2000). Assessment in the inquiry classroom. In *Inquiry: Thoughts, views, and strategies for the K–5 classroom* (Vol. 2, pp. 87–97). Arlington, VA: Division of Elementary, Secondary, and Informal Education.

Hattie, J. (2012). Know thy impact. *Educational Leadership, 70*(1), 18–23.

Hattie, J. (2023). *Visible learning: The sequel—A synthesis of over 2,100 meta-analyses relating to achievement.* New York: Routledge.

Hattie, J., & Clarke, C. (2019). *Visible learning: Feedback.* New York: Routledge.

Heard, G., & McDonough, J. (2009). *A place for wonder: Reading and writing nonfiction in the primary grades.* New York: Routledge.

Henkes, K. (1991). *Chrysanthemum.* New York: Greenwillow Books.

Hough, L. (2022, November 30). *Is it better to ask questions or listen carefully?* Accessed at www.gse.harvard.edu/ideas/ed-magazine/22/11/it-better-ask-questions-or-listen-carefully on February 23, 2024.

Ishikawa, K. (1968). *Guide to quality control.* Tokyo: Union of Japanese Scientists and Engineers.

Jacobs, B. (2022). *Self-regulation and inquiry-based learning in the primary classroom.* Toronto, ON, Canada: Canadian Scholars.

Johnston, P. H. (2004). *Choice words: How our language affects children's learning.* New York: Stenhouse.

Kahlon, R. (n.d.). *Pedagogical documentation.* Accessed at https://sites.google.com/tdsb.on.ca/robkahlon/best-practices/pedagogical-documentation on February 29, 2024.

Katz, S., & Dack, L. A. (2013). *Intentional interruption: Breaking down learning barriers to transform professional practice.* Thousand Oaks, CA: Corwin Press.

Kohn, A. (2006). *Beyond discipline: From compliance to community.* Alexandria, VA: ASCD.

Kuhlthau, C. C., Maniotes, L. K., & Caspari, A. K. (2007). *Guided inquiry: Learning in the 21st century.* Santa Barbara, CA: ABC-CLIO.

Lehman, C. (2012). *Energize research reading and writing: Fresh strategies to spark interest, develop independence, and meet key Common Core standards, grades 4–8.* Portsmouth, NH: Heinemann.

Lewin-Benham, A. (2011). *Twelve best practices for early childhood education: Integrating Reggio and other inspired approaches.* New York: Teachers College Press.

Malaguzzi, L. (1996). *The hundred languages of children: The Reggio Emilia approach to early childhood education.* New York: Ablex.

Mandalios, J. (2013). RADAR: An approach for helping students evaluate Internet sources. *Journal of Information Science, 39*(4), 470–478.

McDowell, M. (2020, December 21). *Making learning targets clear to students: When students clearly understand classroom expectations, they're better able to assess and improve their performance.* Accessed at www.edutopia.org/article/making-learning-targets-clear-students on February 26, 2024.

McTighe, J., & Wiggins, G. (2013). *Essential questions: Opening doors to student understanding.* Alexandria, VA: ASCD.

Meloney, D. (2015, March 5). *Teaching methods: Inquiry with Kath Murdoch.* Accessed at www.teachermagazine.com/au_en/articles/teaching-methods-inquiry-with-kath-murdoch on November 29, 2023.

Murdoch, K. (2015). *The power of inquiry: Teaching and learning with curiosity, creativity and purpose in the contemporary classroom.* Northcote, Victoria, Australia: Seastar Education.

Myller. R. (1990). *How big is a foot?* New York: Yearling.

National Reading Panel. (2013). Teaching children to read. *American Speech, 88*(1), 3–6. https://doi.org/10.1215/00031283-2322610

OER4Schools. (2013, November 11). *Shirley Clarke video on feedback* [Video file]. Accessed at www.youtube.com/watch?v=DGNp0AJte_c on February 27, 2024.

Ogle, D. M. (1986). K-W-L: A teaching model that develops active reading of expository text. *Reading Teacher, 39*(6), 564–570.

Ontario Ministry of Education. (2003). *A guide to effective instruction in reading: Kindergarten to grade 3.* Toronto, Ontario, Canada: Author.

Ontario Ministry of Education. (2010). *Growing success: Assessment, evaluation, and reporting in Ontario schools.* Toronto, Ontario, Canada: Queen's Printer for Ontario. Accessed at www.edu.gov.on.ca/eng/policyfunding/growsuccess.pdf on November 29, 2023.

Ontario Ministry of Education. (2013a). *Inquiry-based learning.* Accessed at www.brainreach.ca/uploads/1/1/2/0/112061741/cbs_inquirybased_9.pdf on February 29, 2024.

Ontario Ministry of Education. (2013b). *Learning for all: A guide to effective assessment and instruction for all students, kindergarten to grade 12.* Toronto, Ontario, Canada: Queen's Printer for Ontario. Accessed at https://files.ontario.ca/edu-learning-for-all-2013-en-2022-01-28.pdf on November 29, 2023.

Ontario Ministry of Education. (2016a). *Growing success: The kindergarten addendum—Assessment, evaluation, and reporting in Ontario schools.* Toronto, Ontario, Canada: Queen's Printer for Ontario. Accessed at www.edu.gov.on.ca/eng/policyfunding/GSKindergartenAddendum2018.pdf on November 29, 2023.

Ontario Ministry of Education. (2016b). *Towards defining 21st century competencies for Ontario: 21st century competencies, foundation document for discussion.* Toronto, Ontario, Canada: Queen's Printer for Ontario.

Ontario Teachers' Federation. (n.d.). *Protocol for analysis of pedagogical documentation.* Accessed at www.otffeo.on.ca/en/wp-content/uploads/sites/2/2018/05/Protocol-for-Analysis-of-Pedagogical-Documentation.pdf on November 29, 2023.

Organisation for Economic Co-operation and Development. (2019). *Student agency for 2030*. Accessed at www.oecd.org/education/2030-project/teaching-and-learning/learning/student-agency/Student_Agency_for_2030_concept_note.pdf on February 23, 2024.

Paul, A. M. (2013, November 4). *How the power of interest drives learning*. Accessed at www.kqed.org/mindshift/32503/how-the-power-of-interest-drives-learning on November 29, 2023.

Paul, R., & Elder, L. (2006). *Critical thinking: Tools for taking charge of your learning and your life*. Upper Saddle River, NJ: Pearson.

Pearson, P. D., & Gallagher, M. (1983, October). The instruction of reading comprehension. *Contemporary Educational Psychology*, *8*(3), 317–344.

Perkins, D. (2022, November 7). *PBL or direct/explicit instruction, what works?* Accessed at https://wegrowteachers.com/pbl-or-direct-explicit-instruction-what-works on February 19, 2024.

Project Zero. (n.d.). *What makes you say that*. Accessed at www.visiblethinkingpz.org/VisibleThinking_html_files/03_ThinkingRoutines/03d_UnderstandingRoutines/WhatMakes/WhatMakes_Routine.html) on March 14, 2017.

Reimer, J., & Watters, D. (2017). *THINQ kindergarten: Inquiry-based learning in the kindergarten classroom*. Toronto, Ontario, Canada: Wave Learning Solutions.

Ritchhart, R., Church, M., & Morrison, K. (2011). *Making thinking visible: How to promote engagement, understanding, and independence for all learners*. Hoboken, NJ: Jossey-Bass.

Rinaldi, C. (2004). *The relationship between documentation and assessment*. Accessed at www.reggioalliance.org/downloads/relationship:rinaldi.pdf on November 30, 2023.

Rothstein, D., & Santana, L. (2011, September). *Make just one change: Teach students to ask their own questions*. Cambridge, MA: Harvard Education Press.

Schwartz, D. L., Tsang, J. M., Blair, K. P. (2016). *The ABCs of how we learn: 26 scientifically proven approaches, how they work, and when to use them*. New York: Norton.

Senge, P. M., Kleiner, A., Roberts, C., Ross, R. B., & Smith, B. J. (1994). *The fifth discipline fieldbook*. New York: Currency.

Stead, T. (2006). *Reality checks: Teaching reading comprehension with nonfiction K–5*. New York: Routledge.

Student Achievement Division. (2012). *Pedagogical documentation: Leading learning in the early years and beyond*. Toronto, Ontario, Canada: Author.

Student Achievement Division. (2015). *Pedagogical documentation revisited: Looking at assessment and learning in new ways*. Accessed at https://rrcanada.org/wp-content/uploads/2016/04/CBS_PedagogicalDocument.pdf on November 29, 2023.

Tanner, K., & McPhee, K. (2015). *A new approach to evaluating information: A reflection on RADAR* [Conference presentation]. 2015 Research on Teaching and Learning Conference, Hamilton, Ontario, Canada. Accessed at https://ir.lib.uwo.ca/wlpres/50 on February 29, 2024.

Timperley, H., Kaser, L., & Halbert, J. (2014). *A framework for transforming learning in schools: Innovation and the spiral of inquiry*. East Melbourne, Victoria, Australia: Centre for Strategic Education.

Trehearne, M. P. (2016). *Multiple paths to literacy, K–2*. n.p.: Miriam P. Trehearne Literacy Consulting.

Vygotsky, L. S. (1962). *Thought and language*. Cambridge, MA: MIT Press.

Vygotsky, L. S. (1987). Thinking and speech. In R.W. Rieber & A. S. Carton (Eds.), *The collected works of L.S. Vygotsky, Volume 1: Problems of general psychology* (pp. 39–285). New York: Plenum Press. (Original work published 1934.)

Watt, J., & Colyer, J. (2014). *IQ: A practical guide to inquiry-based learning*. Don Mills, Ontario, Canada: Oxford University Press.

Watt, J., Fuller, H., & Terro, W. (2017). *THINQ 7–9: Inquiry-based learning in the intermediate classroom*. Toronto, Ontario, Canada: Wave Learning Solutions.

Wesch, M. (2017, May 9). *From knowledgeable to knowledge-able: Learning in new media environments*. Accessed at www.academiccommons.org/2014/09/09/from-knowledgable-to-knowledge-able-learning-in-new-media-environments/ on November 29, 2023.

Wien, C. A. (Ed.). (2008). *Emergent curriculum in the primary classroom: Interpreting the Reggio Emilia approach in schools*. New York: Teachers College Press.

Wiggins, G. (2012). Seven keys to effective feedback. *Educational Leadership*, *70*(1), 10–16.

Wiliam, D. (2011). *Embedded formative assessment*. Bloomington, IN: Solution Tree Press.

Wiliam, D. (2018). *Embedded formative assessment* (2nd ed.). Bloomington, IN: Solution Tree Press.

Willingham, D. T. (2009). *Why don't students like school? A cognitive scientist answers questions about how the mind works and what it means for the classroom*. New York: Wiley.

YouthLearn. (2016). *Inquiry-based learning: An approach to educating and inspiring kids*. Accessed at http://youthlearn.org/wp-content/uploads/Inquiry_Based_Learning.pdf on November 29, 2023.

Index

R

S

T

V

W

Y

Z

Inquiring Minds Want to Learn
Erik M. Francis
Learn how to phrase and pose good questions that will ignite inquiring minds and enrich student learning. Author Erik M. Francis shares a framework for engagement that piques students' interest and then guides students down four pathways of inquiry and questioning that make learning stick.
BKG102

What STEM Can Do for Your Classroom
Jason McKenna
Author and educator Jason McKenna offers examples, tried and tested classroom projects, and collaborative strategies in this innovative resource designed to open up STEM education for K–6 educators in exciting and expansive new ways.
BKG088

Raising the Rigor
Eileen Depka
This user-friendly resource shares questioning strategies and techniques proven to enhance students' critical thinking skills, deepen their engagement, and better prepare them for college and careers. The author also provides a range of templates, surveys, and checklists for planning instruction, deconstructing academic standards, and increasing classroom rigor.
BKF722

The Quest for Learning
Marie Alcock, Michael Fisher, and Allison Zmuda
This resource dives deep into questing, a customizable pedagogy tailored to a student's interests, needs, and abilities. Learn how to use questing to engross students in emotionally gripping learning experiences, engage them with actionable goals, and promote collaboration in online and physical spaces.
BKF718

Inspiring Lifelong Readers
Jennifer McCarty Plucker
Grounded in practices that promote adolescent literacy, inquiry, motivation, inspiration, and engagement, *Inspiring Lifelong Readers* provides secondary teachers with tried-and-true, evidence-based strategies. Discover how you can advance literacy learning so your students become competent, confident, and engaged readers.
BKF947